R-4008-FMP

After High School, Then What?

A Look at the Postsecondary Sorting-Out Process for American Youth

Gus W. Haggstrom, Thomas J. Blaschke,
Richard J. Shavelson

Prepared for the
Assistant Secretary of Defense
(Force Management and Personnel)

PREFACE

This report documents a RAND study of the postsecondary activities of recent high school graduates and dropouts. The study brings together data from several sources to profile America's high school graduating classes during the 1980s and track their educational and vocational pursuits through the first five years after graduation. Special attention is given to college enrollment and persistence patterns as well as to the flows of young people into military service from other postsecondary activities. Projections of numbers of high school graduates by state, race, and sex to the year 2000 are provided to indicate the implications of these flows for the nation's human resources over the next decade.

This research was sponsored by the Office of the Assistant Secretary of Defense (Force Management and Personnel). The research was conducted in the Defense Manpower Research Center, part of RAND's National Defense Research Institute, a federally funded research and development center sponsored by the Office of the Secretary of Defense and the Joint Staff. The report should be of interest to policymakers, educators, and scholars as a comprehensive source of information on America's high school graduates and their postsecondary vocational and educational activities.

SUMMARY

The nation's human resources depend critically on the extent to which young people complete high school and undertake postsecondary education and training that will prepare them for productive careers. During the 1980s, 10 million school-age youth dropped out of high school before graduation; most of them face bleak employment prospects in the years ahead. Another 28 million completed high school and began to sort themselves into educational programs and career paths. Some took entry-level jobs, entered apprenticeship programs, or joined the military. Others enrolled in college or entered vocational-technical schools. Still others took summertime breaks or worked at temporary jobs, many planning to enter college full-time in the fall.

This study was undertaken to examine patterns of military service, college enrollment, and civilian labor force participation among recent high school graduates and dropouts. The main objectives of the study were to profile the high school graduating classes and determine the key factors that affect the postsecondary sorting-out process in the 1980s, paying special attention to the flows of high school graduates into and out of postsecondary educational activities and military service.

The activities that young people pursue after high school are disparate and depend on a multitude of factors. Section I provides an overview of the postsecondary sorting-out process from a human resources perspective. Despite the huge influx of young people into the educational pipeline and labor force during the 1980s, the supply of entry-level workers has not kept pace with the demand for technicians, skilled craftsmen, and college-trained workers, eroding the labor surpluses that existed in many fields in the 1970s and early 1980s. With projections pointing to a 15-percent decline in the size of the 18-year age group between 1990 and 1992, there are mounting concerns about the adequacy of America's human resources to meet the requirements for trained manpower in the 1990s.

As in the past, America looks to its youth and the educational system to fill the gap. Hence, the flows of high school graduates and dropouts into the educational pipeline and the labor force are matters of national concern. Yet, the educational and vocational activities that young people pursue after leaving high school are poorly tracked. Nationally published statistics at best provide only crude indicators of the flows into postsecondary education, military service, and civilian employment, and there is almost no information on the flows across activities as young people redirect their efforts to reflect changes in educational and career goals.

To permit a detailed examination of the postsecondary pursuits of high school graduates in the 1980s, a comprehensive data base was compiled for this study. The primary data source was High School and Beyond (HS&B), a rich longitudinal study of over 26,000 high school seniors in the Classes of 1980 and 1982 who were the subjects of follow-up surveys in 1982, 1984, and 1986. Numerous extensions to this data base were made to enhance its utility for this research and link it to other sources of information on American youth. In particular, supplemental data on the military service activities of the HS&B participants were obtained through the Defense Manpower Data Center.

Also, steps were taken to provide detailed demographic information on the sizes and compositions of high school graduation classes in the 1980s and to circumscribe the school dropout problem. It is a sorry fact that national data bases cannot provide accurate estimates of the numbers of high school graduates and dropouts in any year, let alone the disaggregated estimates by state, race, and sex that are needed to support studies of human resources. Building on existing data from several sources and relying heavily on Census Bureau estimates and projections of age-group sizes, we derived estimates and projections of numbers of high school graduates by state, sex, race, and Hispanic origin for the years 1980–2000. See Section II.

According to estimates for 1986—the last year for which state estimates were available for both public and private schools, the high school graduation rate was 73 percent (71 percent for males, 76 for females), implying that 27 percent of the 18-year-olds in 1986 had already dropped out of school or would do so before graduation. Although high school graduation rates have moved up and down by a few percentage points over the last 25 years, the 1986 rate is almost exactly the same as it was in 1976 and 1965.

Section III examines patterns of postsecondary activities among high school graduates and dropouts during the first year after leaving school. Because many high school graduates take a break before entering college or military service, the focus of attention here is the main activity as of October in the year of graduation. For the purposes of this research, four categories of main activities were identified: full-time student, military service, civilian employment, and "other" (not enrolled full-time and not employed). The full-time student category was divided into three subcategories by type of institution: four-year college (or university), two-year college, and vocational-technical school.

Time series of college entrance and employment rates among high school graduates and dropouts indicate that activity patterns during the first year after leaving school have remained remarkably stable since the early 1970s, with some increases in both college enrollment and military enlistment rates in the early 1980s. Among graduates in the Classes of 1980 and 1982, only 40 percent were enrolled full-time in college in October following graduation, and another 7 to 8 percent were enrolled part-time. Approximately 8 percent of the graduates in these classes entered military service before 1986, but only 3 percent entered within six months after graduation. Except for the fact that military entrants were mostly male, they differed only slightly from their classmates in terms of demographic characteristics. A higher proportion of them came from lower socioeconomic status families and from minority groups, but in terms of measures of academic aptitude, they were on a par with their classmates.

More detailed analyses of HS&B data confirmed findings from previous studies indicating that academic aptitude is the primary factor affecting individual college enrollment decisions of high school graduates. However, about a third of the 1980 and 1982 graduates in the top academic aptitude quartile were not enrolled full-time in college in October following graduation, suggesting that other factors also play important roles in college enrollment decisions. Controlling for differences in academic aptitude and socioeconomic status, we find that graduates from private schools and those of Asian or Pacific Islander descent had significantly higher college entrance rates.

Section IV presents analyses of postsecondary activities during the rest of the five-year period following high school, including estimates of six-month transition rates across main activities. This examination reveals considerable turbulence in activity patterns, much of it into and out of short-term civilian jobs. For college entrants, progress toward degree completion was notably sporadic and drawn out. Among the 1980 graduates who enrolled full-time in a four-year college directly after graduation, only 46 percent had earned bachelor's degrees through February 1986.

In general, our findings indicate that a substantial proportion of high school seniors in the 1980s lacked direction when they left school, and that their subsequent activities were marked by false starts and backtracking. In October following graduation, only about half of the 1980 graduates were pursuing the activities they had planned to pursue as seniors. Their later shifts across activities indicated that many of them were having difficulty finding niches in the adult world. Only one-sixth of the graduates who entered four-year colleges after graduation enrolled continuously until they had completed bachelor's degrees. With half of the college entrants dropping out before they earned degrees, the flow of students through the educational pipeline was greatly impeded. The resulting losses of talent, on top of the huge losses represented by persistently high dropout rates in the secondary schools, point to the conclusion that America made poor use of its human resources during the 1980s and will be hard put to meet its manpower requirements in the 1990s.

ACKNOWLEDGMENTS

The authors would like to thank W. S. Sellman, Director for Accession Policy, Office of the Assistant Secretary of Defense (Force Management and Personnel), for his interest in and sponsorship of this research. We are also indebted to Zahava Doering, former Chief of the Survey and Market Analysis Division at the Defense Manpower Data Center (DMDC), for her help in getting this project under way and her active collaboration during the early stages of the work. Others at DMDC who lent their considerable talents to our work were Jerry Lehnus, John Richards, and Elaine Sellman.

At RAND, we are grateful to Glenn Gotz, who headed the Defense Manpower Research Center during the course of this study, and to Bernard Rostker, Glenn's successor in that role. Thanks also go to John Winkler, who collaborated with us in the initial phases of the study, and to Richard Buddin and Joyce Davidson, who provided formal reviews of the report. Finally, we would like to thank Robert Klitgaard and Laurel McFarland for their comments on earlier drafts of the report.

CONTENTS

PREFACE iii

SUMMARY v

ACKNOWLEDGMENTS ix

FIGURES xiii

TABLES xv

Section
I. INTRODUCTION 1
    The Dwindling Supply of High School Graduates 1
    Labor Market Uncertainties 2
    Tracking High School Graduates and Dropouts 3
    Phases in the Sorting-Out Process 4
    Conceptual Framework 5
    Pathways to Military Service 6

II. SIZING UP AMERICA'S HIGH SCHOOL GRADUATES AND DROPOUTS 9
    The School Dropout Problem 10
    Numbers of Entrants into the Sorting-Out Process 11
    Numbers of High School Graduates 16
    Numbers of Graduates from Private Schools 17
    The Changing Composition of the Graduating Classes 20

III. MAIN ACTIVITIES AFTER LEAVING SCHOOL 23
    Long-Term Trends 23
    Changes in the Sorting-Out Process in the 1970s and 1980s 25
    Enlistments in the All-Volunteer Force 27
    October Activities of Graduates and Dropouts 28
    Individual Differences 32
    Patterns of Main Activities After Graduation 35
    Plans Versus Realizations 38
    Multivariate Analyses of Track Entrance Rates 43

IV. FINDING NICHES IN THE ADULT WORLD 52
    Models and Mavericks 52
    Distributions Across Main Activities 54
    Changing Courses 58
    Student Persistence 58
    Sources of New Entrants 62
    Preservice Activities of Enlistees 63
    Timing of Service Entry 67
    Characteristics of Military Entrants 73

V. CONCLUSIONS 76

Appendix
    A.   ESTIMATING NUMBERS OF HIGH SCHOOL GRADUATES 79
    B.   THE HS&B/DMDC DATA BASE 118

BIBLIOGRAPHY 127

FIGURES

1. Main activities after high school 6
2. Numbers of 18-year-olds and high school graduates, 1970–2000 13
3. Student/employment status in October by year of graduation 30
4. Timing of service entry for HS&B participants in Class of 1980 70
5. Preservice main activities among military entrants in Class of 1980 71

TABLES

1. Estimates and projections of the resident population of ages 17 and 18 as of July 1, 50 states and D.C.: 1970–2000 12
2. Numbers of 17-year-olds by state, sex, race, and Hispanic origin: 1980 14
3. Numbers of high school graduates by control of school and sex, 50 states and D.C.: 1960–1989 16
4. Numbers of high school graduates by control of school and state: 1980–1986 18
5. High school graduation rates by state: 1980–1986 21
6. Full-time freshman enrollments and freshman enrollment rates by sex: Fall 1967 to Fall 1987 26
7. Numbers of nonprior service accessions by sex and high school graduate status: 1972–1987 27
8. Enrollment and employment statuses of recent high school graduates in October, 1967–1987 29
9. Employment statuses of recent high school dropouts in October, 1967–1987 31
10. Percentages of Class of 1961 entering college within five years by sex, socioeconomic status quartile, and academic aptitude quartile 33
11. Percentages of high school graduates enrolled as full-time college students in October by sex, socioeconomic status quartile, and academic aptitude quartile: Classes of 1980 and 1982 34
12. Percentages of high school graduates in military service in October by sex, socioeconomic status quartile, and academic aptitude quartile: Classes of 1980 and 1982 36
13. Estimated percentages of high school graduates by main activity in October: Classes of 1980 and 1982 37
14. Estimated numbers of high school graduates by main activity in October, plans category, and sex: Class of 1980 40
15. Estimated numbers of high school graduates by main activity in October, plans category, and sex: Class of 1982 41
16. Logistic regression results for college entrance and military enlistment proportions: Class of 1981 45
17. Logistic regression results for proportions of seniors planning to enter college or military service: Spring 1980 47
18. Logistic regression results for proportions of sophomores planning to enter college or military service: Spring 1980 48
19. Logistic regression results for proportions of graduates enrolled in college in October: Classes of 1980 and 1982 50
20. Logistic regression results for proportions of male graduates in military service in October: Classes of 1980 and 1982 51
21. Distribution of 1980 high school graduates across main activities: October 1980–October 1985 55
22. Distribution of 1982 high school graduates across main activities: October 1982–October 1985 56
23. Distribution of 1980 high school dropouts across main activities: October 1980–October 1985 57
24. Estimated six-month transition rates across main activities for members of the Class of 1980: October 1980–October 1985 59

25. Estimated six-month transition rates across main activities for members of the Class of 1982: October 1982–October 1985 61

26. Estimated six-month backward transition rates for members of the Class of 1980: October 1980–October 1985 64

27. Estimated six-month backward transition rates for members of the Class of 1982: October 1982–October 1985 66

28. Distribution of military entrants from Class of 1980 across main activities: October 1980–October 1985 68

29. Distribution of military entrants from Class of 1982 across main activities: October 1982–October 1985 69

30. Distribution of lag times between high school graduation and service entry: Classes of 1980 and 1982 72

31. Summary statistics for military entrants by timing of service entry: Classes of 1980 and 1982 74

A.1. Estimated numbers of high school graduates by state and category: 1980–1989 . . 81

A.2. Projected numbers of high school graduates by state and category: 1990–2000 . . . 90

A.3. Estimated numbers of 17-year-olds by state and category: 1980–1989 100

A.4. Projected numbers of 17-year-olds by state and category: 1990–2000 107

A.5. Percentages of 19-year-olds who reported having completed four years of high school by sex, region, race, and Hispanic origin: April 1980 114

A.6. Percentages of high school students enrolled in private schools by region, race, and Hispanic origin: April 1980 117

B.1. Numbers of high school graduates by race, Hispanic origin, control of school, and census division: 1980 120

B.2. Numbers of high school graduates by race, Hispanic origin, control of school, and census division: 1982 121

B.3. Summary statistics for measures of socioeconomic status and academic aptitude by graduation and military service statuses 125

I. INTRODUCTION

As America enters the 1990s, there are mounting concerns about the adequacy of the nation's human resources. These concerns are not new. It has long been recognized that the 18–24 age group would shrink from the early 1980s through the mid-1990s, meaning fewer entry-level workers, fewer students in the educational pipeline, and more competition for high school graduates among the nation's colleges, military services, and civilian employers. With the prospect of greatly reduced numbers of high school graduates in the 1990s and with projections pointing to shortages of college-educated workers in many fields in the late 1990s, there is room to question whether enough young people will pursue the kinds of postsecondary training needed to satisfy the nation's future manpower requirements.

Eight consecutive years of economic expansion from 1982 to 1990, marked by steadily increasing employment, depleted the surplus labor supply that existed in the early 1980s. Reflecting the continual shift from labor surplus to shortage, unemployment rates fell steadily from their peak of 10.8 percent in December 1982, dipping below 5 percent in March 1989 for the first time in 15 years. After years of recruiting success in which the Armed Forces substantially upgraded their enlistment standards, the military began experiencing recruiting difficulties in late 1988. Shortages of college-trained workers—especially teachers and nurses—have been widely reported for some time, and the National Science Foundation (NSF) projects a shortfall of about 500,000 scientists and engineers by the end of the century (Holden, 1989).

Less visible is the reported increasing demand for entry-level technicians, administrative support personnel, and skilled craftsmen, who ordinarily complete high school and some postsecondary training but not a four-year college degree. According to recent projections by the Bureau of Labor Statistics, technicians and related support occupations will show the most rapid growth during the 1990s. These occupations, like most military occupational specialties, draw from the shrinking pool of high school graduates who do not enter four-year college programs after graduation but are qualified to undertake postsecondary education and on-the-job training in technical fields (Kutscher, 1989).

THE DWINDLING SUPPLY OF HIGH SCHOOL GRADUATES

As in the past, the nation will be relying on its high school graduates to fill the gaps, but there will be fewer of them in the 1990s, and there are reasons to doubt that they will sort themselves into postsecondary educational and career paths in sufficient numbers to meet future employment demands. School dropout rates remain high, and many high school graduates have deficiencies in basic skills that severely limit their employment prospects. Only a small proportion of them have the aptitude and resources to complete college programs requisite to filling the nation's most pressing needs for professional and technical workers.

In considering how the nation's manpower requirements will be met in the 1990s, it is natural to look first at the numbers of young people who will be completing school and entering the workforce. Of immediate concern to college and military recruiters is the outlook for greatly reduced numbers of 18-year-olds and high school graduates over the next few years. Census Bureau projections indicate that the 18-year-old age group will shrink by 15 percent between 1989 and 1992. With minorities constituting an increasing proportion of the school age population and with school dropout rates remaining persistently high, especially among Hispanics, the near-term prospect of an upward surge in high school graduation rates appears dim. The clear implication is that the nation's colleges, military services, and civilian employers will be competing for substantially fewer graduates over the next few years.

How many fewer? Which states will be most affected? How will the racial/ethnic mix of the graduating classes change? How will college enrollments and military recruitment be affected? There are serious gaps in the federal data base that make it impossible to answer these questions precisely, but the questions are too important to gloss over. To a certain extent, partial answers can be provided by piecing together existing information on the numbers, characteristics, and activities of recent high school graduates.

In Section II, we take a hard look at the demographics pertaining to high school graduates and dropouts. Drawing on data from several sources and Census Bureau estimates of age group sizes, we provide detailed estimates and projections of numbers of high school graduates by state, sex, and race for the years 1980–2000. These projections point to overall declines of 8, 5, and 2 percent in 1990, 1991, and 1992, followed by gradual increases averaging 2 percent per year from 1993 to 2000. If these projections hold, the total number of graduates from 1990 to 1994 will be 10 percent less than the five-year total for 1985–1989, which would imply a considerable diminution in the educational pipeline for college-trained personnel.

LABOR MARKET UNCERTAINTIES

The main uncertainties underlying assessments of the adequacy of our human resources over the next decade stem from two factors. First, the future growth of the economy cannot be predicted accurately. A deep recession, such as the one in 1981–82, would cut the demand for entry-level workers in most occupations and could send unemployment rates back above 10 percent. Second, even if the future state of the economy were known, scholars could only guess at the timing and extent of shortages in most fields, because the pipeline into and mobility within the labor force are poorly tracked.

Despite the attention given to shortages of college-trained workers in many fields, the national data base for gauging the size and characteristics of the nation's college-trained workforce is in a sorry state. In particular, the extent of the "crisis" in education due to the shortage of qualified teachers cannot be ascertained because of the lack of basic data on the numbers, qualifications, and characteristics of teachers (Haggstrom, Darling-Hammond, and Grissmer, 1988).

The term "crisis" is also being used to describe the outlook for scientists, engineers, and technicians, but reliable statistics on the numbers and employment patterns of workers in these fields do not exist (Panel to Study the NSF Scientific and Technical Personnel Data System, 1989). To underscore the uncertainties that have confounded attempts to use survey data to assess the demand for college-trained workers in technical fields, NSF estimates that the number of employed scientists and engineers grew by over 8 percent per year between 1980 and 1986, reaching 4.6 million in 1986. That figure is half again as large as the Bureau of Labor Statistics estimate of 3.1 million, which is consistent with a much slower 1980–86 growth rate of about 5 percent per year.

On the supply side, the educational pipeline for new entrants into the labor force is also poorly tracked. Between decennial censuses, the primary continuing source of information on the educational and vocational activities of recent high school graduates and dropouts is the Current Population Survey (CPS). This monthly survey fielded by the Census Bureau relies on samples of nearly 56,000 household units each month to gather the raw data supporting the "official" statistics on employment, unemployment, income, educational attainment, enrollment, and living arrangements that appear in *Current Population Reports*, *Employment and Earnings*, and *Monthly Labor Review*.

Although the CPS is conducted and evaluated using state-of-the-art methods, statistics drawn from the CPS are subject to the same errors that beset all population surveys. Because of the sparseness of the CPS sample for gathering information on, say, Hispanic male high school graduates in the Class of 1986, disaggregated estimates of employment, educational attainment, and enrollment derived from the CPS are subject to large sampling errors (U.S. Bureau of the Census, 1988b). Moreover, the CPS is plagued by nonsampling errors due to incomplete population coverage, nonresponse errors, and response errors (Shapiro and Kostanich, 1988). As Sections II and III show, time series on educational attainment and college enrollment derived from the CPS conflict with statistics drawn from other sources.

The National Center for Education Statistics (NCES) gathers data from schools and colleges that provide additional information about the educational pursuits of high school graduates. The earned degrees data compiled annually by NCES provide the counts of college graduates by sex, race, and field of study that appear in the *Digest of Education Statistics*. Comparable counts of high school graduates do not exist, because NCES has no systematic means for gathering data from private schools. At best, existing national statistics provide crude indicators on how many high school graduates enter college, join the military, and enter the labor force each year, but detailed information is missing on who goes where, who persists, and for how long.

TRACKING HIGH SCHOOL GRADUATES AND DROPOUTS

To better understand the implications of demographic trends on the pipeline into the workforce and to guide youth policies bearing on student aid, military recruitment, and national service, we need far more comprehensive information on which students enter the various postsecondary tracks and how, when, and why young people change courses in pursuing their educational and vocational objectives. In short, we need a much better understanding of the *sorting-out process*—the process by which young people with widely differing talents and ambitions choose among competing alternatives such as military service, higher education, civilian employment, or homemaking as they make the transition from youth to adulthood.

One of the difficulties in tracking the activities of young people is that, in essence, there is not a single sorting-out process but myriad processes depending on a variety of factors and individual circumstances that affect student outcomes. Only in the abstract is the sorting-out process for high school graduates the same as it is for dropouts. Although the differences in outcomes may not be as stark for other categories, we clearly need to distinguish the patterns of males vs. females, public school graduates vs. private, rural vs. urban, minority vs. majority, high-achieving students vs. low, rich vs. poor, college-planners vs. others. Many of these categories have several subclasses that merit attention, and there are other categories of students, such as handicapped students, unmarried mothers, and drug addicts, whose postsecondary activities are matters of public concern.

Because there is no such thing as a "typical" high school senior and many young people change paths numerous times before they find their niches, it is not surprising that there is no dominant pattern of postsecondary behavior. The closest approximation is the traditional "lockstep" pattern leading to a college degree: enrollment as a full-time student in a four-year college in the fall after high school graduation, followed by continuous enrollment (except perhaps for summer terms) until graduation four years later. However, as will be seen in Section IV, only about one in six graduates in the Class of 1980 followed that path.

PHASES IN THE SORTING-OUT PROCESS

For the most part, the postsecondary paths are far less direct and marked with flux. This is not to say that they are unpatterned. To characterize the patterns, it is convenient to divide the sorting-out process for a given age cohort into three phases. The first phase is the period before high school graduation, when a substantial proportion of the age cohort make a crucial decision—to drop out of school. As our examination of the "school dropout problem" in Section II will show, the overall proportion of high school dropouts has been around one in four for the last 20 years—a colossal, persistent wastage of talent. That this wastage of talent is not uniform across the nation is evident from the substantial variability in dropout rates across states, sexes, and race/ethnic categories.

The period before graduation is also important to the graduating seniors who make their plans and take steps toward realizing them by applying for admission to college, preparing to enter other training programs, or seeking employment. For some graduates, their plans as seniors constitute blueprints to their future actions at branch points in the sorting-out process; for others, plans are at best vague and dependent on contingencies. Whether the seniors' plans are realized or not, they reflect the seniors' best guesses about their future actions as they approach a critical juncture in their lives.

The second and perhaps most important phase in the sorting-out process occurs right after graduation when the young adults enter their initial postsecondary "tracks" in keeping with their long-term plans. Many graduates take a break of from one to four months after graduation, often for temporary work activity, before they pursue full-time educational or vocational activities consonant with their career goals. The June graduates who plan to complete a four-year degree in the traditional lockstep manner typically defer college entrance until September. Military enlistees also often delay their entry into the service for several months. To allow for these delays, we shall identify each graduate's initial postsecondary track as the main activity pursued in October in the year of graduation. In Section III, we present a detailed examination of the main activities of the Classes of 1980 and 1982 to profile the track memberships and assess the relevance of sex, ability, socioeconomic status, race/ethnicity, and senior plans to college entrance and military enlistment.

The third phase of the sorting-out process is the remainder of the five-year period following high school graduation. Although some high school graduates have definite plans leading to well-defined career objectives and they take direct routes to fulfill them, they may be in the minority. For a substantial portion of graduates, postsecondary activities appear to be less ordered and more dependent on evolving circumstances, such as moving away from home, encountering untoward work or student experiences, or starting a family. For them, sorting out is a process marked by flux, false steps, and changes of plans. Because their day-to-day activities are less tied to specific career goals, they may be more amenable to moving into new endeavors, perhaps to include military service.

CONCEPTUAL FRAMEWORK

To describe the entrants into the postsecondary sorting-out process during the 1980s and to track their subsequent transitions into and out of postsecondary education, military service, and civilian employment, we shall implicitly adopt a "cohort analysis" perspective. The cohorts of primary interest in this study are the successive high school graduating classes and the annual cohorts of school dropouts. For the present discussion, the term "Class of 1985" will refer to the combined cohort consisting of the graduating seniors in 1985 and the dropouts who last attended school in 1985.

Except for the Classes of 1980 and 1982, suitable data do not exist to profile the classes in terms of their sizes, race/ethnic composition, and dispersion across states and school types. To fill this gap, we treat the 17-year age group as of July 1 in the year preceding the graduation year as a synthetic cohort for the purpose of prescribing the sizes and race/ethnic compositions of the senior classes in each state. That is, we treat Census Bureau estimates and projections of sizes of age groups by state, sex, race, and Hispanic origin as proxies for the corresponding numbers of persons of school-leaving age. To estimate high school graduation rates within cohorts of school-leavers, we divide the number of graduates in any year by the number of 17-year-olds in the preceding year.

The Classes of 1980 and 1982 receive special attention in this study, because they are the classes for which there exist detailed longitudinal micro-level data on the activities of large numbers of graduates and dropouts. These data will be used to provide an in-depth examination of the sorting-out process of these two cohorts. We also draw on time series from several sources to examine trends in college entrance rates, military enlistment rates, and rates of employment over the last 20 years. This examination shows that the sorting-out process has been remarkably stable over time, except for the gradual closing of the gap between the sexes in college entrance rates and a trend toward higher enlistment rates in the early 1980s. This stability in the overall rates over time supports the hypothesis that the transition rates for the Classes of 1980 and 1982 have persisted without material change through the 1980s.

The micro-level data on the Classes of 1980 and 1982 come from High School and Beyond (HS&B), a rich longitudinal data base on over 26,000 high school sophomores and seniors in 1980 who were the subjects of follow-up surveys in 1982, 1984, and 1986. On the follow-ups, the HS&B participants were asked to provide information about each episode of employment and educational activity that they had experienced, including the time spans of the activities. Using these data on the students' educational and vocational activities from 1980 through February 1986 and additional data on military service provided by the Defense Manpower Data Center, we have classified each HS&B participant's main activity into one of four categories each month: (1) full-time student, (2) military service, (3) civilian employment, and (4) other (not enrolled full-time and not employed). To characterize these activities more fully, we also encoded subcategories of special interest. For example, the full-time student category has four subcategories corresponding to institutional levels: high school, four-year college, two-year college, and vocational-technical school. See App. B for further details.

Figure 1 provides a schematic representation of the flows of the senior classes into postsecondary tracks and the subsequent transitions across main activities that this classification scheme attempts to capture. Although our data base permits examining month-to-month tran-

6

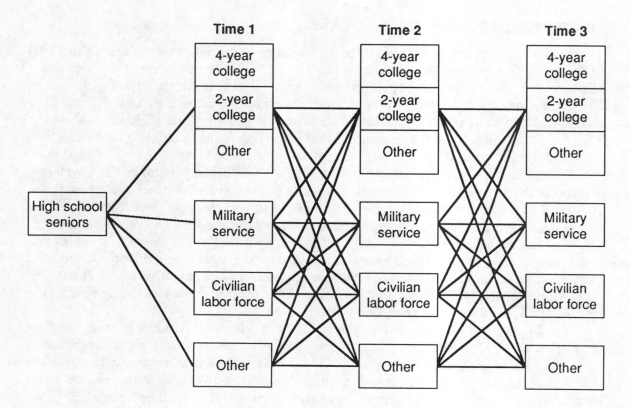

Fig. 1—Main activities after high school

sitions, we only report six-month transition rates in this study, identifying "TIME 1" with October in the year of graduation, "TIME 2" with the following April, and so forth.

In addition to providing the episodic data on employment and education needed to classify the participants' main activities each month, HS&B also provides key background information on the participants and their schools, including individual measures of cognitive ability, socioeconomic status, and postsecondary plans. These data permit examining the extent to which background factors affect young people's educational and vocational decisions at branch points in the sorting-out process.

PATHWAYS TO MILITARY SERVICE

Of special interest to this study are the high school graduates in the 1980s who enlisted in the Armed Forces. The services maintain comprehensive personnel files on their enlistees after they enter the service, but the military has only limited information on the enlistment decision process, i.e., the sequence of events that have led one of every ten graduates (and one of every six males) to enter the service during the 1980s. One of the principal purposes of this study is to gain a better understanding of the pathways to military service among recent high school graduates.

Since 1983, over 90 percent of nonprior service enlistees have been high school graduates. Only a small percentage of the recruits had completed more than a year of college before enlisting, but many had enrolled in college or vocational-technical schools for shorter periods of time. Although the proportion of female recruits has been increasing over time, male recruits continued to outnumber females by about seven to one in 1987. As will be seen in Section IV, the military enlistees from the Classes of 1980 and 1982 were on a par with their classmates in terms of academic ability, but the enlistees had lower socioeconomic status on average, and they were more likely to come from minority groups.

From a human resources perspective, the military plays several roles in the sorting-out process. It not only serves as an employer of about 300,000 new recruits per year but as a huge vocational training institution, providing classroom instruction and on-the-job training for a wide array of occupational specialties. Through the G.I. Bill and the Army College Fund, the military also provides young people opportunities to finance college educations that might otherwise be beyond their means. Here, the fact that a disproportionate number of enlistees come from low-income and minority groups is significant, because these groups are underrepresented in the professional and technical occupations that are expected to evidence shortages in the 1990s.

Because the services are currently seeking to reduce overall force sizes, the services' requirements for new recruits may be somewhat lower in the next few years than in the recent past. However, the military faces a greatly reduced supply of potential recruits and increasing competition with the nation's colleges and civilian employers. If the services continue to restrict their recruiting to high school graduates, their target population will continue to shrink through 1992.

In part, the Armed Forces' demand for high school graduates with high aptitude stems from the need for personnel to undertake technical training in a wide spectrum of occupational specialties and to operate and maintain high-technology weapons systems. Competition with the civilian labor force for youth with aptitudes for such technical areas as electronics, computers, and communications may be increasingly severe over the next few years.

The impending decline in the supply of high school graduates also means that the military will face increasing competition with colleges and universities for high school graduates with college aspirations. In the 1970s, this competition was minimal. The Armed Forces and the colleges were recruiting from two dissimilar subpopulations. From the advent of the All-Volunteer Force in 1972 through 1980, over a third of the recruits were high school dropouts, and few young people enlisted who had college training or planned to complete college. Earlier studies of the potential for military recruiting from two-year colleges and postsecondary vocational schools bore this out, indicating that the military was having little success in recruiting college students (Shavelson, Haggstrom, and Blaschke, 1984).

But during the 1980s, the disjunction between military service and college enrollment became less clear-cut. Aided by rising military pay, better educational incentives, an enhanced public image, and a depressed youth labor market during the 1981–1982 recession, the military made considerable inroads in recruiting high school graduates with college aspirations. Thanks to the Army College Fund and other postservice educational benefits, military service came to be viewed as a viable means to finance a college education. With the enactment of the Montgomery G.I. Bill in 1984, the role of military service as a stepping stone to postservice college and vocational training was expanded, solidified, and given national prominence. On the horizon are other proposals, such as the Citizenship and National Service Act introduced last year by Senator Sam Nunn, that would curtail existing federal student aid programs and substitute educational vouchers similar to the G.I. Bill for one- or two-year stints of military or community service.

As experience with earlier G.I. Bills has shown, sweeping changes like these can result in marked changes in the sorting-out process, including some unplanned side effects. The Army College Fund and the new G.I. Bill undoubtedly help attract recruits, but they also provide strong incentives for enlistees to leave the service to reap the benefits. The person-years gained by bringing additional recruits into the service may be more than offset by later losses of experienced personnel (Haggstrom et al., 1981; Fernandez, 1982). Since the inception of the Montgomery G.I. Bill on July 1, 1985, over 60 percent of eligible recruits (and 80 percent of Army recruits) have signed up for the program, affirming their intent to use the benefits through *nonrefundable* contributions of $1,200. As a consequence, in the 1990s, the services will be facing a double dilemma. They will be losing unusually large numbers of experienced personnel at the same time that their recruiting missions become more difficult due to shrinking applicant pools.

If there is a bright spot in this scenario, it is that the military's losses will be the civilian sector's gain. Just as earlier G.I. Bills contributed to the nation's supply of college-trained personnel, the new G.I. Bill is having the same effect. The numbers of veterans completing college in the next few years will probably not be large enough to forestall anticipated shortages of college-trained personnel, especially in teaching, nursing, science, and engineering. Nonetheless, the shortages will be less than they would otherwise have been, and these programs provide pathways to professional careers for high school graduates from low-income families.

Military personnel also add to college rolls through their educational pursuits while still in service through voluntary off-duty study or in military-sponsored training programs. In a study of the military impact on college enrollments, Hexter and El-Khawas (1988) report that, in 1987, service personnel enrolled in at least 778,000 courses at the postsecondary level. Thus, with the changes that have taken place in the 1980s, the military has become a significant source of college enrollments and, thanks mainly to the new G.I. Bill, a substantial source of student aid for youth from low- and middle-income families.

II. SIZING UP AMERICA'S HIGH SCHOOL
GRADUATES AND DROPOUTS

This section profiles recent entrants into the postsecondary sorting-out process in terms of their numbers, demographic characteristics, and dispersion across states. Trends in cohort sizes and graduation rates are central to examining the flows of high school seniors into postsecondary activities over time, because there is considerable evidence that the transition rates for both high school graduates and dropouts have remained relatively stable over the last 20 years. Therefore, the number of cohort members in a prescribed track at any time following graduation depends mainly on the initial cohort size.

In addition to describing how entire cohorts of high school graduates and dropouts sort themselves into postsecondary tracks, we examine how choices of activities vary across groups of individuals categorized by sex, race, Hispanic origin, ability level, socioeconomic status, and region. To envisage the process, one can think of having a separate flow chart like Fig. 1 for each group. Alternatively, one can partition each of the main activity boxes into smaller boxes corresponding to subpopulations of interest. In either case, tracking student flows over time entails estimating the subpopulation sizes at the outset and then monitoring their subsequent transitions across activities.

Unfortunately, providing detailed profiles of recent entrants into the sorting-out process necessitates a certain amount of guesswork, because the national data base on high school graduates and dropouts is in a sorry state. The National Center for Education Statistics (NCES), for example, cannot provide reasonably accurate estimates of the numbers of high school graduates or dropouts for any year, let alone the kinds of disaggregated data by state, sex, race, and school affiliation that are needed to profile the nation's youth, track their educational progress, and examine their potential for meeting the nation's future manpower needs.

To help fill the information gap, we have pieced together data from several sources, relying heavily on Census Bureau estimates and projections of age group sizes by state, age, and race to provide data on the cohorts of young people of school-leaving age in each state. The products of this effort include estimates of high school graduation rates by state, and estimates and projections of numbers of high school graduates by state, sex, race, and control (public or private) for the years 1980 to 2000.

Several government publications, including the *Digest of Education Statistics* (NCES, 1989) and the *Statistical Abstract of the United States* (U.S. Bureau of the Census, 1989), provide tables pertaining to numbers of high school graduates, dropout rates, and educational attainment. However, the published data are inadequate for assessing the magnitude and dimensions of the school dropout problem or for providing basic data on the sizes and compositions of the graduating classes. They are even less adequate for monitoring the postsecondary sorting-out process to examine the extent to which today's graduates are acquiring the skills to become tomorrow's managers, technicians, and teachers. In the absence of detailed, reliable information on the numbers of high school graduates and dropouts each year, the flows of students through the nation's schools and colleges are essentially unknown, making it difficult to measure the extent and severity of the dropout problem, assess the implications of the shrinking college age group, or analyze policies bearing on youth problems, such as student aid, military recruiting, and national service.

THE SCHOOL DROPOUT PROBLEM

High dropout rates have long been a matter of national concern, in part because dropping out has been linked with other high-profile youth problems—illiteracy, lack of basic skills, teenage pregnancy, drug abuse, and crime. The prevalent concern is that dropouts are ill equipped to make their way in American society and thus apt to become part of a self-perpetuating underclass, locked in poverty and prone to lifelong patterns of unemployment, welfare dependency, and criminal activity (Carnegie Council on Policy Studies in Higher Education, 1979).

While these concerns may be exaggerated, there is little doubt that the postsecondary activities of dropouts differ considerably from those of graduates in the same age group. High school graduation is a prerequisite for entrance into most postsecondary educational programs, and many employers, including the military services, use high school completion as a criterion in screening applicants for entry-level jobs and training programs. Hence, the educational and career opportunities open to dropouts may be severely limited.

It is not surprising that, as a group, high school dropouts fare poorly in the labor market. Among persons of age 16 to 24 who were not enrolled in school in October 1989, only two-thirds of the dropouts were in the civilian labor force (i.e., currently employed or seeking work), as compared with 87 percent of the high school graduates in the same category. Among those in the labor force, the unemployment rate was 20.5 percent for the dropouts, more than double the 8.5 percent rate for the high school graduates in the same category (Bureau of Labor Statistics, 1989b).

However, the causes and consequences of dropping out are by no means well understood, partly because of definitional and data problems that confound analyses of the dropout problem (Pallas, 1986). Despite the absence of uniform definitions of dropouts and the lack of hard data that permit comparisons of graduation and dropout rates across states, races, and genders, there is a continual stream of irreconcilable statistics on dropouts that add to what Chester Finn, former Assistant Secretary for Educational Research and Development, characterized as the "high school dropout puzzle" (Finn, 1987).

In part, the puzzle persists because two seemingly well-grounded methods for gauging the magnitude of the dropout problem yield radically different estimates. One method relies on the educational attainments reported by participants in the Current Population Survey. In 1987, 85 percent of all persons of age 20 to 24 reported having completed four years of high school, as did 88 percent of those of age 25 to 29 (U.S. Bureau of the Census, 1988a). These figures suggest that only about one of every eight Americans fails to complete high school.

By contrast, graduation rates derived from state data on numbers of high school graduates indicate that the above figures misrepresent the magnitude of the dropout problem by a factor of two. Our analysis of the state data in Appendix A supports the contention that, roughly speaking, one of every four 17-year-olds in the 1980s dropped out of school before graduating, a figure that has remained essentially unchanged for the last 20 years.

Although part of the disparity between the two sets of dropout rate estimates can be ascribed to definitional problems (e.g., recipients of "high school equivalency" certificates may classify themselves as graduates), the numbers still do not add up. At least part of the difference seems to be due to the nonresponse and response errors that plague population surveys, i.e., nonrespondents to the CPS are more likely to be high school dropouts, and the dropouts who respond are more likely to be misclassified (or to misclassify themselves) on educational attainment. Overreporting of educational attainment is not new; it was documented on the post-enumeration studies of both the 1950 and 1960 censuses (Folger and Nam, 1967).

Adding to the confusion about dropout statistics, the Department of Education reports high school dropout rates by state that "cover public schools only, and are calculated by dividing the number of high school graduates by the ninth-grade enrollment four years earlier" (*Chronicle of Higher Education*, September 6, 1989, pp. 6, 96). These estimates have dubious validity, because they exclude private school students, dropouts before grade nine, and returnees who take more than four years to complete grades 9–12. Moreover, the disparities in the reported rates across neighboring states are too wide to be credible, perhaps because the states use different criteria in reporting ninth-grade enrollments. In 1987, when the reported national rate was 29 percent, Michigan's rate was listed at 38 percent, whereas the rates reported by its three neighboring states—Wisconsin, Indiana, and Ohio—were just 15, 26, and 17 percent respectively. South Dakota's 20 percent rate exceeded that of its six neighbors by from 6 to 11 percentage points.

The definitional difficulties will be skirted in this study by treating dropout rates as complements of high school graduation rates, i.e., if the graduation rate in a given state is 75 percent, the dropout rate is defined to be 25 percent. The graduation rates are defined by dividing the number of high school graduates from regular day schools by the size of an age group that serves as a proxy for the number of young people who graduate from or drop out of school each year. At the national level, the number of 18-year-olds as of July 1 serves that purpose. However, at the state level, because there is substantial interstate migration among 18-year-olds, the number of 17-year-olds as of July 1 in the previous year serves the purpose better.

NUMBERS OF ENTRANTS INTO THE SORTING-OUT PROCESS

Table 1 shows Census Bureau estimates and projections of the numbers of 17- and 18-year-olds in the resident population as of July 1 each year from 1970 to 2000. The near term projections for 1990–1992 indicate that the number of 18-year-olds fell by 8 percent in 1990 and will continue to fall by 5 and 2 percent in 1991 and 1992, followed by a pattern of gradual increases from 1993 through the rest of the 1990s. See Fig. 2.

It is well known that the sizes of college age groups have declined over the 1980s. What seems to have been overlooked is that the decline has been far from uniform. In fact, the number of 18-year-olds rose steadily from 1986 to 1989. As Fig. 2 shows, the three-year decline in the numbers of 18-year-olds beginning in 1990 will be much steeper than the decline during the early 1980s. Despite the gradual increases projected for the late 1990s, the average size of the 18-year-old cohorts during the 1990s will be 11 percent smaller than the average for the 1980s.

Since high school graduation rates as well as postsecondary enrollment, employment, and enlistment rates vary considerably across regions and races, disaggregated estimates corresponding to the national estimates in Table 1 are needed to infer the ramifications of these trends on college enrollments and the youth labor market. Hence, we have compiled disaggregated estimates of age group sizes by state, race, and sex for 1980–2000. These estimates depend primarily on revised Census Bureau estimates of the resident population as of the 1980 census and are linked to their estimates and projections for the years 1986–2010 by state, race, and sex (U.S. Bureau of the Census, 1988c). See Appendix A.

Our interest in these disaggregated estimates is driven by the need for analogous estimates of numbers of high school graduates in the same categories to support our analyses of

12

Table 1

ESTIMATES AND PROJECTIONS OF THE RESIDENT POPULATION OF AGES 17 AND 18 AS OF JULY 1, 50 STATES AND D.C.: 1970–2000
(In thousands)

Year	17-year-olds			18-year-olds		
	Total	Male	Female	Total	Male	Female
1970	3845	1955	1890	3756	1888	1868
1971	3952	2007	1944	3859	1942	1917
1972	4035	2052	1984	3952	1986	1965
1973	4092	2079	2012	4029	2029	2000
1974	4251	2163	2089	4085	2061	2024
1975	4272	2173	2100	4237	2141	2096
1976	4274	2171	2103	4250	2150	2101
1977	4266	2169	2097	4238	2140	2098
1978	4344	2211	2133	4230	2141	2089
1979	4276	2176	2099	4303	2183	2119
1980	4222	2161	2062	4228	2142	2087
1981	4163	2133	2030	4160	2108	2052
1982	3993	2041	1952	4103	2083	2020
1983	3778	1934	1844	3938	1996	1942
1984	3677	1881	1796	3726	1890	1835
1985	3603	1846	1757	3628	1840	1788
1986	3675	1883	1792	3554	1805	1749
1987	3760	1930	1831	3624	1841	1783
1988	3837	1971	1866	3709	1885	1824
1989	3532	1812	1720	3783	1925	1858
1990	3345	1717	1628	3483	1770	1713
1991	3267	1679	1589	3299	1676	1622
1992	3343	1719	1624	3222	1639	1583
1993	3291	1690	1601	3296	1678	1618
1994	3440	1769	1671	3245	1650	1595
1995	3468	1781	1687	3391	1727	1665
1996	3576	1836	1740	3418	1738	1680
1997	3703	1900	1802	3524	1792	1733
1998	3758	1930	1828	3649	1855	1794
1999	3803	1953	1850	3704	1884	1819
2000	3819	1963	1856	3747	1906	1842

SOURCES: U.S. Bureau of the Census (1982, 1988b, 1988c, and unpublished estimates).

High School and Beyond. To that end, we have modified the Census Bureau estimates to provide estimated age group sizes for the same five race/ethnicity categories that are reported in HS&B—one for persons of Hispanic origin of all races and four others for non-Hispanics in the main census race categories: white, black, Asian and Pacific Islander, and native American (American Indians, Eskimos, and Aleuts). For the sake of brevity, the term "non-Hispanic" will be suppressed henceforth, and these four categories will be referred to as "White," "Black," "Asian," and "Indian" in the tables below.

While the size of the 18-year age group serves as a satisfactory base for calculating national high school graduation rates, it does not serve nearly as well in defining state graduation rates. The reason is that the states are differentially affected by the migration that occurs among 18-year-olds as they leave high school and move to attend college, seek

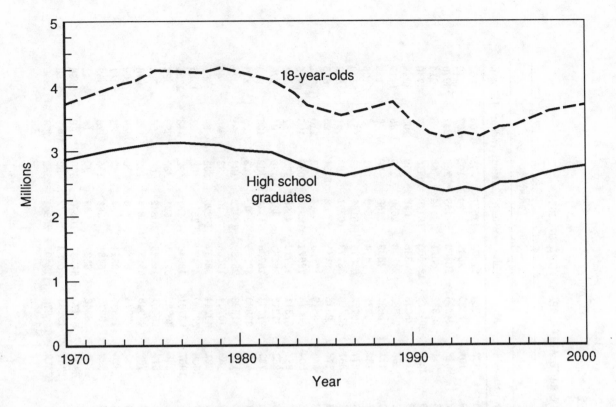

Fig. 2—Numbers of 18-year-olds and high school graduates, 1970–2000

employment, or enter the military. In particular, the District of Columbia experiences considerable immigration of 18-year-olds each year, so that the size and racial mix of the District's 18-year age group do not mirror the 17-year age group, which better reflects the size and racial composition of the District's high school population. Hence, in lieu of using the 18-year age group size as a base for calculating state high school graduation and dropout rates, we have substituted the number of 17-year-olds as of July 1 in the previous year, except for 1980, where we use the census data for the 17-year age group as of April 1.

Table A.3 in Appendix A provides estimates of the numbers of 17-year-olds by state for the years 1980–1989. The corresponding projections for 1990–2000 are listed in Table A.4. Breakdowns by sex and race/Hispanic category are provided for all years. Table 2 lists the disaggregated estimates for 1980.

During the 1980s, there was a continual shift toward increased minority representation in the school age population; this trend will continue into the 1990s. In 1980, the percentages of 17-year-olds in the five race/Hispanic categories were: White, 76.2; Black, 14.0; Asian/Pacific Islander, 1.4; Native American, 0.7; Hispanic, 7.7. The corresponding estimated percentages for 1990 are 70.1, 15.8, 2.7, 1.2, and 10.2. By the year 2000, they will become 67.5, 15.7, 3.5, 1.5, and 11.8. Thus, although minority representation has increased and will continue to increase through 2000, the changes in the race/Hispanic mix of the high school age population have been gradual.

Table 2

NUMBERS OF 17-YEAR-OLDS BY STATE, SEX, RACE, AND HISPANIC ORIGIN: 1980

State	Total	Male						Female					
		All	White	Black	Asian	Indian	Hispanic	All	White	Black	Asian	Indian	Hispanic
Alabama	74987	38193	25896	11705	89	70	433	36794	24775	11527	73	56	363
Alaska	7588	4008	2856	107	105	839	101	3580	2502	90	102	807	79
Arizona	49699	25305	17097	841	267	1852	5248	24394	16452	759	266	1847	5070
Arkansas	43594	22262	17319	4585	61	86	211	21332	16511	4444	68	95	214
California	426119	218898	133795	19825	11264	1809	52205	207221	128360	19149	10315	1657	47740
Colorado	52429	26756	21110	1061	277	168	4140	25673	20336	958	259	156	3964
Connecticut	58411	29729	25438	2650	149	36	1456	28682	24548	2530	150	35	1419
Delaware	11675	5854	4591	1111	31	10	111	5821	4529	1156	18	6	112
D. of Columbia	10508	5233	535	4512	47	7	132	5275	484	4649	31	5	106
Florida	163278	83506	58167	15473	440	149	9277	79772	55375	15156	442	150	8649
Georgia	105809	54980	36973	16856	206	64	881	50829	33772	16261	163	51	582
Hawaii	16951	8606	2306	80	5420	26	774	8345	2141	62	5281	25	836
Idaho	17620	9078	8326	36	62	109	545	8542	7985	14	62	110	371
Illinois	215191	110147	83227	18641	1157	118	7004	105044	78524	18940	1039	106	6435
Indiana	104554	53043	47084	4703	195	74	987	51511	45712	4598	150	57	994
Iowa	55121	27908	26998	450	134	63	263	27213	26265	481	130	61	276
Kansas	42796	21762	19354	1431	126	128	723	21034	18725	1428	132	136	613
Kentucky	71050	37670	33738	3386	94	34	418	33380	30216	2805	63	23	273
Louisiana	83775	42077	26430	14184	234	118	1111	41698	25869	14472	184	94	1079
Maine	21895	11191	11018	26	36	49	62	10704	10565	16	33	46	44
Maryland	81622	41408	29030	11037	551	69	721	40214	28137	10825	535	66	651
Massachusetts	106765	54696	50097	2599	425	67	1508	52069	47498	2571	403	62	1535
Michigan	180279	91578	76545	12159	532	375	1967	88701	73940	12137	492	348	1784
Minnesota	81154	41497	39859	535	327	431	345	39657	38141	521	283	373	339
Mississippi	51871	26570	15171	10947	74	61	317	25301	14045	10842	66	56	292
Missouri	92799	47851	40877	5925	222	119	708	44948	38236	5845	192	102	573
Montana	15441	8063	7359	9	35	520	140	7378	6785	5	30	449	109
Nebraska	29288	14949	13847	630	66	86	320	14339	13311	554	68	89	317
Nevada	14335	7463	5826	622	167	156	692	6872	5461	588	136	128	559
New Hampshire	16791	8545	8432	28	21	10	54	8246	8121	39	30	14	42
New Jersey	138595	71222	54358	10652	718	58	5436	67373	51031	10470	570	46	5256
New Mexico	27176	13893	6175	279	82	1271	6086	13283	5932	222	82	1281	5766
New York	322169	163299	117641	25486	2537	323	17312	158870	112401	25944	2332	298	17895

15

Table 2—continued

State	Total	Male						Female					
		All	White	Black	Asian	Indian	Hispanic	All	White	Black	Asian	Indian	Hispanic
North Carolina	109453	55808	39105	15222	222	677	582	53645	37532	14717	213	651	532
North Dakota	12607	6361	5984	16	29	294	38	6246	5910	15	25	252	44
Ohio	202028	102793	89572	11448	350	90	1333	99235	85919	11532	357	91	1336
Oklahoma	55860	29120	23706	2471	203	1996	744	26740	21734	2247	197	1928	634
Oregon	46187	23686	21706	408	371	292	909	22501	20795	418	342	268	678
Pennsylvania	213609	109234	95307	11566	549	81	1731	104375	90472	11612	492	72	1727
Rhode Island	16836	8474	7886	318	50	27	193	8362	7766	331	58	32	175
South Carolina	62325	32396	20206	11563	94	46	487	29929	18280	11184	84	40	341
South Dakota	13751	7065	6367	10	24	613	51	6686	6078	10	20	532	46
Tennessee	84545	43371	34392	8399	114	41	425	41174	32527	8162	95	36	354
Texas	268566	137581	82054	18962	997	332	35236	130985	78680	18142	852	284	33027
Utah	27185	13955	12440	224	218	278	795	13230	11999	114	212	271	634
Vermont	9747	4965	4901	12	11	8	33	4782	4727	4	9	6	36
Virginia	99692	50787	38183	11205	520	74	805	48905	36405	11146	528	76	750
Washington	74296	38037	33746	1109	1066	632	1484	36259	32412	1029	981	582	1255
West Virginia	34355	17499	16639	703	25	8	124	16856	15995	722	28	9	102
Wisconsin	93134	47414	43976	2168	200	324	746	45720	42458	2092	197	322	651
Wyoming	8337	4328	3932	32	20	72	272	4009	3636	35	20	72	246
United States	4223848	2160114	1647577	298407	31214	15240	167676	2063734	1570010	293570	28890	14359	156905

NUMBERS OF HIGH SCHOOL GRADUATES

Table 3 lists estimates of the numbers of high school graduates for 1960–1989 by control of school and sex. The estimates for the years before 1980 are taken from NCES (1989a, 1989b) and earlier publications in the same series; the sources of the more recent estimates are listed in Appendix A. The graduation rates in the last two columns are calculated by expressing the number of graduates as a percentage of the number of 17-year-olds as of July 1 in the previous year.

High school graduation rates have changed by only a few percentage points in the last 20 years, but there was a continual decline for both sexes during the 1970s followed by steady increases in the early 1980s. Graduation rates for females have typically dominated the male rates by 4–6 percentage points.

The most reliable recent data on numbers of high school graduates by state are for 1986, when the overall graduation rate was 73.4 percent (70.8 percent for males, 76.2 percent for

Table 3

NUMBERS OF HIGH SCHOOL GRADUATES BY CONTROL OF SCHOOL
AND SEX, 50 STATES AND D.C.: 1960–1989
(In thousands)

Year	High School Graduates	Control		Sex		Graduation Rate	
		Public	Private	Male	Female	Male	Female
1960	1858	1627	231	895	963	63.4	70.9
1961	1964	1725	239	955	1009	66.7	73.1
1962	1918	1678	240	938	980	66.8	72.5
1963	1943	1710	233	956	987	65.2	70.0
1964	2283	2008	275	1120	1163	66.0	71.3
1965	2658	2360	298	1311	1347	71.6	76.8
1966	2665	2367	298	1323	1342	73.9	78.3
1967	2672	2374	298	1328	1344	74.2	78.4
1968	2695	2395	300	1338	1357	73.6	77.1
1969	2822	2522	300	1399	1423	74.8	79.4
1970	2889	2589	300	1430	1459	75.2	78.4
1971	2937	2637	300	1454	1483	74.4	78.5
1972	2999	2699	300	1486	1513	74.0	77.8
1973	3030	2730	300	1497	1533	73.0	77.3
1974	3063	2763	300	1507	1556	72.5	77.3
1975	3123	2823	300	1537	1586	71.1	75.9
1976	3137	2837	300	1547	1590	71.1	75.7
1977	3130	2840	290	1536	1594	70.8	75.8
1978	3115	2825	290	1525	1590	70.3	75.8
1979	3097	2817	280	1513	1584	68.4	74.3
1980	3021	2748	274	1485	1536	68.8	73.2
1981	3001	2725	276	1474	1527	68.2	74.0
1982	2984	2705	279	1470	1514	68.9	74.6
1983	2871	2598	274	1411	1460	69.1	74.8
1984	2764	2495	269	1363	1401	70.5	76.0
1985	2683	2414	269	1322	1361	70.3	75.8
1986	2645	2382	263	1307	1339	70.8	76.2
1987	2694	2426	284	1331	1363	70.7	76.1
1988	2753	2482	271	1362	1391	70.6	76.0
1989	2807	2533	275	1390	1418	70.5	76.0

females). Given that the estimated numbers of graduates have consistently run less than three-fourths the numbers of 17-year-olds since the mid-1970s, we can only conclude that one of every four 17-year-olds dropped out of school before graduation. The fact that the youth population contains such a high proportion of high school dropouts implies a colossal wastage of human resources, but this reality has been blurred by national statistics on educational attainment indicating that the dropout problem is far less serious. As was noted earlier, in 1987, 85 percent of the population of age 20 to 24 reported having completed four years of high school, as did 88 percent of those of age 25 to 29.

Although part of the discrepancy between educational attainment statistics and graduation rates may result from survey respondents overstating their educational attainments, a more likely explanation is that many high school dropouts pursue postsecondary educational programs that are difficult to quantify in years of educational attainment. In particular, an increasing number of high school dropouts obtain General Educational Development (GED) credentials—428,000 were issued in 1986 as compared with 333,000 in 1976 (NCES, 1988). And many high school dropouts pursue postsecondary training programs in community colleges and vocational-technical schools. In responding to surveys, many of them probably classify themselves as having completed 12 years of school and perhaps one or more years of college, thereby confounding national statistics on educational attainment. Although the Armed Forces maintain the distinction between high school diploma graduates and GED recipients in setting enlistment standards, the blurring of high school graduate status in the labor market has undoubtedly become more pervasive over time.

NUMBERS OF GRADUATES FROM PRIVATE SCHOOLS

Reliable counts of high school graduates have not existed for many years. The NCES routinely gathers state data on public high school graduates and publishes them in the *Digest of Education Statistics* (NCES, 1989). But NCES has undertaken no systematic effort to collect complete data on numbers of graduates from private schools since the mid-1960s. The often cited data for 1980, which were derived from a sample survey using an out-of-date sampling frame, do not accord with state data from other sources.

To provide better information on private high school graduates and more detailed state data on the flows of students through public schools, the Western Interstate Commission for Higher Education compiled a data base on enrollments by grade level and numbers of graduates, both public and private, for the academic years 1978–79 through 1985–86. Although some states were unable to provide time series of private school graduates, WICHE published the time series that were available as well as their best estimates for 1986 (WICHE, 1988).

Our tabulations of WICHE's state estimates by census division for the states with no missing values showed small, relatively uniform increases in the private/public ratio from 1980 to 1986. Led by the consistency of this pattern both within and across regions, we estimated the missing 1980–1985 values in the WICHE time series by using their 1986 estimates and applying the assumption that the private/public ratios for 1980–1986 in the "missing states" were proportional to the overall ratios for the nonmissing states in the same region.

The resulting state estimates for both public and private schools are given in Table 4. They indicate that the numbers of private school graduates changed little from 1980 to 1986, while the public schools were producing fewer and fewer graduates. Private schools

Table 4

NUMBERS OF HIGH SCHOOL GRADUATES BY CONTROL OF SCHOOL AND STATE: 1980–1986

State	Public School Graduates							Private School Graduates						
	1980	1981	1982	1983	1984	1985	1986	1980	1981	1982	1983	1984	1985	1986
Alabama	45190	44894	45409	44352	42021	40002	39620	3453	3353	3467	3299	3221	3175	3235
Alaska	5223	5343	5477	5622	5457	5184	5464	89	92	105	114	116	113	110
Arizona	28633	28416	28049	26530	28332	27877	27533	777	780	855	856	952	959	875
Arkansas	29052	29577	29710	28447	27049	26342	26227	907	952	969	844	859	840	805
California	249217	242172	241343	236897	232199	225448	229026	22309	21217	24581	25097	25434	25695	23124
Colorado	36804	35897	35494	34875	32954	32255	32621	2370	2337	2566	2668	2626	2632	2458
Connecticut	37683	38369	37706	36204	33679	32126	33571	7423	7515	7530	7790	7539	7484	7341
Delaware	7582	7349	7144	6924	6410	5893	5791	1472	1654	1654	1635	1662	1609	1608
D. of Columbia	4959	4848	4871	4909	4073	3940	3875	1182	1129	1160	1139	973	975	987
Florida	87324	88755	90736	86871	85908	81140	83029	9357	9297	9715	9063	9234	9031	9507
Georgia	61621	62963	64489	63293	60718	58654	59082	4089	4085	4276	4089	4042	4043	4190
Hawaii	11493	11472	11563	10757	10454	10092	9958	2520	2522	2385	2494	2494	2424	2510
Idaho	13187	12679	12560	12126	11732	12148	12059	232	237	228	223	263	243	238
Illinois	135579	136795	136534	128814	122561	117027	114319	19137	19803	20268	20047	19374	19027	18451
Indiana	73143	73381	73984	70549	65710	63308	59817	4203	5226	4218	4559	3638	4297	4029
Iowa	43445	42635	41509	39569	37248	36087	34279	3148	3231	3107	3076	2957	2974	2795
Kansas	30890	29397	28298	28316	26730	25983	25587	1617	1578	1562	1732	1580	1577	1608
Kentucky	41203	41714	42531	40478	39645	37999	37288	4244	4158	4182	4124	3891	3714	3608
Louisiana	46297	46199	39895	39539	39400	39742	39965	8634	8372	8104	7124	7510	7816	8357
Maine	15445	15554	14764	14600	13935	13924	13006	1816	1841	1827	1840	1870	1797	1767
Maryland	54270	54050	54621	52446	50684	48299	46700	6576	6843	6957	6907	6756	6876	6738
Massachusetts	73802	74831	73414	71219	65885	63411	60360	11872	12310	12301	12273	11611	11601	11162
Michigan	124316	124372	121030	112950	108926	105908	101042	11788	11757	11614	10460	10900	11345	10742
Minnesota	64908	64166	62145	59015	55376	53352	51988	4296	4277	4284	4098	4217	4178	4161
Mississippi	27586	28083	28023	27271	26324	25315	25134	2351	2339	2386	2262	2250	2241	2289
Missouri	62265	60359	59872	56420	53388	51290	49204	5815	6509	5966	6379	6000	6137	5663
Montana	12135	11634	11162	10689	10224	10016	9761	434	462	454	391	322	354	318
Nebraska	22410	21411	21027	19986	18674	18036	17845	2384	2307	2377	2187	2197	2043	1953
Nevada	8473	9069	9240	8979	8726	8572	8784	300	306	359	370	370	383	391
New Hampshire	11722	11552	11669	11470	11478	11052	10648	1580	1592	1638	1656	1695	1694	1650
New Jersey	94564	93168	93750	90048	85569	81547	78781	16642	16768	17187	16977	16498	16323	15939
New Mexico	18424	17915	17635	16530	15914	15622	15468	709	1182	1091	1235	1390	1308	1417
New York	204064	198465	194605	184022	174762	166752	162165	31873	31772	32251	32060	31139	30843	30428

Table 4—continued

State	Public School Graduates							Private School Graduates						
	1980	1981	1982	1983	1984	1985	1986	1980	1981	1982	1983	1984	1985	1986
North Carolina	70862	69395	71210	68783	66803	67245	65865	2832	2711	2843	2676	2678	2791	2813
North Dakota	9928	9924	9504	8886	8569	8146	7610	803	711	722	715	701	586	539
Ohio	144169	143503	139899	133524	127837	122281	119561	15000	14540	14698	14600	14540	13692	13244
Oklahoma	39305	38875	38347	36799	35254	34626	34452	636	615	620	580	572	582	596
Oregon	29939	28729	28780	28099	27214	26870	26286	1371	1499	1455	1466	1590	1503	1460
Pennsylvania	146458	144645	143356	137494	132412	127226	122871	24188	24557	24185	22835	22332	22440	22134
Rhode Island	10864	10719	10545	10533	9652	9201	8749	1807	1823	1827	1877	1759	1859	1761
South Carolina	38697	38347	38647	37570	36800	34500	34500	2346	2272	2341	2217	2238	2172	2235
South Dakota	10689	10385	9864	9206	8638	8206	7870	755	746	686	698	666	743	512
Tennessee	49845	50648	51447	46704	44711	43293	43263	3125	3105	3223	2851	2812	2820	2899
Texas	171449	171665	172085	168897	161580	159234	161150	9005	8814	9030	8636	8513	8687	9044
Utah	20035	19886	19400	19350	19606	19890	19774	247	234	267	233	268	299	299
Vermont	6733	6424	6513	6011	6002	5769	5794	992	968	1000	949	969	967	982
Virginia	66621	67126	67809	65571	62177	60959	63113	3931	3872	3998	3767	3681	3737	3980
Washington	50402	50046	50148	45809	44919	45431	45805	2526	2592	2624	2779	2821	2937	2937
West Virginia	23369	23580	23589	23561	22613	22262	21870	1007	720	763	735	696	651	676
Wisconsin	69332	67743	67357	64321	62189	58851	58340	6901	7949	6889	6716	6352	6314	6182
Wyoming	6072	6161	5999	5909	5764	5687	5587	158	162	176	183	186	188	171
United States	2747678	2725285	2704758	2597744	2494885	2414020	2382457	273529	275693	278971	273581	268954	268719	262918

accounted for approximately 9 percent of the nation's high school graduates in 1980 and 10 percent in 1986.

Table 5 shows the high school graduation rates by state that result from expressing each state's total number of high school graduates as a percentage of the number of 17-year-olds in the previous year. Led by the stability in the U.S. graduation rates from 1984 to 1986 and by the flatness of the public school rates through 1987 (see Appendix A), we extended the state estimates for both public and private schools through 1989 by incorporating the assumption that the estimated state graduation rates for 1987 would persist through 1989 and applying the state rates to the Census Bureau estimates of the 17-year age group sizes by state, sex, and race for 1987–1989. Since the scheme could be readily extended into the 1990s using Census Bureau projections of age group sizes, the same procedure was used to generate projections of numbers of graduates for the years 1990–2000. See Table A.2 in Appendix A.

THE CHANGING COMPOSITION OF THE GRADUATING CLASSES

To estimate the composition of graduating classes by state, sex, race, and Hispanic origin, we relied heavily on the percentages of persons of age 19 who reported having completed four years of high school in the 1980 census. Treating the 1980 regional high school completion rates by sex, race, and Hispanic origin as first approximations for high school graduation rates and applying them to each state's numbers of 17-year-olds in those categories, we derived preliminary estimates of the number of graduates in each cell. These preliminary estimates were then rescaled using iterative proportional fitting so that the numbers of graduates in the various categories summed to the state total for that year.

The procedure for estimating the number of private school graduates in each category was similar in that, as a first approximation for each state, we used regional estimates of the percentages of high school students of each race that were enrolled in private schools as of the 1980 census. These preliminary estimates were then rescaled to conform to the state totals.

Table B.1 shows the estimated composition of the 1980 graduating class by census division, control of school, sex, and race/Hispanic category. According to these estimates, the percentages of high school graduates in the five race/Hispanic categories were: White, 81.6; Black, 11.2; Asian/Pacific Islander, 1.5; Native American, 0.5; Hispanic, 5.1. The analogous estimated percentages for the Class of 1990 are 76.7, 12.9, 2.7, 0.9, and 6.8. For the Class of 2000, the projected percentages are 74.0, 13.2, 3.6, 1.1, and 8.0. Thus, the estimated percentage of graduates from minority groups increased from 18.4 percent in 1980 to 23.3 percent in 1990, and it is projected to increase to 26.0 percent in 2000.

In addition to the shift in the race/Hispanic composition of the graduating classes, another noteworthy demographic trend is the shift toward increasing numbers of graduates from southern and western states. As can be seen from Table 5, the percentages of 1980 graduates in the four census regions were: Northeast, 23.2; North Central, 28.7; South, 30.8; West, 17.3. The corresponding estimated percentages for 1990 are 20.6, 26.4, 33.9, and 19.1. In 2000, they are projected to become 19.1, 24.5, 34.2, and 22.2.

Since minority students are less likely to attend private schools and since private schools account for smaller proportions of graduates in the South and West, both of these demographic trends portend smaller proportions of private school graduates in the 1990s.

Table 5

HIGH SCHOOL GRADUATION RATES BY STATE: 1980–1986

State	Year						
	1980	1981	1982	1983	1984	1985	1986
Alabama	64.9	64.3	66.0	66.8	66.8	66.3	67.0
Alaska	70.0	71.6	73.2	77.9	78.3	75.7	79.8
Arizona	59.2	58.7	58.3	56.8	63.1	62.1	60.5
Arkansas	68.7	70.0	71.5	71.2	73.9	74.8	75.2
California	63.7	61.8	63.0	64.4	66.8	66.6	67.6
Colorado	74.7	72.9	73.8	76.1	77.6	77.0	77.4
Connecticut	77.2	78.6	78.7	79.9	77.3	77.9	83.1
Delaware	77.6	77.1	76.3	77.3	75.8	72.7	75.8
D. of Columbia	58.4	56.9	57.4	58.8	52.0	53.7	56.2
Florida	59.2	60.1	62.2	61.6	64.1	61.5	63.9
Georgia	62.1	63.4	65.8	66.6	66.1	64.6	65.8
Hawaii	82.7	82.6	78.3	74.9	78.4	81.0	83.5
Idaho	76.2	73.3	74.4	76.1	77.3	81.1	81.9
Illinois	71.9	72.8	74.2	73.8	75.5	74.9	75.8
Indiana	74.0	75.2	76.0	76.4	75.8	75.3	73.6
Iowa	84.5	83.2	82.8	83.8	85.0	86.7	86.1
Kansas	76.0	72.4	71.2	75.5	76.8	78.7	80.3
Kentucky	64.0	64.6	67.2	67.3	70.8	69.9	70.3
Louisiana	65.6	65.1	58.0	58.4	62.5	64.8	67.5
Maine	78.8	79.4	77.5	80.9	81.3	82.6	80.0
Maryland	74.9	74.6	76.2	76.1	77.2	76.5	75.6
Massachusetts	80.2	81.6	81.6	83.1	80.3	80.4	78.7
Michigan	75.5	75.5	74.7	72.6	74.6	74.6	72.8
Minnesota	85.3	84.3	83.7	84.2	85.0	87.2	87.7
Mississippi	57.7	58.6	59.5	59.8	62.4	61.8	62.3
Missouri	73.4	72.1	72.4	72.6	74.7	74.6	74.3
Montana	81.4	78.3	76.7	77.6	82.0	83.5	85.5
Nebraska	84.7	81.0	81.6	81.8	83.6	85.0	86.9
Nevada	61.2	65.4	67.6	68.3	68.4	68.0	70.3
New Hampshire	79.2	78.3	80.2	81.9	83.4	80.5	77.3
New Jersey	80.2	79.3	81.3	81.9	81.3	81.0	81.1
New Mexico	70.4	70.3	69.2	67.5	71.3	73.1	75.0
New York	73.2	71.5	71.3	70.6	69.9	69.9	70.7
North Carolina	67.3	65.9	68.4	68.5	69.9	70.9	69.3
North Dakota	85.1	84.4	83.1	82.7	87.4	86.2	86.6
Ohio	78.8	78.2	77.9	78.3	79.9	78.3	79.0
Oklahoma	71.5	70.7	70.8	71.4	74.8	76.4	76.3
Oregon	67.8	65.4	66.9	69.2	70.5	71.9	72.2
Pennsylvania	79.9	79.2	79.7	79.7	80.8	80.6	80.3
Rhode Island	75.3	74.5	74.5	77.4	73.5	72.3	69.2
South Carolina	65.9	65.2	66.5	66.9	69.3	67.2	67.8
South Dakota	83.2	80.9	77.8	77.0	80.0	83.5	81.6
Tennessee	62.7	63.6	65.6	61.8	62.6	62.4	63.8
Texas	67.2	67.2	68.4	69.4	70.1	69.5	69.8
Utah	74.6	74.0	73.8	77.3	81.5	80.3	80.1
Vermont	79.3	75.8	78.4	75.9	78.8	78.1	79.6
Virginia	70.8	71.2	73.0	73.3	73.7	74.3	77.8
Washington	71.2	70.8	72.3	70.2	73.1	75.9	76.5
West Virginia	71.0	70.7	72.3	75.6	77.1	77.7	76.7
Wisconsin	81.9	81.3	81.4	82.0	83.8	82.4	85.7
Wyoming	74.7	75.8	75.7	79.0	81.9	83.7	82.5
United States	71.5	71.0	71.7	71.9	73.2	73.0	73.4

According to the projections in Table A.2, there will be a gradual reduction in the percentage of private school graduates over time—from 9.9 percent in 1986 to 9.6 in 2000.

In summary, the compositions of the high school graduating classes changed during the 1980s to reflect greater minority representation in most states and more rapid growth in the South and West. These trends will persist through the 1990s. However, the major changes that we foresee in the near term do not pertain to the compositions of the graduating classes but to their overall sizes. The high school graduating classes are projected to shrink by 15 percent between 1989 and 1992. The consequences of those changes depend critically on how the graduates sort themselves into postsecondary paths.

III. MAIN ACTIVITIES AFTER LEAVING SCHOOL

This section examines patterns of postsecondary activities followed by high school graduates and dropouts during the first year after leaving school. We begin with a summary of trends pertaining to the numbers of graduates and dropouts who enter the three main postsecondary tracks—college, military service, and civilian employment. Time series from several sources are presented to provide an overview of young people's educational and vocational pursuits, and to examine a long-standing contention that, except for disruptions for military service during times of war, postsecondary sorting-out patterns have been relatively stable for many years.

Then, drawing on a large panel study of over 26,000 seniors in the Classes of 1980 and 1982, we present analyses of the seniors' main activities in October following graduation to show how individuals from varying backgrounds sort themselves into postsecondary tracks. Primary attention is given to examining the relevance of sex, race, Hispanic origin, socioeconomic status, academic aptitude, and economic factors on decisions to enter college or enlist in the Armed Forces.

LONG-TERM TRENDS

For the most part, previous studies of the postsecondary sorting-out process were restricted to educational pursuits. Some noteworthy exceptions are Johnston and Bachman (1972), who examined enlistment behavior during the Vietnam Conflict; Ornstein (1976), who used retrospective data to study entrance into the labor force; and Hosek and Peterson (1985) and Hosek, Peterson, and Eden (1986), who studied enlistment behavior during 1979 among males of age 17–22.

Studies of college attendance patterns before 1970 pointed to ever-increasing educational attainment among college-age youth. Although consistent time series on college enrollment by level and sex were not available before World War II, the data on earned degrees indicated continual increases in college enrollment rates and degree attainments from 1900 to 1940, except during World War I.

More detailed analyses of enrollment patterns from 1940 to 1970 revealed wide fluctuations in college enrollment patterns, especially for men. During the early stages of World War II, the Korean War, and the Vietnam Conflict, college entrance rates dropped as millions of Americans postponed or interrupted their educational and career pursuits to enter the military. The most pronounced disruptions were during World War II, when most able-bodied young men either enlisted or were inducted into military service, decimating college enrollments between 1941 and 1945. After the war, more than two million veterans swamped the college campuses, many of them staying on to complete bachelor's and advanced degrees under the G.I. Bill. Whereas colleges had awarded 129,000 degrees to men in 1940 and less than half that many in 1944, the number soared to 376,000 in 1950 (Adkins, 1975).

College enrollment patterns for men were also greatly affected during the Korean War. With almost 500,000 inductions per year from 1951 to 1953, college entrance rates dropped sharply. After the war, nearly 1.2 million veterans entered college under the Korean G.I. Bill, swelling college enrollments and stimulating degree production through the early 1960s.

Despite these disruptions of normal college attendance patterns during World War II and the Korean War, there was a remarkable finding in the mid-1960s that patterns of educational attainment beyond high school and persistence through college had been very stable across age groups since the early 1900s. In a widely quoted paper based on their analysis of educational attainment data in the 1940 and 1960 censuses, Jaffe and Adams (1964) wrote:

> Roughly half of all the white men who graduate from high school go on to college. Roughly 4 in 10 white women and nonwhite students who graduate from high school go on to college.... One assumption is that a larger proportion of high school graduates now goes on to college. We find, on the contrary, that the proportion continues to be the same.... We find that slightly over half the men are receiving their degrees and about 4 in 10 women are completing four years. These proportions continue long-standing trends.

Whether this very simple characterization of college entrance and persistence patterns held for the period before 1960 is debatable, but their contention about the long-term stability of college entrance rates became untenable during the 1960s when the rates increased markedly, especially for women. Folger, Astin and Bayer, (1970), in their report for the Commission on Human Resources and Advanced Education, presented data from several sources indicating that college entrance rates rose substantially in the late 1950s and early 1960s. A subsequent study for the Carnegie Commission on Higher Education reported consistently rising college entrance rates during the 1950s and 1960s for women and parallel increases for men after allowing for the surges of veterans into college following World War II and the Korean War (Haggstrom, 1971). That study also showed that college persistence and degree completion rates for women increased during the 1960s, bringing their rates up to the male levels, which remained relatively stable during the 1950s and 1960s despite the clear-cut effects of the Korean and Vietnam Wars on college enrollment.

As the U.S. heightened its military commitment to the Vietnam Conflict in the mid-1960s, normal college attendance patterns were again disrupted. College entrance rates fell slightly in 1966 as over 500,000 enlistees and 300,000 inductees entered military service. Opposition to the draft and U.S. military policies in Vietnam mounted over the next three years. With draft calls continuing to run between 200,000 and 300,000 from 1967 to 1969, college enrollments were stimulated as many men took advantage of the draft deferments available for full-time college students. Other men sought exemption from the draft through reserve participation, leading to long waiting lists of men trying to enlist in reserve and National Guard units.

The uncertainties that beset college age males subject to the draft were lessened when the first draft lottery was implemented in December 1969. With greatly reduced numbers of draft calls in 1970 and 1971, the phasing out of student deferments, and the advent of the All-Volunteer Force in 1972, the wartime effects on college enrollment dwindled in the 1970s except for the large numbers of veterans attending college.

In addition to the Vietnam Conflict, another important factor affecting college enrollments in the late 1960s was the aftereffect of the postwar baby boom. High school graduating classes underwent very rapid growth in the middle and late 1960s (see Table 3). As the postwar baby boomers graduated from high school and entered college, enrollments soared. The number of college degrees awarded at the bachelor's level and above more than doubled between 1960 and 1970, reaching 1,071,000 in 1970. Because degree production during the late 1960s was so much higher than it had been in previous decades, the stock of persons in the U.S. holding college degrees also increased rapidly, from 1.6 million in 1960 to 2.8 million in 1970 (Adkins, 1975), leading to an oversupply of college-trained personnel in the 1970s, especially in the field of education.

There were other factors on the horizon in the late 1960s that may have affected post-secondary pursuits. The economy slipped into a minor recession in December 1969 that lasted for 11 months. Although this recession was not as severe as the later recession of 1973–1975, the fact that it occurred following a nine-year period of rapid economic expansion and at the same time that the Vietnam Conflict was winding down may have heightened its effects on young people's educational and career pursuits.

CHANGES IN THE SORTING-OUT PROCESS IN THE 1970s AND 1980s

Before the implementation of the draft lottery in December 1969, young men had been subject to the draft through age 26, with older men being called first. Various kinds of deferments were available before 1970, the most common being for college attendance. Before these deferments were phased out beginning in 1970, college age men could forestall the uncertainties of the draft by maintaining full-time student status, which led more men to complete bachelor's and advanced degrees during the late 1960s and early 1970s than there might otherwise have been.

The draft lottery of 1969 and those that followed in 1970 and 1971 for men turning 19 years of age were significant, because they permitted college age men to plan their futures with almost complete certainty that their educational and vocational pursuits would not be interrupted for military service. Only those with low random selection numbers faced imminent induction, and they could avoid being called to active duty by enlisting in one of the active reserve components. Many young men with low random selection numbers exercised that option during the first six months of 1970.

The extent to which these changes influenced postsecondary pursuits is difficult to ascertain, but the evidence points to a turning point in the sorting-out process in 1970 as the pressure exerted by the draft on enrollments at all levels lost its force. Johnston and Bachman (1972) reported that concerns about the draft were central considerations affecting high school seniors' plans in 1969. Although it seems doubtful that the draft could have had an appreciable effect on high school completion rates, high school graduation rates began their decade-long decline in 1970, dropping from a peak of 77 percent in 1969 to a low of 71 percent in 1981. See Table 3.

There was also a marked change in college enrollment patterns in the late 1960s and early 1970s. While freshman enrollment rates for women continued to increase during the 1970s, those for men went down. See Table 6. The freshman enrollment rates were determined by expressing the number of full-time freshman enrollments as a percentage of the number of high school graduates in the same year, as reported in Table 3.[1]

These differences between the male and female rates underscore the huge gender gap in college enrollment patterns that existed in 1970. Men outnumbered women in the 1970 freshman class by about four to three, and almost the same ratio held for bachelor's degree

---

[1]The "freshman enrollments" reported here are for first-time students, i.e., entering students who have not previously attended other institutions of higher education. We chose to use *full-time* freshman enrollments, instead of *total* enrollments, in calculating the enrollment rates to make them more comparable with college entrance rates reported later in this report. Also, the rates shown should not be interpreted as the percentages of graduates in a specific year who entered college as full-time students that year. Any fall freshman class includes many entering freshmen from previous years' graduating classes, as well as students who were not members of any graduating class (e.g., foreign students and students who did not earn high school diplomas). Also, some entering freshmen do not enroll for the first time during the fall term. The rates are given mainly to indicate college entrance trends during the 1970s and 1980s. They can, however, also be regarded as rough estimates of the percentages of the graduates in each class who entered college as full-time students at some stage following graduation.

Table 6

FULL-TIME FRESHMAN ENROLLMENTS AND FRESHMAN ENROLLMENT
RATES BY SEX: FALL 1967 TO FALL 1987

Year	Full-Time Freshman Enrollment (in Thousands)			Freshman Enrollment Rate		
	Total	Male	Female	Total	Male	Female
1967	1335	761	574	50.0	57.3	42.7
1968	1471	847	624	54.6	63.3	46.0
1969	1525	876	649	54.0	62.6	45.6
1970	1567	896	691	54.2	62.7	47.4
1971	1606	896	710	54.7	61.6	47.9
1972	1574	858	716	52.5	57.7	47.3
1973	1607	867	740	53.1	57.9	48.3
1974	1673	896	777	54.6	59.5	49.9
1975	1763	942	821	56.5	61.3	51.8
1976	1663	855	808	53.0	55.3	50.8
1977	1681	840	841	53.7	54.7	52.8
1978	1651	817	834	53.0	53.5	52.5
1979	1706	840	866	55.1	55.5	54.7
1980	1749	862	887	57.9	58.0	57.7
1981	1738	852	886	57.9	57.8	58.0
1982	1688	837	851	56.6	56.9	56.2
1983	1678	825	853	58.4	58.5	58.4
1984	1613	786	827	58.4	57.7	59.0
1985	1602	775	827	59.8	58.6	60.8
1986	1590	769	821	60.1	58.8	61.3
1987	1627	779	848	60.3	58.5	62.2

SOURCE: NCES (1989a, Table 159).

recipients that year (NCES, 1989a). These disparities vanished during the 1970s and early 1980s as the freshman enrollment rates for women followed a relatively steady upward path and the rates for men remained relatively stable except for a dip in the late 1970s. The cross-over year for degree completions was 1982, when there were more bachelor's degrees awarded to women than men for the first time since World War II.

The large numbers of Vietnam veterans returning to college in the early 1970s inflated the male freshman enrollment rates somewhat from 1970 to 1975, exaggerating the gender gap. The 10-percent difference in 1975 shrank to nearly zero in 1980, after which time the rates remained nearly the same for both sexes through 1983. A possible explanation for the rate divergence that began in 1984 is that a larger proportion of male high school graduates postponed college entrance for a few years. It is notable that the year of divergence was the year in which the Montgomery G.I. Bill was enacted, indicating that the effects of military service on college attendance patterns did not end with the creation of the All-Volunteer Force.

ENLISTMENTS IN THE ALL-VOLUNTEER FORCE

Table 7 shows the numbers of persons who entered the service as enlisted personnel by sex and high school graduate status for the years 1972–1987. The "military enlistment rates" are calculated by expressing the number of nonprior service accessions each year as a percentage of the number of 18-year-olds as of July 1 in the same year. For the high school graduate accessions, the base for the enlistment rate was taken to be the number of high school graduates in the same year.

Table 7

NUMBERS OF NONPRIOR SERVICE ACCESSIONS BY SEX AND
HIGH SCHOOL GRADUATE STATUS: 1972–1987

	All Accessions			HSG Accessions		
Year	Total	Male	Female	Total	Male	Female
NUMBERS OF NONPRIOR SERVICE ACCESSIONS (IN THOUSANDS)						
1972	396	382	14	266	253	13
1973	428	408	20	281	262	19
1974	391	360	31	237	209	28
1975	415	378	37	277	244	33
1976	397	366	31	269	241	28
1977	381	351	30	270	242	28
1978	308	270	38	232	198	34
1979	310	269	41	223	186	37
1980	356	307	49	242	200	42
1981	321	280	41	260	222	38
1982	298	265	33	256	224	32
1983	302	266	36	281	246	35
1984	305	269	36	284	249	35
1985	287	250	37	266	230	36
1986	299	263	36	275	239	36
1987	296	260	36	276	240	36
MILITARY ENLISTMENT RATES						
1972	10.0	19.2	0.7	9.0	17.0	0.9
1973	10.6	20.1	1.0	9.4	17.5	1.2
1974	9.6	17.5	1.5	7.8	13.9	1.8
1975	9.8	17.7	1.8	9.0	15.9	2.1
1976	9.3	17.0	1.5	8.6	15.6	1.8
1977	9.0	16.4	1.4	8.6	15.8	1.8
1978	7.3	12.6	1.8	7.4	13.0	2.1
1979	7.2	12.3	1.9	7.2	12.3	2.3
1980	8.4	14.3	2.3	8.0	13.5	2.7
1981	7.7	13.3	2.0	8.7	15.1	2.5
1982	7.3	12.7	1.6	8.6	15.2	2.1
1983	7.7	13.3	1.9	9.8	17.4	2.4
1984	8.2	14.2	2.0	10.2	18.3	2.5
1985	7.9	13.6	2.1	9.9	17.4	2.6
1986	8.4	14.6	2.1	10.4	18.3	2.7
1987	8.2	14.1	2.0	10.2	18.0	2.6

Although not all enlistees enter the service at age 18 and not all high school graduates enter the service the same year they graduate, the enlistment rates serve as crude estimates of the percentages of the cohorts who enter military service. The rates in the table indicate that the proportion of 18-year-olds entering the military has remained quite stable over the 1980s, but the proportion of male high school graduates who enter military service has risen substantially—from around 12 percent in 1979 to over 18 percent in 1984.

It is noteworthy that the large increases in the enlistment rates occurred in the early 1980s when the numbers of graduates were either changing little or declining. In particular, the 34 percent increase in the number of male high school graduate accessions between 1979 and 1984 occurred during a period in which the corresponding numbers of high school graduates went down by 10 percent. While the rates do not take into account the time lags between high school graduation and service entrance (a topic that we return to in Section IV), it is clear from this table that, during the 1980s, more and more male high school graduates included military service in their postsecondary career paths. For a thorough treatment of the geographic and demographic attributes of enlistees during the 1980s, see *Population Representation in the Military Services: Fiscal Year 1987*, Office of the Assistant Secretary of Defense (Force Management and Personnel), August 1988.

OCTOBER ACTIVITIES OF GRADUATES AND DROPOUTS

To provide a more definitive examination of trends in postsecondary activities during the first few months after leaving school, we turn to national statistics on the enrollment and employment statuses of high school graduates and dropouts as of October in the year that they left school. See Table 8. These statistics, which are derived from time series published in the *Handbook of Labor Statistics* (Bureau of Labor Statistics, 1989a), refer to activities reported in the October Current Population Survey. Because the CPS is a household survey designed to provide information on the civilian noninstitutional population, the activities of graduates who entered the military before October are not included. Also, because the statistics are based on survey data, the estimates are subject to sampling and response errors.[2]

The time series of enrollment rates in Table 8 evidence many of the same patterns that were apparent in the freshman enrollment rates in Table 6, even though the numerators in these rates are quite different. Whereas the numerator for the freshman enrollment rate includes all full-time entering students regardless of when they completed high school, the numerator of the enrollment rate reported in Table 8 is restricted to freshmen who graduated from high school the same year but includes both part-time and full-time students.

Both time series indicate that college entrance rates for male graduates dropped in the aftermath of the Vietnam Conflict, rebounded in the early 1980s, and then remained stable from 1984 to 1987. The two time series for women show slightly different patterns, in that the college entrance rates in Table 8 do not show the pronounced upward trend during the 1970s that is evident in Table 6. However, both Tables 6 and 8 support the conclusion that the gender gap in college entrance rates shrank during the 1970s, leading to approximate parity in the male and female rates in the early 1980s.

---

[2]The standard errors of the enrollment rates reported in Table 8 are approximately 2.0 percent (U.S. Bureau of the Census, 1988b). The numbers of graduates reported here are estimated totals based on CPS responses. Even though these estimates exclude high school graduates in military service, they tend to run somewhat higher than the estimates in Appendix A derived from state data.

Table 8

ENROLLMENT AND EMPLOYMENT STATUSES OF RECENT HIGH SCHOOL
GRADUATES IN OCTOBER, 1967–1987

| | Total | | Enrolled | | Not Enrolled | | | | | |
| | | | | | Employed | | Unemployed | | Others | |
Year	Male	Female	Male	Female	Male	Female	Male	Female	Male	Female
NUMBERS OF GRADUATES (IN THOUSANDS)										
1967	1142	1384	658	653	379	422	40	115	65	194
1968	1184	1422	748	696	345	437	39	83	52	206
1969	1352	1490	812	704	449	480	37	83	54	223
1970	1343	1414	741	686	458	383	68	118	76	227
1971	1371	1502	789	747	451	420	73	108	58	227
1972	1423	1542	751	708	538	519	75	107	59	208
1973	1463	1602	733	695	596	561	63	100	71	246
1974	1498	1611	740	738	576	551	105	126	77	196
1975	1522	1674	801	819	534	492	126	129	61	234
1976	1461	1540	692	774	584	473	118	115	67	178
1977	1495	1661	781	818	555	566	93	116	66	161
1978	1500	1679	767	827	598	575	75	118	60	159
1979	1491	1689	753	817	584	581	95	136	59	155
1980	1518	1593	712	824	585	500	138	116	83	153
1981	1490	1563	816	830	472	455	114	139	88	139
1982	1508	1592	739	829	499	427	161	170	109	166
1983	1390	1574	721	841	442	440	152	150	75	143
1984	1429	1583	800	862	434	430	130	126	65	165
1985	1286	1380	754	785	346	353	112	116	74	126
1986	1300	1402	732	720	396	422	97	106	74	154
1987	1278	1369	746	757	409	378	65	106	59	127
PERCENTAGES OF GRADUATES										
1967	100.	100.	57.6	47.2	33.2	30.5	3.5	8.3	5.7	14.0
1968	100.	100.	63.2	48.9	29.1	30.7	3.3	5.8	4.4	14.5
1969	100.	100.	60.0	47.2	33.2	32.2	2.7	5.6	4.0	15.0
1970	100.	100.	55.2	48.5	34.1	27.1	5.1	8.3	5.6	16.1
1971	100.	100.	57.6	49.7	32.9	28.0	5.3	7.2	4.2	15.1
1972	100.	100.	52.8	45.9	37.8	33.7	5.3	6.9	4.1	13.5
1973	100.	100.	50.1	43.4	40.7	35.0	4.3	6.2	4.9	15.4
1974	100.	100.	49.4	45.8	38.5	34.2	7.0	7.8	5.1	12.2
1975	100.	100.	52.6	48.9	35.1	29.4	8.3	7.7	4.0	14.0
1976	100.	100.	47.4	50.3	40.0	30.7	8.1	7.5	4.5	11.5
1977	100.	100.	52.2	49.2	37.2	34.1	6.2	7.0	4.4	9.7
1978	100.	100.	51.1	49.3	39.9	34.2	5.0	7.0	4.0	9.5
1979	100.	100.	50.5	48.4	39.1	34.4	6.4	8.0	4.0	9.2
1980	100.	100.	46.9	51.7	38.5	31.4	9.1	7.3	5.5	9.6
1981	100.	100.	54.8	53.1	31.7	29.1	7.6	8.9	5.9	8.9
1982	100.	100.	49.0	52.1	33.1	26.8	10.7	10.7	7.2	10.4
1983	100.	100.	51.9	53.4	31.8	28.0	10.9	9.5	5.4	9.1
1984	100.	100.	56.0	54.4	30.4	27.2	9.1	8.0	4.5	10.4
1985	100.	100.	58.6	56.9	26.9	25.6	8.7	8.4	5.8	9.1
1986	100.	100.	56.3	51.4	30.5	30.1	7.5	7.6	5.7	11.0
1987	100.	100.	58.4	55.3	32.0	27.6	5.1	7.7	4.6	9.3

The employment status rates in Table 8 show no clear-cut trends during the 20-year period, with only minor changes in the employment and unemployment percentages during recession years (1970, 1974–1975, 1980, and 1981–1982). As Fig. 3 shows, the overall proportions of graduates in the four student and employment categories changed little from 1970 through 1987, indicating that the graduates' choices of postsecondary activities were not very sensitive to labor market conditions.

The same cannot be said for the school dropouts. Table 9 shows the corresponding employment status breakdowns for "recent high school dropouts," a term that refers to persons who dropped out of school between October of the reference year and October of the previous year. There was a 13-percent decline in the male employment rate in the 1980 recession, with commensurate rises in the unemployment and out-of-labor-force percentages. With the exception of the 1986 blip (which may be a statistical artifact due to sampling errors), employment rates for male dropouts did not recover in the 1980s despite the effects of overall economic expansion in the mid and late 1980s.

Table 9 shows that female dropouts have made some gains in labor force participation over the last 20 years. Whereas 60 percent of these women were out of the labor force in 1970, the percentage dropped to 42 percent in 1987. However, a large part of the gains showed up, not in the employed column, but in the unemployed category. Unlike the male rates, the female employment rates did not undergo marked changes during recession years.

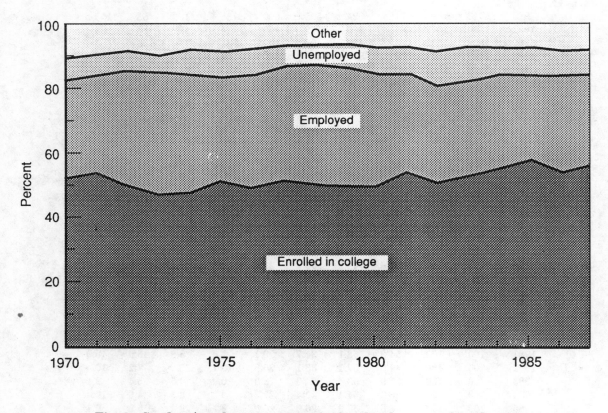

Fig. 3—Student/employment status in October by year of graduation

Table 9

EMPLOYMENT STATUSES OF RECENT HIGH SCHOOL DROPOUTS IN OCTOBER, 1967–1987

	Total		Employed		Employment Status			
					Unemployed		Others	
Year	Male	Female	Male	Female	Male	Female	Male	Female
NUMBERS OF DROPOUTS (IN THOUSANDS)								
1967	320	294	208	101	49	33	63	160
1968	310	300	203	102	46	39	61	159
1969	341	320	238	99	41	27	62	194
1970	370	342	209	109	83	26	78	207
1971	354	303	210	96	76	34	67	174
1972	372	362	235	103	71	50	66	208
1973	444	346	273	134	87	30	84	183
1974	444	369	276	115	90	65	78	190
1975	364	373	197	108	103	54	64	211
1976	420	329	234	92	92	53	94	184
1977	443	389	270	148	89	62	84	178
1978	479	360	292	125	92	66	95	168
1979	400	412	256	140	60	80	84	193
1980	428	331	217	115	95	58	117	157
1981	363	350	191	98	78	86	94	166
1982	355	313	154	92	118	57	83	164
1983	329	268	167	91	81	38	81	139
1984	323	277	167	91	84	45	72	141
1985	321	291	163	103	98	49	60	139
1986	290	254	166	90	50	52	74	112
1987	274	228	125	82	77	49	72	96
PERCENTAGES OF DROPOUTS								
1967	100.	100.	65.0	34.4	15.3	11.2	19.7	54.4
1968	100.	100.	65.5	34.0	14.8	13.0	19.7	53.0
1969	100.	100.	69.8	30.9	12.0	8.4	18.2	60.6
1970	100.	100.	56.5	31.9	22.4	7.6	21.1	60.5
1971	100.	100.	59.5	31.6	21.5	11.2	19.0	57.1
1972	100.	100.	63.2	28.4	19.1	13.9	17.7	57.7
1973	100.	100.	61.5	38.6	19.6	8.6	18.9	52.9
1974	100.	100.	62.2	31.2	20.3	17.6	17.5	51.2
1975	100.	100.	54.1	29.0	28.3	14.5	17.5	56.6
1976	100.	100.	55.7	28.0	21.9	16.1	22.3	56.0
1977	100.	100.	60.9	38.1	20.1	15.9	19.0	46.0
1978	100.	100.	61.0	35.0	19.2	18.3	19.8	46.6
1979	100.	100.	64.0	33.9	15.0	19.4	21.0	46.6
1980	100.	100.	50.6	34.8	22.2	17.5	27.2	47.7
1981	100.	100.	52.6	28.0	21.5	24.6	25.9	47.4
1982	100.	100.	43.4	29.4	33.2	18.2	23.4	52.4
1983	100.	100.	50.8	34.0	24.6	14.2	24.6	51.9
1984	100.	100.	51.7	32.9	26.0	16.2	22.3	50.9
1985	100.	100.	50.8	35.4	30.5	16.8	18.7	47.8
1986	100.	100.	57.2	35.5	17.2	20.5	25.5	43.9
1987	100.	100.	45.6	36.0	28.1	21.5	26.3	42.4

A comparison of the employment statuses of recent graduates in Table 8 with those of dropouts in Table 9 makes it clear that dropouts fare poorly in the labor market relative to graduates who do not enter college. Among the dropouts, 54 percent of the men and 64 percent of the women were unemployed or out of the labor force in 1987 whereas, among recent graduates not enrolled in college, the jobless rates were 23 percent for males and 38 percent for females. These statistics underscore the concern that a large proportion of high school dropouts, who constitute one-fourth of America's college age youth, face bleak employment prospects after they leave school.

INDIVIDUAL DIFFERENCES

Except for the closing of the gender gap in college entrance rates during the 1970s and the trend toward higher enlistment rates among men in the early 1980s, the time series reported in this section indicate that the sorting-out process among high school graduates has been quite stable since the advent of the All-Volunteer Force in 1972. Although time series based on national statistics are useful for examining overall trends, they often raise more questions than they answer. When one considers the myriad opportunities, constraints, preferences, and norms that shape young people's activities after leaving high school, national statistics provide little illumination as to who does what, when, and why. In essence, the sorting-out process is individualistic in nature, with each young person facing a unique set of options depending on his or her abilities, attitudes, and circumstances.

While we cannot hope to characterize how particular individuals with specific traits make the transition from youth to adulthood, there is a middle road between examining national statistics and looking at individual behavior, namely, studying the postsecondary activities of relatively homogeneous subgroups of young people. Led by previous investigations as to what factors are most important in determining postsecondary behavior, we turn to an examination of differences in postsecondary pursuits across subgroups of individuals categorized by sex, race, Hispanic origin, academic aptitude, socioeconomic status, postsecondary plans, school control, degree of urbanization, and location. Our main data base, High School and Beyond, provides individual measures on these factors for over 28,000 seniors and 30,000 sophomores in Spring 1980, as well as comprehensive longitudinal data on the postsecondary activities of nearly 12,000 seniors and 15,000 sophomores in the same classes. See Appendix B.

There have been hundreds of studies devoted to examining the determinants of college entry and progress toward bachelor's and higher degrees. Folger, Astin and Bayer (1970) provide an excellent review of the literature before 1970, including supplemental analyses of Project TALENT, a large-scale longitudinal study of over 100,000 high school students in 1960. Manski and Wise (1983) provide a more recent review plus a thorough analysis of college attendance patterns based on the National Longitudinal Study of the High School Class of 1972 (NLS72). The main finding that runs through this literature is that academic aptitude, as measured by performance on cognitive tests or in terms of classroom performance, is of primary importance in determining who goes to college, but sex and socioeconomic status also play important roles.

Table 10 shows the extent to which college entrance rates depended on these factors in the early 1960s. Derived from the Project TALENT five-year follow-up survey, the entries in the table are the estimated percentages of seniors in the Class of 1961 who attended college within five years after leaving high school (Flanagan et al., 1971). Using the same data,

Table 10

PERCENTAGES OF CLASS OF 1961 ENTERING COLLEGE
WITHIN FIVE YEARS BY SEX, SOCIOECONOMIC STATUS
QUARTILE, AND ACADEMIC APTITUDE QUARTILE

Academic Aptitude Quartile	Socioeconomic Status Quartile				
	Lowest	Second	Third	Highest	Total
Lowest					
Males	14	29	35	42	25
Females	14	24	27	33	22
Second					
Males	34	45	47	76	48
Females	12	23	35	58	28
Third					
Males	59	65	78	90	74
Females	22	38	74	78	49
Highest					
Males	81	81	95	96	91
Females	47	65	72	95	77
Total					
Males	32	53	69	86	58
Females	18	36	51	78	43

Folger, Astin and Bayer (1970) estimated that 49 percent of the males and 35 percent of the females in the Class of 1961 entered college within a year after leaving school.

The two major successors to Project TALENT—NLS72 and HS&B—provided better data for analyzing student flows after high school and achieved much higher follow-up response rates. Like Project TALENT, NLS72 and HS&B began with large-scale base year studies of students selected at random from over 1000 high schools. In both cases, the selected students were administered a battery of cognitive tests, and considerable background information was obtained from the students themselves, their parents, and their schools. Follow-up surveys for NLS72 were conducted in 1973, 1974, 1976, 1979, and 1986; those for HS&B were fielded in 1982, 1984, and 1986. Of the two panel studies, HS&B obtained more detailed information on the participants' postsecondary activities by eliciting separate items on each episode of employment and schooling that the student had experienced since the previous follow-up. To provide reliable information on the military service and reserve participation of HS&B participants, the Defense Manpower Data Center supplemented our data files with extracts of service-related information on the enlistees, including dates of service entry and separation.

Using data from both sources, we classified each HS&B participant's main activity into one of four categories each month from January 1980 through February 1986: (1) full-time student, (2) military service, (3) civilian employment, and (4) not employed. Each of these categories was subdivided further to permit finer breakdowns of the participants' main activities. In particular, the full-time student category was divided into four subcategories corresponding to levels of schooling—high school, four-year college, two-year college, and vocational-technical school.

To prescribe "college entrance rates" for the Classes of 1980 and 1982, we combined the estimated percentages of graduates who were enrolled full-time in two- or four-year colleges as of October in the year of graduation. Table 11 shows how these rates depend on sex, academic aptitude, and socioeconomic status.

Although the measures of academic aptitude and socioeconomic status derived from HS&B are quite different from those used in Project TALENT (see Appendix B), the dependence of the college entrance rates on those factors in Table 11 is as clear-cut as it was in Table 10 for the Class of 1961.[3] However, the levels of the rates in Tables 10 and 11 are not

Table 11

PERCENTAGES OF HIGH SCHOOL GRADUATES ENROLLED AS
FULL-TIME COLLEGE STUDENTS IN OCTOBER BY SEX,
SOCIOECONOMIC STATUS QUARTILE, AND ACADEMIC
APTITUDE QUARTILE: CLASSES OF 1980 AND 1982

| Academic Aptitude Quartile | Socioeconomic Status Quartile | | | | |
	Lowest	Second	Third	Highest	Total
	CLASS OF 1980				
Lowest					
Males	14	14	16	35	17
Females	16	18	24	33	20
Second					
Males	22	25	36	45	31
Females	28	27	37	60	35
Third					
Males	32	44	47	50	46
Females	35	42	44	65	48
Highest					
Males	42	56	69	66	61
Females	49	66	67	75	66
Total					
Males	25	32	43	55	39
Females	28	34	43	65	41
	CLASS OF 1982				
Lowest					
Males	7	10	14	29	12
Females	11	16	26	39	18
Second					
Males	17	24	25	35	25
Females	19	26	28	51	30
Third					
Males	29	36	44	63	45
Females	28	40	54	69	49
Highest					
Males	46	59	67	83	69
Females	55	58	72	80	71
Total					
Males	20	29	40	63	39
Females	21	32	45	67	41

---

[3]Although the overall rates were about the same for the Classes of 1980 and 1982, there are notable differences in the rates for individual cells that merit comment, especially those corresponding to the highest and lowest quartiles. These differences may be statistical artifacts stemming from the fact that the classification of HS&B participants into SES and test score quartiles was less reliable for the senior cohort (Class of 1980) than for the sophomores; SES scores or test scores (or both) were missing for 17 percent of the seniors but only 6 percent of the sophomores.

comparable, because those in Table 11 refer to full-time enrollment in a particular month following graduation, whereas those in Table 10 refer to both full-time and part-time enrollment at any time within five years after graduation.

Table 12 shows the analogous percentages of graduates in military service as of October in the year of graduation. Only 2.6 percent of the Class of 1980 and 2.3 percent of the Class of 1982 were on active duty as of that month. Because the majority of military entrants in the Classes of 1980 and 1982 delayed their entries into service for several months, these percentages do not reflect the prevalence of military duty among the Classes of 1980 and 1982. According to our estimates from the HS&B/DMDC files, 7.9 percent of the Class of 1980 and 7.6 percent of the Class of 1982 had served on active duty through February 1986. These estimates are in line with the enlistment rates reported in Table 7 (namely, 8.0 percent in 1980, 8.6 percent in 1982), which were derived by expressing the number of nonprior service accessions in any year as a percentage of the number of high school graduates in the same year.

Whereas Table 11 indicates that college entrance is more closely related to academic aptitude than to SES, Table 12 suggests that the opposite is true for military service. With military entrance rates for males in the lowest SES quartile running three or four times higher than those for males in the highest SES quartiles, it is clear from Table 12 that a disproportionate number of the enlistees who entered the military right after high school came from lower SES backgrounds.

PATTERNS OF MAIN ACTIVITIES AFTER GRADUATION

To show that postsecondary activity patterns also vary considerably across subgroups of youth categorized by sex, race, control of school, and location, we turn to an examination of October activities for other categories of students based on the weighted HS&B data. Table 13 shows the estimated percentages of high school graduates in each of the main activity categories. To facilitate interpretation, the small number of graduates who were either still in high school in October or whose HS&B records did not permit us to classify their main activities that month were allocated proportionately across activities. The numbers of cases in these two categories were small—1.6 and 5.9 percent respectively for the Class of 1980, 0.2 and 3.9 percent for the Class of 1982.

For the most part, the estimated track entrance rates for the two classes follow similar patterns. The most pronounced change between 1980 and 1982 was in the "Other" category consisting of graduates who were not full-time students and not employed. The overall increase from 14.6 percent in 1980 to 19.3 percent in 1982 is close to the increase from 15.8 to 19.5 percent in the jobless rates reported in Table 8 for recent high school graduates not enrolled in college. These increases reflect the tightening of the job market for entry-level workers during the 1981–1982 recession.

Combining the four-year and two-year college rates in Table 13, we see that the full-time college enrollment rates in October for the Classes of 1980 and 1982 were 40.5 and 39.9 percent respectively. Since the analogous part-time college enrollment rates for the two classes were 7.8 and 7.2 percent, the overall college enrollment rates in October following graduation were 48.3 and 47.1 percent.[4] These estimates accord very well with the estimates

---

[4]The difference between these estimates is not statistically significant. The standard errors of the estimates (and the analogous estimates for full-time enrollments) are approximately 0.7 each, and the standard error of their difference is about 1.0. In calculating these *college* enrollment rates, we excluded enrollments in vocational and technical schools to maintain comparability with enrollment statistics cited in government publications. If one

Table 12

PERCENTAGES OF HIGH SCHOOL GRADUATES IN MILITARY SERVICE
IN OCTOBER BY SEX, SOCIOECONOMIC STATUS QUARTILE, AND
ACADEMIC APTITUDE QUARTILE: CLASSES OF 1980 AND 1982

Academic Aptitude Quartile	Socioeconomic Status Quartile				
	Lowest	Second	Third	Highest	Total
CLASS OF 1980					
Lowest					
Males	8.5	6.7	4.3	4.2	6.5
Females	1.0	1.6	0.1	0.4	0.9
Second					
Males	4.9	6.7	6.5	2.6	5.6
Females	0.9	0.9	0.5	0.8	0.8
Third					
Males	4.7	3.9	2.4	1.8	2.9
Females	0.8	1.7	0.1	0.2	0.6
Highest					
Males	9.3	0.9	2.0	2.2	3.3
Females	0.5	0.1	0.8	0.3	0.4
Total					
Males	7.3	5.1	3.8	2.4	4.5
Females	0.8	1.2	0.4	0.4	0.7
CLASS OF 1982					
Lowest					
Males	5.3	4.4	3.9	2.5	4.4
Females	0.6	0.2	0.0	0.0	0.3
Second					
Males	11.4	4.9	3.8	2.8	5.7
Females	0.8	0.9	0.5	0.4	0.7
Third					
Males	6.5	7.0	3.9	1.2	4.3
Females	0.1	0.8	0.6	0.0	0.4
Highest					
Males	4.3	4.7	2.7	1.0	2.6
Females	0.0	0.0	1.1	0.9	0.7
Total					
Males	6.9	5.2	3.5	1.5	4.2
Females	0.5	0.5	0.6	0.5	0.5

in Table 8 derived from the Current Population Survey—49.4 percent in 1980, 50.6 in 1982 (with standard errors of about 1.4). While the latter rates show a slight increase between 1980 and 1982, the decrease of 1.2 percent in the estimates derived from HS&B data is consistent with the decrease in the freshman enrollment rates reported in Table 6.

It is noteworthy that the distribution of graduates across main activities in 1980 accords very closely with the analogous distribution for the Class of 1972 reported by Kanouse et al. (1980, p. 17). Their estimated percentages in the three full-time student categories were 30.0, 13.3, and 6.7 percent, and their estimates for military service, civilian employment, and

includes the graduates who were enrolled in vocational-technical schools in October (6.5 percent in 1980, 5.7 in 1982), the overall October enrollment rates for the Classes of 1980 and 1982 were 54.8 and 52.8 percent.

Table 13

ESTIMATED PERCENTAGES OF HIGH SCHOOL GRADUATES BY MAIN ACTIVITY
IN OCTOBER: CLASSES OF 1980 AND 1982

| | | Main Activity in October Following Graduation | | | | | |
| | | Student | | | Military | Civilian | |
Category	Number in 1000s	4-year	2-year	Voc-tech	Service	Employment	Other
		CLASS OF 1980					
All	3021	29.4	11.1	5.3	2.6	37.1	14.6
Male	1485	28.3	11.0	5.0	4.5	39.4	11.8
Female	1536	30.4	11.1	5.6	0.7	34.9	17.3
Control of school							
Public	2748	28.4	11.3	5.5	2.8	37.6	14.5
Private	274	44.7	8.3	3.9	0.6	27.3	15.1
Race/Hispanic origin							
White	2466	31.3	11.1	5.6	2.2	37.3	12.4
Black	341	24.0	8.1	3.8	4.6	30.7	28.8
Asian/Pacific Islander	45	37.3	19.2	2.3	3.1	22.9	15.2
Native American	15	13.2	13.9	5.8	3.8	42.2	21.1
Hispanic	154	17.8	12.2	4.9	3.0	43.2	18.7
Census division							
New England	182	35.1	7.5	5.8	2.0	40.6	8.9
Middle Atlantic	518	36.0	8.9	4.2	2.1	33.3	15.6
East North Central	604	33.2	8.4	7.4	2.6	35.0	13.3
West North Central	263	33.6	9.6	9.9	2.7	31.8	12.4
South Atlantic	448	28.7	10.6	4.4	3.4	36.2	16.8
East South Central	177	26.2	13.7	7.4	3.3	30.2	19.3
West South Central	305	25.5	10.0	3.2	2.3	44.7	14.2
Mountain	149	22.5	9.8	4.5	2.2	46.8	14.2
Pacific	375	20.0	21.7	2.2	2.3	38.7	15.0
		CLASS OF 1982					
All	2984	28.5	11.4	4.7	2.3	33.9	19.3
Male	1470	28.3	10.5	3.8	4.2	35.6	17.6
Female	1514	28.7	12.2	5.5	0.5	32.2	20.9
Control of school							
Public	2705	26.6	11.6	4.7	2.4	34.7	19.9
Private	279	48.4	9.8	4.0	1.1	25.4	11.3
Race/Hispanic origin							
White	2423	29.9	11.6	4.9	2.2	35.0	16.4
Black	344	23.7	9.0	3.2	3.4	23.3	37.4
Asian/Pacific Islander	49	43.8	14.9	2.2	0.3	22.3	16.4
Native American	16	12.4	8.4	4.8	1.9	39.4	33.1
Hispanic	152	18.1	12.4	4.6	2.3	36.6	25.9
Census division							
New England	181	36.1	9.0	5.5	3.3	34.8	11.2
Middle Atlantic	505	36.0	10.3	4.4	2.6	27.9	18.8
East North Central	596	30.2	8.1	5.4	2.9	35.0	18.4
West North Central	251	31.9	9.8	8.8	1.6	34.4	13.6
South Atlantic	457	24.2	11.4	4.8	2.4	33.9	23.3
East South Central	181	22.9	12.7	2.7	2.2	34.8	24.7
West South Central	299	25.6	9.2	4.1	1.2	37.4	22.4
Mountain	146	26.0	8.5	4.3	1.7	40.5	19.0
Pacific	368	21.8	22.9	2.0	2.0	33.3	18.0

the "Other" category were 2.5, 37.6, and 9.8 percent. The concordance of the 1972 and 1980 rates underscores the stability of the overall college entrance rates during the 1970s and early 1980s. A comparison of the 1972 and 1980 rates for males and females separately confirms the closing of the gender gap during the 1970s. The 1972 female percentages reported by Kanouse et al. for the full-time student categories were 29.1, 12.6, and 8.5 percent, and those for males were 31.0, 14.0, and 4.9. Noting the reduction in the full-time vocational-technical percentage for females from 8.5 percent in 1972 to 5.6 in 1980, we see that part of the narrowing of the gender gap in college entrance rates between 1972 and 1980 reflected a shift of female enrollments from vocational-technical schools (e.g., for health services and secretarial training) into community colleges.

Although the differences in the 1980 and 1982 track entrance rates across categories of graduates are not as marked as those between the first and fourth quartiles in academic aptitude or SES, the differences are still sizable. Private school graduates were much more likely to enroll full-time in four-year colleges in October than public school graduates. Among minority groups, the full-time college enrollment rates in October ranged from a low of 30 percent for Hispanics to a high of 58 percent for Asian/Pacific Islander graduates, whereas the white non-Hispanic rates were around 42 percent in both years.

The differences in track entrance rates across census divisions show that postsecondary sorting-out patterns vary considerably across the country. In terms of full-time college enrollment rates, the Middle Atlantic states (New Jersey, New York, and Pennsylvania) had the highest rate in 1982 at 46 percent, more than ten points above the rates for the southern divisions and the Mountain states. Although the Pacific states (Alaska, California, Hawaii, Oregon, and Washington) had a relatively high rate of 45 percent in 1982, they ranked lowest in terms of four-year college enrollment rates, with only 22 percent of the Class of 1982 attending four-year colleges full-time in October. These variations in enrollment patterns across regions and race/Hispanic origin categories are important in analyzing subsequent educational attainments because of the very different persistence patterns across institutional categories.

Table 13 shows that the proportion of graduates in military service in October also varied widely across subgroups of high school graduates. In addition to the pronounced gender gap in the military service rates, there were substantial differences between public and private school graduates and between blacks and whites. As will be seen from multiple regression analyses later in this section, part of these differences are attributable to differences in socioeconomic status across categories.

PLANS VERSUS REALIZATIONS

The HS&B base year surveys for both the seniors and sophomores included the question "What is the one thing that most likely will take the largest share of your time in the year after you leave high school?" The responses to this item, when contrasted with the same students' activities following graduation, shed light on the timing and stability of plans formulated prior to graduation. Given the multitude of personal factors that affect choices of postsecondary activities and the infeasibility of assessing them accurately via population surveys, one can regard the plans reported by the seniors themselves as the most informed guesses as to how those factors will play out in the months following graduation. Hence, they provide important information about the decisionmaking processes of young people as they approach a key juncture in their lives.

However, senior plans do not provide very reliable predictors. Only about half of the senior HS&B participants' main activities in October matched the plans that they reported in the spring. While this discordance of plans and realizations can be dismissed as indicating that some seniors do not treat survey questions seriously, scholars who have studied this phenomenon explain it differently, saying that plans made in high school tend to be unreasonable and unstable (Flanagan et al., 1971). Studies of educational attainment objectives and career aspirations have consistently shown that many high school seniors have unrealistic expectations, and that others skew their responses to conform to socially acceptable norms (Kanouse et al., 1980).

One explanation for the instability of high school students' plans is that they are affected by changes in the students' circumstances and attitudes. For seniors who have found more ups than downs in their high school experiences, who have doubts about the personal benefits of further education, or who have only vague notions as to where they are going and how they will get there, it is understandable that their plans might fluctuate over time, perhaps depending on day-to-day developments in their personal relationships with friends, parents, and teachers. On the other hand, these uncertainties may not exist for some seniors who have long-standing plans supported by their families and tailored to their desires, talents, and resources.

Johnston and Bachman (1972) found that plans made in grades 10 and 11 to get a job or enter the military were poor predictors of later behavior, but that college plans made in those grades were more reliable. They concluded that the decision to go to college is made fairly early for most students who attend college, but that "the decision to get a job or enter the service is typically made very late in high school or even subsequent to graduation. . . . Military service and work often become first choices only after it is realized that continued education is an unsuitable or impossible goal to achieve" (Johnston and Bachman, 1972, p. 30).

We concur with the view that decisions regarding postsecondary activities are sequential in nature and that educational goals play an important role in determining those activities. However, we contend that decisions to enter the military or to take jobs in the civilian sector, especially those entailing lengthy periods of classroom or on-the-job training, may represent first steps in well-formulated plans to achieve concrete educational goals rather than digressions from those objectives. In particular, individuals who enter the military right after high school may not be opting away from educational pursuits but entering technical training programs consistent with their career goals or accepting temporary diversions to pave the way for subsequent college attendance funded through postservice educational benefits. If most students have well-orchestrated plans of this nature, the concordance of their plans and outcomes should demonstrate the coherence of their plans. However, as we shall now see, there is plenty of evidence to show that high school students' plans are erratic.

Tables 14 and 15 show how well seniors' plans accord with their October activities based on the weighted HS&B data for the Classes of 1980 and 1982. The top halves of these tables show the estimated numbers of graduates in each of the cells that result from crossing the plans and activity categories. The bottom halves of these tables are similar to Table 13 in that they show the track entrance rates for each plans category. The entries along the diagonal are the percentages of graduates who were pursuing the same main activity in October that they had checked in responding to the plans item. Hence, they are measures of the reliability of senior plans as predictors of October activities.

Only about two-thirds of the seniors in both classes who planned to devote most of their time to four-year college attendance were actually pursuing that activity full-time in October.

Table 14

ESTIMATED NUMBERS OF HIGH SCHOOL GRADUATES BY MAIN ACTIVITY
IN OCTOBER, PLANS CATEGORY, AND SEX: CLASS OF 1980

Plans Category and Sex	Main Activity in October Following Graduation						
	Student			Military Service	Civilian Employment	Other	Total
	4-year	2-year	Voc-tech				
NUMBERS OF GRADUATES (IN THOUSANDS)							
Student, 4-year							
Male	344.7	44.5	14.1	6.7	87.5	49.2	546.8
Female	412.2	30.6	15.2	0.8	86.2	64.8	609.9
Student, 2-year							
Male	13.5	75.3	13.0	3.1	59.0	17.1	180.9
Female	18.9	97.1	21.2	0.7	84.1	33.9	256.0
Student, voc-tech							
Male	2.6	6.8	23.6	2.2	34.7	12.6	82.6
Female	3.4	11.2	29.4	0.6	38.8	23.7	107.1
Military service							
Male	2.8	2.1	1.0	32.5	13.3	5.2	56.9
Female	0.1	1.4	0.5	6.0	8.0	4.0	19.9
Civilian employment							
Male	14.4	18.2	12.9	11.4	277.2	56.5	390.4
Female	10.5	15.5	10.0	1.4	223.7	87.1	348.2
Not employed							
Male	8.5	5.5	3.5	2.9	49.8	15.0	85.3
Female	3.5	4.0	4.2	0.0	43.6	25.1	80.4
Unknown							
Male	33.4	11.4	6.2	8.3	63.3	19.5	142.0
Female	18.6	10.5	5.7	1.2	52.2	26.7	115.0
Total							
Male	419.8	163.8	74.2	67.1	584.8	175.1	1484.8
Female	467.3	170.5	86.1	10.7	536.5	265.3	1536.4
PERCENTAGES OF GRADUATES							
Student, 4-year							
Male	63.0	8.1	2.6	1.2	16.0	9.0	100.0
Female	67.6	5.0	2.5	0.1	14.1	10.6	100.0
Student, 2-year							
Male	7.4	41.6	7.2	1.7	32.6	9.5	100.0
Female	7.4	37.9	8.3	0.3	32.9	13.3	100.0
Student, voc-tech							
Male	3.1	8.2	28.6	2.8	42.0	15.3	100.0
Female	3.2	10.5	27.4	0.6	36.2	22.1	100.0
Military service							
Male	4.8	3.7	1.8	57.2	23.3	9.1	100.0
Female	0.4	7.0	2.4	29.9	40.3	20.0	100.0
Civilian employment							
Male	3.7	4.7	3.3	2.9	71.0	14.5	100.0
Female	3.0	4.5	2.9	0.4	64.2	25.0	100.0
Not employed							
Male	10.0	6.5	4.1	3.4	58.4	17.6	100.0
Female	4.3	5.0	5.2	0.0	54.3	31.2	100.0
Unknown							
Male	23.5	8.0	4.4	5.8	44.6	13.7	100.0
Female	16.2	9.2	5.0	1.1	45.4	23.2	100.0
Total							
Male	28.3	11.0	5.0	4.5	39.4	11.8	100.0
Female	30.4	11.1	5.6	0.7	34.9	17.3	100.0

Table 15

ESTIMATED NUMBERS OF HIGH SCHOOL GRADUATES BY MAIN ACTIVITY
IN OCTOBER, PLANS CATEGORY, AND SEX: CLASS OF 1982

Plans Category and Sex	Main Activity in October Following Graduation						
	Student			Military Service	Civilian Employment	Other	Total
	4-year	2-year	Voc-tech				
NUMBERS OF GRADUATES (IN THOUSANDS)							
Student, 4-year							
Male	341.3	32.9	6.3	2.2	63.5	42.4	488.6
Female	372.9	40.2	7.3	1.3	65.6	60.7	547.9
Student, 2-year							
Male	21.4	70.1	7.6	2.3	41.8	27.2	170.4
Female	23.1	102.0	18.8	0.0	76.2	34.4	254.4
Student, voc-tech							
Male	1.5	6.5	17.9	1.1	27.0	16.6	70.5
Female	2.1	9.0	31.9	0.0	36.2	25.9	105.0
Military service							
Male	2.2	1.4	2.7	34.8	22.0	18.2	81.4
Female	1.2	0.4	0.2	4.0	7.5	3.7	17.0
Civilian employment							
Male	30.4	24.5	13.6	12.8	269.5	98.8	449.5
Female	20.8	19.4	16.6	1.0	229.6	108.2	395.6
Not employed							
Male	4.5	7.0	3.8	2.9	45.2	18.2	81.6
Female	4.1	6.5	5.2	0.7	38.3	36.7	91.5
Unknown							
Male	14.2	12.1	3.7	6.1	54.5	37.7	128.3
Female	10.8	6.9	3.9	0.7	33.6	46.4	102.2
Total							
Male	415.4	154.3	55.4	62.2	523.6	259.2	1470.1
Female	434.9	184.4	83.8	7.6	486.9	316.0	1513.6
PERCENTAGES OF GRADUATES							
Student, 4-year							
Male	69.9	6.7	1.3	0.4	13.0	8.7	100.0
Female	68.1	7.3	1.3	0.2	12.0	11.1	100.0
Student, 2-year							
Male	12.6	41.1	4.5	1.3	24.5	15.9	100.0
Female	9.1	40.1	7.4	0.0	30.0	13.5	100.0
Student, voc-tech							
Male	2.1	9.2	25.4	1.5	38.3	23.5	100.0
Female	2.0	8.6	30.4	0.0	34.4	24.7	100.0
Military service							
Male	2.7	1.7	3.3	42.8	27.1	22.4	100.0
Female	7.0	2.4	1.1	23.7	43.9	21.9	100.0
Civilian employment .							
Male	6.8	5.5	3.0	2.8	60.0	22.0	100.0
Female	5.2	4.9	4.2	0.3	58.0	27.4	100.0
Not employed							
Male	5.5	8.5	4.6	3.6	55.4	22.3	100.0
Female	4.5	7.1	5.6	0.7	41.9	40.1	100.0
Unknown							
Male	11.1	9.4	2.9	4.8	42.5	29.4	100.0
Female	10.6	6.8	3.8	0.6	32.9	45.4	100.0
Total							
Male	28.3	10.5	3.8	4.2	35.6	17.6	100.0
Female	28.7	12.2	5.5	0.5	32.2	20.9	100.0

For the Class of 1980, the same two-thirds figure applied to those with "Civilian employment" plans, but the figure dropped to around three-fifths for the Class of 1982. This drop was partially offset by a rise in the "Other" category (not employed and not enrolled full-time), presumably as a result of reduced employment opportunities during the 1981–1982 recession.

The seniors in the "Military service" plans category were those who checked "Going into regular military service (or service academy)" in responding to the plans item. Only 50 percent of the 1980 graduates and 40 percent of 1982 graduates who checked this response were on active duty in October following graduation, but the percentages were higher for the males (57 and 43 percent). Allowing for the fact that some enlistees delay their service entry several months after enlistment, we have also estimated the percentages of the graduates with military plans who served on active duty at any time following graduation through February 1986, the last month for which we have follow-up data. Those estimates were 66 percent for the Class of 1980 (73 percent for males, 44 percent for females) and 64 percent for the Class of 1982 (69 for males, 39 for females).

Shifting attention to the top halves of Tables 14 and 15, we note that, of the estimated 77,800 graduates in the Class of 1980 on active duty in October, only 38,500 (49 percent) reported plans to enter the service. The analogous percentage for the Class of 1982 was somewhat higher at 56 percent, perhaps due to the decrease in civilian employment opportunities during the 1981–1982 recession. The remainder of the enlistees on active duty in October following graduation were drawn disproportionately from the other plans categories, with the largest representation coming from the seniors who planned to take jobs in the civilian sector. These figures and those for the other plans categories suggest that, for a substantial portion of the seniors, plans regarding postsecondary activities fluctuate over time as the seniors' personal circumstances change and they gain additional information, perhaps through employment and educational experiences during the summer following graduation.

The fact that about half of the seniors were not pursuing main activities in October consistent with their plans reported in the spring indicates that the time around high school graduation is a period of considerable uncertainty and flux for many seniors. In the absence of firm plans regarding postsecondary activities, they may simply treat a survey item about "plans" as one about "hopes" or "desires." As Table 14 shows, the number of 1980 seniors who reported plans to enroll full-time in four-year colleges exceeded the actual number of graduates in that category by about 30 percent.

Whether senior plans represent vague guesses, unfounded hopes, or well-conceived blueprints for future actions, they merit examination either as the students' best informed guesses about postsecondary activities or as indicators of desired activities. While some of these assessments may be unrealistic, senior plans still provide indications of future behavior that can be treated as proxies for preferences or aggregated across subgroups of seniors to examine group behavior. The marginal entries in Tables 14 and 15 indicate that the distribution of seniors across plans categories conforms quite well with the distribution of main activities in October, and the concordance of the two distributions can be improved further by allowing for exaggerated college attendance plans. Given that the HS&B base year data on senior plans are more numerous, more representative, and more complete than the follow-up data on postsecondary outcomes, we have augmented our multivariate analyses of main activities by performing similar analyses using the plans data.

MULTIVARIATE ANALYSES OF TRACK ENTRANCE RATES

To examine the factors that influence young people's choices of postsecondary activities, we turn to multiple regression analyses of track entrance rates based on the HS&B/DMDC data. There are three types of information available for this purpose: (1) school-level estimates by HS&B school adminstrators of the proportions of the 1981 graduates from their schools who entered college, vocational-technical schools, and military service; (2) plans data for the students who participated in the HS&B base year surveys in Spring 1980; and (3) individual data on the postsecondary activities of members of the Classes of 1980 and 1982 derived from the HS&B follow-up surveys.

The school-level data on track entrance rates were provided by school adminstrators in responding to HS&B school survey questionnaires fielded in February 1982. The questions regarding the postsecondary activities of their graduates were Items 2–4 on the questionnaire:

2. To the best of your knowledge, about what percentage of the entire 1980–1981 graduating class is now enrolled in a regular two-year or four-year college? ____ %

3. To the best of your knowledge, about what percentage of the 1980–1981 graduating class went on to post-secondary education or training of some kind OTHER THAN A JUNIOR COLLEGE OR FOUR-YEAR COLLEGE (for example, beauty school, vocational-technical school, or business school)? Do not include military service. ____ %

4. To the best of your knowledge, about what percentage of the 1980–1981 graduating class went into military service? ____ %

The responses to Items 2 and 4 provide school-level estimates of college entrance and military enlistment rates for the Class of 1981. Although Item 2 asks for estimates of current college enrollment rates (as of February 1982), most school survey respondents would not have had up-to-date information to provide these estimates. Assuming that the school administrators attempted to provide estimates of college entrance rates for the fall term following graduation and that many of them had to rely on senior plans data to provide these estimates, we shall treat these data as rough estimates of the college entrance rates for the Class of 1981. The overall weighted college entrance rate based on the estimates is 50.3 percent, which is about 10 percent above the full-time college enrollment rate in October for the Classes of 1980 and 1982 (see Table 13) and 2–3 percent above the analogous rate that includes part-time enrollments.

If the school estimates are reasonably good proxies for the actual college entrance and military enlistment rates, they provide extensive data for examining how the rates vary across school types and locations. The 987 HS&B schools for which these data are available were chosen to provide representative samples of the nation's public and private high schools, and these schools accounted for over 350,000 graduates in the Class of 1981. However, the school-level data are *estimates* of the college entrance and enlistment rates for these schools, not the actual proportions. To the extent that the school estimates reflect senior plans rather than their actual activities, they are subject to the same biases that affect the plans data.

To analyze the reported college entrance rates for the Class of 1981 and the corresponding planned entrance rates derived from the base year survey of seniors and sophomores in the HS&B schools, we fitted logistic regression equations of the form

$$p = 1/[1 + \exp(-\Sigma_{j=1}^{k}\beta_j x_j)]$$

to the grouped data points (p_i, X_i), $i = 1, 2, \ldots, n$, where p_i is the reported entrance rate (or plans rate) for the i-th school and X_i is a vector of independent variable values x_{ij} for the i-th school. Under this formulation, the logit of the dependent variable p defined by $\text{logit}(p) = \log[p/(1 - p)]$ is assumed to be a linear function of the k independent variables x_j, $j = 1, \ldots, k$, where $x_1 = 1$.[5]

Some of the independent variables used in the school-level analyses are listed in Table 16. In selecting schools to participate in HS&B, Frankel et al. (1981) stratified by school type, identifying four types of public schools (regular, alternative, Cuban, and other Hispanic) and five types of private schools (regular Catholic, black Catholic, Hispanic Catholic, elite private, and other non-Catholic). Preliminary analyses incorporating separate indicators for the strata revealed no significant differences within the three main categories—public, Catholic, and other private. Using the public school category as the benchmark (omitted) category from which increments for the other categories would be estimated, we kept two indicator variables in the equations, one for Catholic and one for other private schools. The regional and urban/rural indicators are those reported on the HS&B school file. The North Central and urban categories serve as benchmark categories in the equations.

The student attributes included as independent variables in the school-level fitted equations are the student minority percentages and the mean values of SES (socioeconomic status), TEST (a measure of academic aptitude), and family income for the base year participants in the school. To allow for the effects of local economic conditions in the vicinity of the schools, three state-level economic characteristics were included: (1) the estimated average unemployment rate in the state in 1981; (2) estimated per capita income in thousands of dollars; and (3) average hourly earnings of production workers on manufacturing payrolls. See Appendix B for further details.

Table 16 lists the regression coefficients and t-statistics for the logistic regression equations fitted to three dependent variables. First is the estimated college entrance rate. Next is the analogous military enlistment rate, which is designated in the table by "U" for "unconditional." Like the college entrance rate, this is the school-reported proportion of 1981 graduates that entered military service (Item 4). The third rate is the military enlistment rate among the graduates who did not enter college. This (conditional) rate, denoted by "NC" for "noncollege," is relevant in treating military enlistment as a two-stage procedure in which a high school graduate first decides whether to enter college or not; if he does not enter college,

---

[5]The standard method for fitting a logistic regression equation to grouped data is to estimate the parameters using the minimum logit chi square estimates b_j of β_j (Cox, 1970; Haggstrom, 1983), which entails replacing the school rates p_i by their (modified) logits and applying weighted least squares with weights $w_i = N_i p_i(1 - p_i)$ where N_i is the class size for the i-th school. This case is nonstandard in the sense that decisions to enter college by graduates in the same school cannot be assumed to be independent, because the decisions are arrived at jointly and depend on unobserved factors. The minimum logit chi square procedure, unlike other commonly applied methods (i.e., maximum likelihood and discriminant function techniques), affords protection against intragroup correlation and reporting errors.

Table 16

LOGISTIC REGRESSION RESULTS FOR COLLEGE ENTRANCE AND MILITARY ENLISTMENT PROPORTIONS: CLASS OF 1981

	College Entrance		Military Enlistment(U)		Military Enlistment(NC)	
	b	t	b	t	b	t
Constant	−5.326	−9.1	−.997	−1.5	−2.907	−4.1
Control of school						
Catholic	.494	5.4	−.548	−3.7	−.146	−0.9
Other private	.372	1.7	−.145	−0.5	.019	0.1
Region						
Northeast	.063	0.9	.207	2.5	.242	2.6
South	−.152	−2.1	.250	3.0	.200	2.1
West	−.300	−4.5	.311	3.9	.188	2.1
Degree of urbanization						
Suburban	.050	1.0	.137	2.3	.135	2.0
Rural	−.056	−0.9	.235	3.3	.190	2.4
Minority percentages						
Black	.005	4.8	.004	3.5	.007	5.3
Asian/Pacific Islander	.012	3.0	−.011	−2.4	−.004	−0.8
Native American	−.003	−0.5	−.003	−0.4	−.009	−1.1
Hispanic	.008	6.8	−.003	−1.9	.002	1.1
Student attributes						
SES/100	.866	6.6	−.124	−0.8	.246	1.5
TEST/100	.176	2.5	−.167	−2.0	−.038	−0.4
Family income/1000	−.001	−0.1	−.013	−1.4	−.009	−0.9
State economic factors						
Unemployment rate (%)	.014	0.8	−.082	−3.7	−.061	−2.5
Per capita income/1000	.071	2.5	−.043	−1.4	−.001	−0.0
Wage rate in mfg.	−.098	−2.7	.071	1.7	.001	0.0
Number of schools	987		987		986	
Number of graduates	353,474		353,474		175,587	
Number of entrants	177,887		14,308		14,308	
Entrance rate (%)	50.3		4.0		8.1	
R squared	0.38		0.16		0.07	
F statistic	27.9		13.5		5.4	

he then decides whether to enlist or enter one of the other noncollegiate tracks.[6] Analysis of the noncollege enlistment rate serves to identify school and student attributes that tend to increase the likelihood of enlistment in lieu of civilian employment, vocational-technical school enrollment, apprenticeship programs, and other noncollegiate activities.

The logistic regression results in Table 16 identify control of school, location, minority percentages, and socioeconomic status as important factors affecting college entrance and enlistment rates for the Class of 1981. Both categories of private schools show higher college entrance rates and lower enlistment rates than the public schools after controlling for differences due to other factors. Since the overall college entrance rate for public schools was

[6]Under the assumption that military enlistment (M) and college entrance (C) are mutually exclusive events following graduation, the probability P(M) of enlisting is the probability of not entering college, 1 − P(C), times the conditional probability P(M|NC).

about 40 percent in 1981 (see Table 13), the regression coefficient of .494 for Catholic schools implies that the estimated "effect" of Catholic school enrollment on college entrance is a shift of .494 on the logit scale, which represents an increment of 12 percent above the public school rate. This illustrates the fact that shifts on the logit scale for probabilities between .4 and .6 are about four times as large as the corresponding increments on the probability scale.

Table 16 shows that graduates' choices of main activities after graduation are also affected by community and regional factors. The coefficients for the regional indicators imply lower college entrance rates for the South and West and lower enlistment rates in the North Central (omitted) region than in the other regions. Other things equal, students from rural schools tend to have lower college entrance rates and higher enlistment rates than those from urban and suburban schools.

The minority percentages and the mean values of SES, TEST, and family income are interrelated in ways that make it difficult to assess their separate effects using school-level data. Mean SES is the dominant predictor among these factors in accounting for differences across schools in reported college entrance rates. However, as will be seen below, academic aptitude is the dominant factor for explaining individual behavior.

When one considers the huge sample sizes represented by the school-level data, perhaps the most surprising finding to emerge from this analysis is that mean family income and the state economic factors are at best only marginally significant predictors. Collectively, they explain only a small proportion of the variability in the school rates that remains unaccounted for by the other factors listed in Table 16.[7] Although the state unemployment rate is a statistically significant predictor of school enlistment rates (t = −3.7), the coefficient has the "wrong" sign, indicating that, other things equal, enlistment rates are lower in states having high unemployment rates. This anomalous finding casts doubt on the validity of the school-reported estimates of the 1981 graduates' track entrance rates.

Table 17 shows the corresponding regression results when the school estimates of college entrance and enlistment rates for the Class of 1981 are replaced by the corresponding *planned* entrance rates derived from the individual plans reported by the HS&B seniors in Spring 1980. These results are similar to those in Table 16 in that they identify control of school, minority percentages, and SES as significant predictors of college entrance and enlistment plans, but there are notable differences.

First, the measure of academic aptitude, TEST, emerges as the dominant predictor of both college entrance plans and plans to enlist, especially among the graduates who did not plan to attend college. Second, wage rates in manufacturing show up as statistically significant predictors of both college entrance and enlistment plans, indicating that graduates in states having high wage rates are more likely to plan to work after leaving high school than to enter college or enlist in military service. Third, the regional indicators in Table 17, unlike those in Table 16, evidence little explanatory power, showing that the other factors account for most of the regional variations in senior plans.

The highly significant coefficients for the minority percentages (except for Native Americans) indicate that, other things equal, more minority students plan to enter college. Among minority students who do not plan to enter college, more report plans to enlist. However, as we observed earlier, matches between college plans and realizations are less frequent for minority students, so that the increases implicit in the regression coefficients may not translate into increased fall enrollment rates for minority students.

---

[7]The proportions of residual variance explained by the four income and economic factors are 1.1, 0.4, and 0.6 percent respectively for the three regression equations reported in Table 16.

Table 17

LOGISTIC REGRESSION RESULTS FOR PROPORTIONS OF SENIORS PLANNING
TO ENTER COLLEGE OR MILITARY SERVICE: SPRING 1980

	College Entrance		Military Enlistment(U)		Military Enlistment(NC)	
	b	t	b	t	b	t
Constant	−6.993	−15.4	−1.297	−2.0	−4.314	−6.4
Control of school						
Catholic	.422	7.3	−.433	−4.6	−.166	−1.6
Other private	.309	2.8	−.353	−2.4	−.122	−0.7
Region						
Northeast	.002	0.0	.156	2.0	.179	2.3
South	.049	0.9	−.008	−0.1	.049	0.6
West	−.012	0.2	.109	1.4	.113	1.4
Degree of urbanization						
Suburban	−.028	−0.6	.020	0.3	.010	0.1
Rural	.000	0.0	.217	3.2	.214	3.1
Minority percentages						
Black	.011	12.5	.005	4.6	.012	9.6
Asian/Pacific Islander	.012	2.9	.010	2.5	.015	3.7
Native American	.001	0.4	−.001	−0.3	.002	0.5
Hispanic	.011	11.3	−.001	−1.1	.005	3.4
Student attributes						
SES/100	.762	7.3	−.323	−2.3	−.010	−0.1
TEST/100	.582	9.6	.115	1.4	.495	5.6
Family income/1000	.000	0.0	−.009	−1.0	−.005	−0.6
State economic factors						
Unemployment rate (%)	.018	1.3	.008	0.4	.022	1.1
Per capita income/1000	.045	2.1	.060	2.0	.083	2.6
Wage rate in mfg.	−.060	−2.2	−.140	−3.7	−.175	−4.4
Number of schools	987		987		981	
Number of seniors	26,941		26,941		12,909	
Number planning activity	14,032		915		915	
Percent planning activity	52.1		3.4		7.1	
R squared	0.60		0.17		0.19	
F statistic	62.9		15.0		13.5	

Table 18 sheds more light on the planning process by providing the same type of analyses for the sophomores who participated in the HS&B base year survey in Spring 1980. Since the sophomore plans item was the same as the one for the seniors, the sophomore data can be contrasted with the senior data to provide information about the evolution of postsecondary plans. The percentage of sophomores planning to devote most of their time to college attendance the year after high school was 46.8 percent, which is in line with the senior figure (52.1 percent), considering that some of the sophomores will drop out of school before graduating. The proportion of sophomores planning to enlist during the year after graduation was 3.6 percent, which accords very well with the 3.4 percent figure for the seniors.

A comparison of the regression coefficients in Tables 17 and 18 shows a remarkable amount of agreement, the main exception being the rural schools coefficient for plans to enter

Table 18

LOGISTIC REGRESSION RESULTS FOR PROPORTIONS OF SOPHOMORES
PLANNING TO ENTER COLLEGE OR MILITARY SERVICE: SPRING 1980

	College Entrance		Military Enlistment(U)		Military Enlistment(NC)	
	b	t	b	t	b	t
Constant	-7.937	-18.9	-.912	-1.4	-.431	-6.2
Control of school						
Catholic	.308	5.9	-.119	-1.3	.048	0.5
Other private	.097	1.0	-.067	-0.4	.105	0.6
Region						
Northeast	-.006	-0.1	.078	1.0	.097	1.2
South	.094	1.9	-.025	-0.3	.036	0.4
West	-.107	-2.2	-.117	-1.5	-.195	-2.4
Degree of urbanization						
Suburban	-.014	-0.4	.018	0.3	.025	0.4
Rural	-.067	12.3	.116	1.7	.099	1.4
Minority percentages						
Black	.010	12.3	.004	3.2	.010	7.5
Asian/Pacific Islander	.020	4.8	.005	1.0	.014	2.4
Native American	.002	0.7	-.008	-1.5	-.006	-1.2
Hispanic	.010	11.4	.003	2.2	.009	6.6
Student attributes						
SES/100	.873	9.2	-.064	-0.4	.283	1.8
TEST/100	.679	9.9	-.263	-2.6	.173	1.6
Family income/1000	-.182	-0.3	-.006	-0.7	-.117	-0.2
State economic factors						
Unemployment rate (%)	.020	2.1	.013	0.9	.024	1.5
Per capita income/1000	.017	2.0	.030	1.2	.035	1.3
Wage rate in mfg.	-.061	-2.8	-.069	-2.0	-.100	-2.8
Number of schools	999		999		995	
Number of sophomores	27,859		27,859		14,826	
Number planning activity	13,033		1,011		1,011	
Percent planning activity	46.8		3.6		6.8	
R squared	0.59		0.15		0.14	
F statistic	82.3		10.0		12.0	

college. This concordance of the sophomore and senior plans data suggests that, whereas individual plans may be unstable and erratic, there is considerable stability in the distribution of planned activities over time, at least back to the sophomore year in high school.

Shifting from school-level data to individual data on the main activities of the HS&B participants in October following graduation, we fitted logistic regression equations separately by sex to the HS&B activities data to examine the effects of student and school attributes on individual decisions to enter college or military service. Tables 19 and 20 present these results for the same set of independent variables as before except that individual student attributes are used in lieu of school averages. Family income was omitted because of its lack of explanatory power and because values of family income were unavailable for a substantial number of graduates.[8]

With a few exceptions, the patterns of the regression coefficients in Table 19 for college enrollment in October are similar for males and females, and they are consistent with the patterns for the college plans data. These results pinpoint academic aptitude as the predominant factor affecting college entrance. The TEST scores that served as measures of academic aptitude measures for this study had overall means of 510 and 521 for the Classes of 1980 and 1982, and a standard deviation of 88 in both years. See Appendix B for further details.

The dependence of the college entrance rates on sex, SES quartiles, and TEST score quartiles was displayed in Table 12. Except for certain categories of student, that table provides a convenient summary of the extent to which the likelihood of college entrance depends on student characteristics. Two exceptional categories are Asian/Pacific Islander graduates, who have substantially higher college entrance rates after controlling for other factors, and Native Americans, who have much lower college entrance rates. Other things equal, graduates from private schools had higher college entrance rates, and graduates from rural schools had lower college entrance rates than those from suburban schools.

The corresponding logistic regression results for military entrance are presented in Table 20. Only the equations for male graduates are listed, because the corresponding equations for females were based on too few enlistments and were nonrevelatory. For males, the coefficient on SES is negative and statistically significant in all four equations, indicating that low SES graduates were more likely to be on active duty in October after graduation. Table 12 provides estimates of enlistment rates by sex, SES quartile, and TEST quartile that support this finding.

Other things equal, black male graduates in the Classes of 1980 and 1982 were more likely to enlist than white non-Hispanic males. The other regression coefficients for minority groups were too erratic to support a similar conclusion for nonblack minorities.

There is some evidence in Table 20 of changes in enlistment patterns between 1980 and 1982. The South and Asian/Pacific Islander coefficients showed marked changes, and the urban/rural differences became less pronounced. Another noteworthy change was the coefficient on TEST, indicating that military enlistment became more attractive to graduates with above average academic aptitude in 1982.

---

[8]Because of the nature of the sample allocation scheme for the HS&B follow-up surveys (see Appendix B), the graduates who participated in the follow-ups were not representative samples of students from their schools. This ruled out the use of school-level averages to permit fitting logistic regression equations by minimum logit chi square. Instead, the equations reported here were fitted by maximum likelihood.

Table 19

LOGISTIC REGRESSION RESULTS FOR PROPORTIONS OF GRADUATES
ENROLLED IN COLLEGE IN OCTOBER: CLASSES OF 1980 AND 1982

| | Class of 1980 | | | | Class of 1982 | | | |
| | Males | | Females | | Males | | Females | |
	b	t	b	t	b	t	b	t
Constant	−.390	−7.3	−.433	−8.3	−.322	−7.0	−.252	−5.5
Control of school								
Catholic	.297	2.6	.428	4.3	.555	7.0	.308	4.4
Other private	.238	1.3	.285	1.9	1.027	5.9	.468	2.7
Region								
Northeast	−.202	−1.8	−.039	−0.4	.000	0.0	.151	1.6
South	−.064	−0.6	.054	0.5	.168	1.6	−.033	−0.3
West	−.190	−1.8	−.086	−0.9	.157	1.6	.095	1.0
Degree of urbanization								
Suburban	.009	0.1	−.030	−0.4	.151	1.9	.215	3.0
Rural	−.209	−2.3	−.181	−2.2	−.018	−0.2	.066	0.8
Minority status								
Black	.110	1.2	.039	0.5	−.261	−2.9	.174	2.1
Asian/Pacific Islander	.585	3.5	.514	3.2	.470	2.9	.609	4.0
Native American	−.438	−1.8	−.025	−0.1	−.610	−2.9	−.797	−3.4
Hispanic	−.088	−0.9	−.145	−1.6	−.391	−4.4	−.235	−2.8
Student attributes								
SES/100	.046	0.7	.162	2.5	−.184	−2.7	.105	1.6
TEST/100	.579	9.3	.566	8.8	.554	9.0	.296	4.8
State economic factors								
Unemployment rate (%)	.016	0.6	−.015	−0.6	.011	0.6	−.018	−0.9
Per capita income/1000	.150	3.4	.068	1.7	.059	1.7	.021	0.7
Wage rate in mfg.	−.141	−2.5	−.013	−0.3	.026	0.6	.011	0.2
Number of graduates	4906		5707		5504		5994	
Number enrolled	1884		2239		2284		2603	
Percent enrolled	38.4		39.2		41.5		43.4	
R squared	0.17		0.20		0.26		0.19	
Chi square statistic	344.0		400.5		562.6		404.4	

Table 20

LOGISTIC REGRESSION RESULTS FOR PROPORTIONS OF MALE GRADUATES
IN MILITARY SERVICE IN OCTOBER: CLASSES OF 1980 AND 1982

| | On Active Duty (U) | | | | On Active Duty (NC) | | | |
| | 1980 | | 1982 | | 1980 | | 1982 | |
	b	t	b	t	b	t	b	t
Constant	−.361	−0.3	−1.250	−1.2	−.835	−0.7	−1.596	−1.5
Control of school								
Catholic	−.765	−2.0	−.287	−1.4	−.585	−1.5	.021	0.1
Other private	−.618	−1.0	−.806	−0.7	−.454	−0.7	−.125	−0.1
Region								
Northeast	−.026	−0.1	−.169	−0.7	−.045	−0.2	−.183	−0.7
South	.282	1.2	−.570	−2.3	.277	1.2	−.570	−2.2
West	−.158	−0.6	−.204	−0.9	−.174	−0.7	−.129	−0.6
Degree of urbanization								
Suburban	.027	0.2	.167	0.9	.023	0.1	.246	1.3
Rural	.338	2.0	.161	0.8	.248	1.4	.170	0.8
Minority status								
Black	.547	3.1	.699	3.9	.586	3.2	.634	3.4
Asian/Pacific Islande	.431	1.1	−.819	−1.4	.713	1.8	−.598	−1.0
Native American	.390	0.9	.221	0.5	.244	0.6	−.015	−0.0
Hispanic	.385	1.9	.322	1.6	.341	1.7	.200	1.0
Student attributes								
SES/100	−.285	−2.1	−.443	−2.9	−.308	−2.1	−.542	−3.5
TEST/100	−.152	−1.2	.282	2.1	.060	0.5	.505	3.6
State economic factors								
Unemployment rate (%)	.000	0.0	.052	1.1	.006	0.1	.060	1.3
Per capita income/100	−.011	−0.1	.061	0.1	.024	0.3	.030	0.4
Wage rate in mfg.	−.105	−0.9	−.203	−1.8	−.141	−1.2	−.213	−1.9
Number of male graduates	4906		5504		3022		3220	
Number on active duty	286		244		286		244	
Percent on active duty	5.8		4.4		9.5		7.6	
R squared	0.07		0.03		0.06		0.03	
Chi square statistic	118.0		62.3		75.8		43.4	

IV. FINDING NICHES IN THE ADULT WORLD

This section examines the main activities of high school graduates and dropouts during the turbulent five years after leaving school. During this period of transition from adolescent dependency to adult self-sufficiency, young people are likely to make several critical decisions that will affect the rest of their lives. Some will marry and have children. Most will leave their parents' homes, complete their initial phases of postsecondary education, enter the labor market, and gain some measure of financial independence.

In going their separate ways after leaving high school, young people undergo a sequence of social, educational, and work experiences that lead many of them to change their objectives and redirect their pursuits. The discordance between seniors' plans and their postgraduation activities demonstrates that many, if not most, high school seniors have only vague notions as to where they are headed and how they will get there. Their activities during the first few months after leaving school are tentative first steps along educational and career paths that may be mapped out ahead of time but, more likely, will be determined sequentially, depending on contingencies and unforeseen events. Lacking clear-cut objectives and being subject to myriad factors that can deflect them from their pursuits, many of them will experience numerous diversions and setbacks before they find their niches in the adult world.

MODELS AND MAVERICKS

There is no such thing as a typical high school senior or a dominant pattern of postsecondary behavior. Although some high school graduates have well-formulated courses of action leading to concrete career objectives and they follow direct routes in pursuit of those goals, the patterns followed by most high school graduates are less direct.[1] Given that 40 percent of the high school seniors in Spring 1980 expected to enter professional careers and that 46 percent expected to complete a bachelor's degree (Peng, Fetters, and Kolstad, 1981), one would think that the dominant pattern of postsecondary behavior would be the traditional "lockstep" pattern through college—enrollment in a four-year college in the summer or fall term after graduation followed by a continuous pattern of enrollments until graduation, except perhaps for summertime breaks. However, Carroll (1989) reports that only 16 percent of the 1980 graduates followed that pattern.

For most high school graduates, postsecondary activities appear to be less ordered and more dependent on evolving circumstances. Perhaps the closest thing to a "model" for postsecondary behavior is based on the premise that, as young people mature, they develop self-concepts (or self-images) based on their previous experiences, their relationships with others, and personal assessments of their interests, capabilities, and aspirations. Their notions of themselves include perceptions of what they will become. Those perceptions, in turn, imply educational, career, and lifestyle objectives that guide their decisions and lead them to

---

[1]Some economists hypothesize that young people's choices of postsecondary activities can be explained in terms of utility-maximizing behavior. For example, in deciding whether to take a job after high school or enter college, a high school graduate weighs the "utilities" of the two actions and chooses the action that has the higher utility. The argument is made that, although the utilities cannot be observed, the choices that individuals make reveal preferences that can be analyzed to determine how the individuals' utility functions depend on personal attributes and other factors that affect their preferences. See Manski and Wise (1983) for formulations along those lines.

undertake activities in preparation for their perceived adult roles. As their personal circumstances change and they gain additional information about themselves and the options and constraints that affect their behavior, they modify their plans and activities accordingly.

The first full-time job after high school or the first episode of postsecondary education represents an incursion into the adult world and a major step toward independence. As such, it can be a very telling experience for gauging one's talents, limitations, and ambitions, and for illuminating the promises and pitfalls associated with a particular course of action. Since few entry-level jobs and freshman experiences live up to their expectations, the first few months after high school are a time of uncertainty and reappraisal, especially for young people who have qualms about their objectives or capabilities.

As we saw in Section III, senior plans are unreliable predictors of the activities pursued in October following graduation. The matches between plans and realizations are somewhat better for the seniors who plan to enter four-year colleges, perhaps because college attendance is consonant with a wide range of career and lifestyle objectives, and because "getting a college education" is widely viewed as an integral part of the maturation and acculturation process in American society. The bachelor's degree represents the culmination of that process, which relegates the two-year colleges and vocational-technical schools to, at best, a transitory role for students who aspire to complete four or more years of college. Since many students enter two-year colleges to pursue vocational courses of study and only a small proportion of the students in academic programs complete college degrees, the distinction between two-year college attendance and enrollment in noncollegiate educational programs may be immaterial in this regard.

Except for summertime breaks, most young people remain in school or college until they have completed their initial educational objectives. Once they leave student status, most of them enter the labor force and remain there indefinitely, perhaps with intermittent episodes of unemployment. There are two main exceptions to this pattern: (1) military personnel, some of whom enter the service before they enter college to avail themselves of the G.I. Bill or other educational benefits; and (2) women with children, who may remain out of the labor force and educational activities for long periods of time to devote most of their time to homemaking.

Within this overall pattern, there are three groups of young people whose postsecondary patterns are quite distinct—high school dropouts, graduates who do not enter college in the fall following graduation, and college entrants. As we showed in Section II, about one in four young people drop out of school before graduating, a figure that has remained virtually unchanged for 25 years. College entrance rates also remained quite stable during the 1970s and early 1980s (see Table 8), and data on earned degrees indicate that college completion rates changed little during this period. About 40 percent of the graduates in the Classes of 1980 and 1982 were enrolled in college full-time in October following graduation (see Table 13). We estimate that another 20 percent entered or will enter college at other times, and half of the college entrants will eventually complete a bachelor's degree, so that about 30 percent of each class (and 22 percent of each age group) will earn college degrees.

These are rough estimates, but they are consistent with college entrance rates based on first-time freshmen enrollments (see Table 7) and college completion rates determined by dividing the number of bachelor's degrees awarded each year by the number of high school graduates five years earlier. The latter ratios remained stable at 30–32 percent from 1975 through 1985 but rose slightly during the late 1980s—from 31 percent in 1984 to 34 percent in 1988.[2] These ratios may exaggerate college completion rates among high school graduates, because the numerators include degrees awarded to foreign students and Americans who did not earn high school diplomas, and some college graduates earn more than one bachelor's degree.

Nevertheless, the 30 and 22 percent figures are lower than college completion rates based on self-reported educational attainment data. According to estimates derived from the Current Population Survey, 25.8 percent of the persons of age 30 to 34 in March 1987 reported having completed four or more years of college, and 87.1 percent said they had completed high school (U.S. Bureau of the Census, 1988a). If we take these estimates at face value, it follows that 30 percent of the high school graduates of age 30–34 had already completed four or more years of college, and some persons in that age group will earn bachelor's degrees after reaching 35 years of age.

DISTRIBUTIONS ACROSS MAIN ACTIVITIES

The estimated 30-percent college completion rate for the Classes of 1980 and 1982 exceeds the 29-percent estimate of the proportion of the graduates from those classes who were enrolled full-time in four-year colleges in October, and it is almost twice as high as the 16-percent estimate for the proportion of graduates who followed a lockstep pattern in completing bachelor's degrees in four years or less (Carroll, 1989). The implication of these statistics is that almost half of the graduates who entered four-year colleges right after graduation either dropped out or "stopped out" (i.e., temporarily quit), and those who dropped out were replaced by others who pursued less direct routes to college completion. This indicates that there is a lot of turbulence in educational activities, even among the high school graduates who complete college degrees.

Table 21 shows the estimated proportion of graduates in the Class of 1980 in each of the main activity categories at six-month intervals after graduation, beginning with October 1980. Table 22 shows the corresponding table for the Class of 1982.[3] Not surprisingly, the two tables show very similar patterns. As we observed in Section III, the most pronounced changes between 1980 and 1982 were the increases in the "Other" category consisting of graduates who were not enrolled full-time and not employed. The increases in this category are in line with the increases in jobless rates among recent high school graduates during the 1981–1982 recession. See Table 8.

With that exception, the patterns for the two classes are very similar. During the first three years after graduation, the proportion of graduates enrolled full-time in four-year colleges remained quite stable, as the students who dropped out were replaced by entrants from

---

[2]Table 3 lists estimated numbers of high school graduates for the years 1960–1989. For the analogous time series on bachelor's degrees, see NCES (1989a, p. 221). Using NLS72 data, NCES estimates that 28 percent of the graduates in the Class of 1972 had completed a bachelor's degree as of June 1986 (*Ibid.*, p. 279).

[3]The entries in these tables and those displayed in later tables were obtained by first using the weighted HS&B data to estimate the total number of graduates, N(i,j;t), who moved from the i-th main activity category at the beginning of the t-th time period to the j-th category at the end of the period. In estimating these totals, a separate activity category was included for those participants whose main activities were unclassified. Once those estimates were obtained for each of the time periods (t = 1, 2, . . . , 11), they were combined with the analogous estimates of transitions between senior plans categories and main activities as of October 1980 (see Table 14), which served as initial estimates for t = 0. To allocate the estimated totals for the unclassified categories into the six main activity cells, a sequential scheme was adopted in which the estimated number of graduates whose activities were unclassified at any time t were first divided into six categories according to their classifications at time t – 1. Then, in each of the six categories, the cases in the unclassified category at time t were allocated across the other categories proportional to the numbers of transitions into classified activities during time t.

Table 21

DISTRIBUTION OF 1980 HIGH SCHOOL GRADUATES ACROSS MAIN ACTIVITIES: OCTOBER 1980–OCTOBER 1985

	Percentage in Main Activity					
	Student			Military	Civilian	
Month	4-year	2-year	Voc-tech	Service	Employment	Other
MALES						
Oct 1980	28.3	11.0	5.0	4.5	39.4	11.8
Apr 1981	26.9	10.7	5.0	6.2	40.0	11.2
Oct 1981	26.9	10.2	4.9	6.8	41.7	9.5
Apr 1982	26.0	8.7	3.6	7.9	40.4	13.4
Oct 1982	27.8	5.8	2.8	8.2	44.3	11.2
Apr 1983	27.6	5.4	2.8	8.5	45.9	9.8
Oct 1983	28.2	3.2	2.4	8.1	48.9	9.1
Apr 1984	21.9	2.0	1.6	7.3	49.7	17.4
Oct 1984	14.9	1.4	1.8	7.0	62.0	12.9
Apr 1985	12.1	1.3	2.1	6.8	67.4	10.2
Oct 1985	8.0	0.9	2.4	6.0	72.3	10.3
FEMALES						
Oct 1980	30.4	11.1	5.6	0.7	34.9	17.3
Apr 1981	29.2	10.3	5.3	0.9	37.8	16.5
Oct 1981	27.9	9.4	3.8	1.0	42.1	15.7
Apr 1982	26.7	8.0	2.7	1.2	41.0	20.4
Oct 1982	27.3	5.0	2.5	1.2	45.4	18.5
Apr 1983	26.8	4.5	2.4	1.2	46.9	18.2
Oct 1983	26.3	2.8	1.8	1.1	50.8	17.2
Apr 1984	19.0	2.0	1.5	1.2	49.3	26.9
Oct 1984	11.2	1.6	2.3	1.2	62.7	21.1
Apr 1985	8.9	1.6	2.6	1.1	67.6	18.3
Oct 1985	5.3	1.1	2.3	1.1	71.2	19.1
BOTH SEXES						
Oct 1980	29.4	11.1	5.3	2.6	37.1	14.6
Apr 1981	28.1	10.5	5.2	3.5	38.9	13.9
Oct 1981	27.4	9.8	4.3	3.9	41.9	12.7
Apr 1982	26.3	8.3	3.2	4.4	40.8	17.0
Oct 1982	27.6	5.4	2.6	4.6	44.9	14.9
Apr 1983	27.2	5.0	2.6	4.8	46.4	14.1
Oct 1983	27.2	3.0	2.1	4.6	49.9	13.2
Apr 1984	20.4	2.0	1.6	4.2	49.5	22.2
Oct 1984	13.0	1.5	2.1	4.0	62.3	17.1
Apr 1985	10.5	1.4	2.3	3.9	67.5	14.4
Oct 1985	6.7	1.0	2.3	3.5	71.7	14.8

other tracks. As of April 1983 (almost three years after graduation), 27 percent of the Class of 1980 were enrolled full-time in four-year colleges. Over the same period, the proportion of graduates in military service almost doubled—from 2.6 percent in October 1980 to 4.8 percent in April 1983. As we shall see, there was an almost continuous flow of enlistees into military service over the course of the five-year period.

Table 22

DISTRIBUTION OF 1982 HIGH SCHOOL GRADUATES ACROSS MAIN
ACTIVITIES: OCTOBER 1982–OCTOBER 1985

| | Percentage in Main Activity | | | | | |
| | Student | | | Military | Civilian | |
Month	4-year	2-year	Voc-tech	Service	Employment	Other
			MALES			
Oct 1982	28.3	10.5	3.8	4.2	35.6	17.6
Apr 1983	27.6	10.3	4.0	6.5	36.0	15.5
Oct 1983	26.6	10.7	4.2	7.3	39.3	12.0
Apr 1984	22.7	6.9	2.9	8.0	41.7	17.9
Oct 1984	25.0	4.3	2.2	8.4	46.7	13.4
Apr 1985	24.6	3.7	2.1	8.8	49.8	10.9
Oct 1985	23.5	2.3	2.2	7.3	53.7	10.9
			FEMALES			
Oct 1982	28.7	12.2	5.5	0.5	32.2	20.9
Apr 1983	27.5	11.8	5.5	0.7	35.5	18.9
Oct 1983	26.5	10.2	4.7	0.8	39.7	18.1
Apr 1984	24.2	7.0	3.1	0.8	40.4	24.5
Oct 1984	25.0	4.4	2.7	0.9	47.8	19.2
Apr 1985	24.4	3.8	2.6	1.0	49.6	18.6
Oct 1985	22.2	2.4	2.0	0.8	54.7	17.9
			BOTH SEXES			
Oct 1982	28.5	11.4	4.7	2.3	33.9	19.3
Apr 1983	27.6	11.1	4.8	3.6	35.8	17.2
Oct 1983	26.5	10.4	4.5	4.0	39.5	15.1
Apr 1984	23.5	6.9	3.0	4.4	41.0	21.2
Oct 1984	25.0	4.4	2.5	4.6	47.2	16.3
Apr 1985	24.5	3.8	2.4	4.8	49.7	14.8
Oct 1985	22.8	2.4	2.1	4.0	54.2	14.4

As the young adults completed their initial phases of education and military service, most of them entered the civilian labor force. In October 1985—five years after graduation, 72 percent of the Class of 1980 were employed full-time in civilian jobs, 4 percent were in the military, and 7 percent were still enrolled full-time in four-year colleges. Anticipating that most of the latter would undertake full-time employment after graduation, we see that the full-time employment rate was approaching 80 percent as the Class of 1980 entered the second five-year period after graduation.

As Table 23 shows, the pattern of activities for the dropouts from the Class of 1980 was markedly different from that of the graduates. These estimates pertain to a special subgroup of dropouts, namely, those who remained in school through part of their senior year, and who chose to participate in the HS&B follow-up surveys. Hence, this table may not present an

Table 23

DISTRIBUTION OF 1980 HIGH SCHOOL DROPOUTS ACROSS MAIN
ACTIVITIES: OCTOBER 1980–OCTOBER 1985

| | Percentage in Main Activity | | | | | |
| | Student | | | Military | Civilian | |
Month	4-year	2-year	Voc-tech	Service	Employment	Other
MALES						
Oct 1980	0.7	7.3	3.7	3.8	49.0	35.5
Apr 1981	0.7	13.2	4.5	4.7	48.8	28.0
Oct 1981	1.2	1.2	4.0	4.8	71.2	17.7
Apr 1982	0.8	0.7	2.4	4.5	67.5	24.0
Oct 1982	0.5	11.0	0.7	5.3	59.5	23.0
Apr 1983	0.5	11.0	0.7	6.0	57.4	24.4
Oct 1983	1.0	10.5	4.3	4.9	56.1	23.3
Apr 1984	0.8	9.7	0.1	4.5	64.1	20.7
Oct 1984	0.0	0.0	2.9	4.5	69.8	22.8
Apr 1985	0.0	11.2	2.8	4.3	62.3	19.4
Oct 1985	0.5	0.0	1.7	4.2	76.2	17.3
FEMALES						
Oct 1980	0.0	3.2	0.4	0.0	44.0	52.4
Apr 1981	0.0	0.0	6.1	0.0	42.5	51.4
Oct 1981	0.0	0.0	7.8	0.0	44.5	47.7
Apr 1982	0.0	0.0	8.4	0.0	50.0	41.6
Oct 1982	0.0	0.0	2.1	0.0	50.4	47.5
Apr 1983	0.0	0.0	0.0	0.0	60.4	39.6
Oct 1983	0.0	0.2	3.7	0.0	46.6	49.4
Apr 1984	0.0	0.0	3.2	0.0	39.9	56.9
Oct 1984	0.0	3.0	3.2	0.0	43.1	50.8
Apr 1985	0.0	0.2	3.6	0.0	50.9	45.4
Oct 1985	2.2	0.0	3.5	0.0	49.9	44.4
BOTH SEXES						
Oct 1980	0.4	5.7	2.4	2.3	47.0	42.3
Apr 1981	0.4	7.9	5.2	2.8	46.3	37.4
Oct 1981	0.7	0.7	5.5	2.9	60.5	29.7
Apr 1982	0.5	0.4	4.8	2.7	60.5	31.1
Oct 1982	0.3	6.6	1.3	3.2	55.8	32.8
Apr 1983	0.3	6.6	0.4	3.6	58.6	30.5
Oct 1983	0.6	6.4	4.0	2.9	52.3	33.8
Apr 1984	0.5	5.8	1.4	2.7	54.4	35.2
Oct 1984	0.0	1.2	3.0	2.7	59.1	34.0
Apr 1985	0.0	6.8	3.1	2.6	57.7	29.8
Oct 1985	1.2	0.0	2.4	2.5	65.6	28.2

accurate picture of the employment patterns for the general population of school dropouts.[4] However, it is clear from a comparison of Tables 21 and 23 that the overall activity patterns

[4]As partial evidence on this score, the proportions of dropouts enrolled full-time in two-year colleges (7.9 percent in April 1981) are much higher than the corresponding proportions for dropouts from the Class of 1982, which ran less than 2 percent in all periods. With that exception, however, the overall patterns of main activities were quite similar for the two cohorts.

for dropouts are starkly different from those for graduates, not only in terms of educational activities but in terms of employment status. Among young adults not enrolled in college, there was a much higher percentage of dropouts in the "Other" category, demonstrating the prevalence of joblessness among school dropouts. Nevertheless, 80 percent of the male dropouts and 50 percent of the females had full-time jobs in October 1985.

CHANGING COURSES

The preceding tables mask the turbulence in activities that young people experience as they wend their ways along career and educational paths. To capture that turbulence, we shift to an examination of the six-month transition rates between main activities during the five-year period following graduation. Table 24 lists the transition rates separately by sex for the Class of 1980. Table 25 presents analogous rates for the Class of 1982.

The entries in these tables are the percentages of graduates who made the transition from one activity (the "Start" state) to a second activity (the "End" state) during each of the six-month intervals from October following graduation through October 1985. Here, the main activities are designated by "S4," "S2," etc., with the same ordering as before, so that "CE" refers to "Civilian Employment." For the Class of 1980, the first time period (t = 1) is from October 1980 to April 1981; the last period (t = 10) is from April to October 1985. For example, the first two entries 92.8 and 0.7 in Table 24 for t = 1 indicate that 92.8 percent of the males enrolled full-time in a four-year college in October 1980 were also enrolled in a four-year college in April 1981, and 0.7 percent were enrolled in two-year colleges as of that date.

Restricting attention to the block of entries for transitions from four-year college attendance (S4), we see that most transitions occurred 3-1/2 years or more after leaving school, which would ordinarily signify the completion of requirements for a bachelor's degree. The exits were mainly into civilian employment and the "Other" category, marking the completion of the initial phase of college attendance and entry into the civilian labor force.

Looking at the other blocks of transition rates in Tables 24, we note that military service (M) consistently had the highest six-month persistence (or continuation) rates for males at about 95 percent, with lower rates beyond the three-year point as early entrants completed their initial tours of duty and left the service. In both classes, the female transition rates differed little from those for males, except for lower continuation rates for women in the military during the first three years and higher rates thereafter.

STUDENT PERSISTENCE

The high transition rates out of full-time student status indicate that college entrants experience considerable flux in pursuing their educational goals. As Tables 24 and 25 show, students in two-year colleges and vocational-technical schools have low persistence rates, reflecting the fact that vocational-technical courses of study are usually of limited duration, and two-year colleges have high attrition among students pursuing academic programs. The higher transition rates into four-year colleges at the end of the second and third year after high school show that some two-year college students make the transition to continue working toward their bachelor's degrees. But, for both sexes, the transition rates into four-year colleges are lower than the rates into the civilian employment and "Other" categories.

Table 24

ESTIMATED SIX-MONTH TRANSITION RATES ACROSS MAIN ACTIVITIES FOR MEMBERS OF THE CLASS OF 1980: OCTOBER 1980–OCTOBER 1985

Activity		Percent Making Transition During Period									
Start	End	1	2	3	4	5	6	7	8	9	10
						MALES					
S4	S4	92.8	88.2	82.1	89.0	95.5	94.1	70.3	56.8	77.3	59.4
S4	S2	0.7	2.5	0.6	0.9	0.4	0.4	0.1	0.1	0.0	0.0
S4	SV	0.2	0.4	1.0	0.6	0.1	0.4	0.4	2.9	0.5	1.1
S4	M	0.3	0.3	0.5	0.2	0.1	0.6	0.2	1.3	0.4	0.6
S4	CE	4.4	6.4	7.9	6.1	3.3	3.9	11.9	31.3	18.8	33.4
S4	O	1.6	2.1	7.9	3.2	0.7	0.5	17.2	7.6	3.0	5.5
S2	S4	0.9	6.0	4.1	18.9	5.2	18.9	3.0	13.3	4.8	4.9
S2	S2	88.3	76.4	63.6	47.8	82.8	50.1	45.6	42.3	80.5	57.7
S2	SV	0.0	1.2	0.2	1.1	0.1	2.4	1.5	0.0	0.0	0.7
S2	M	0.7	0.5	0.9	0.3	0.2	0.8	0.3	1.8	0.0	0.1
S2	CE	7.0	12.2	19.0	26.2	7.4	20.6	31.8	35.8	10.9	28.0
S2	O	3.1	3.7	12.1	5.6	4.3	7.2	17.7	6.9	3.7	8.6
SV	S4	0.0	2.3	7.7	4.5	1.1	1.5	6.5	1.7	1.6	1.0
SV	S2	0.3	0.1	3.7	0.8	0.1	0.0	1.2	0.0	0.0	0.0
SV	SV	85.4	67.6	52.8	46.6	84.4	59.6	41.5	45.9	82.7	59.0
SV	M	0.8	0.1	0.1	0.0	1.1	0.3	0.0	2.2	0.0	0.0
SV	CE	11.9	25.5	21.4	36.3	11.5	34.3	27.6	42.7	11.7	30.4
SV	O	1.6	4.4	14.4	11.7	1.8	4.2	23.2	7.5	4.1	9.5
M	S4	0.1	0.6	0.0	0.0	0.4	0.0	0.4	0.4	0.0	2.0
M	S2	0.2	0.1	0.0	0.0	0.0	0.2	0.0	1.5	0.0	0.0
M	SV	0.0	0.0	0.0	0.0	0.6	0.0	0.2	0.2	0.0	0.0
M	M	95.0	96.2	97.6	94.4	94.0	88.3	84.7	83.7	91.2	82.3
M	CE	3.9	2.5	2.0	4.1	3.4	7.2	11.6	10.7	6.2	13.6
M	O	0.9	0.7	0.4	1.5	1.6	4.3	3.1	3.5	2.5	2.2
CE	S4	1.1	3.7	4.8	4.3	1.3	1.9	2.7	2.2	0.6	0.8
CE	S2	1.5	2.4	2.9	2.0	0.7	0.7	0.8	0.6	0.1	0.3
CE	SV	1.3	2.2	1.4	1.2	0.6	0.7	0.8	0.5	0.7	1.2
CE	M	3.4	1.4	1.8	1.0	1.0	0.4	0.5	0.5	0.5	0.3
CE	CE	85.9	83.7	76.4	82.6	91.5	90.7	82.0	89.1	94.4	92.3
CE	O	6.8	6.6	12.7	8.9	4.9	5.6	13.2	7.1	3.6	5.1
O	S4	1.0	7.5	12.3	8.4	0.5	3.2	5.6	5.9	1.2	0.9
O	S2	1.4	3.1	6.5	4.3	1.7	0.7	1.0	0.6	0.8	0.0
O	SV	1.5	3.2	2.1	2.7	1.0	1.4	0.9	1.1	0.6	1.7
O	M	2.9	1.9	2.1	2.0	2.8	2.4	1.1	1.3	0.9	0.8
O	CE	28.2	33.8	34.9	39.9	31.6	36.1	39.3	49.7	40.6	40.6
O	O	65.0	50.5	42.1	42.7	62.5	56.2	52.1	41.4	55.9	56.0
						FEMALES					
S4	S4	93.4	87.5	80.4	89.9	95.7	92.1	64.0	49.5	76.2	48.3
S4	S2	0.9	1.8	0.4	0.5	0.2	0.3	1.2	0.2	0.3	0.0
S4	SV	0.5	1.1	0.6	0.9	0.1	0.7	0.7	2.9	0.1	0.7
S4	M	0.1	0.2	0.2	0.0	0.0	0.0	0.0	0.0	0.0	0.0
S4	CE	3.9	6.8	9.6	6.1	3.0	5.6	15.0	38.2	18.2	41.3
S4	O	1.2	2.6	8.9	2.6	0.9	1.4	19.1	9.2	5.2	9.7
S2	S4	0.4	5.0	3.1	12.2	2.1	12.9	3.6	11.7	0.2	6.4
S2	S2	83.5	73.7	59.5	49.8	82.9	51.3	38.5	43.0	72.3	51.7
S2	SV	0.8	2.3	1.5	2.1	1.2	3.5	1.3	7.5	0.0	0.0
S2	M	0.0	0.0	0.0	0.1	0.0	0.0	0.8	0.0	0.0	0.1
S2	CE	11.6	13.8	21.3	27.4	7.5	24.8	38.7	26.2	16.9	27.7
S2	O	3.7	5.3	14.6	8.4	6.2	7.5	17.2	11.6	10.6	14.0

Table 24—continued

Activity		Percent Making Transition During Period									
Start	End	1	2	3	4	5	6	7	8	9	10
SV	S4	2.0	1.7	7.0	2.9	0.0	3.0	10.1	4.6	0.0	0.4
SV	S2	1.0	1.9	3.9	0.2	0.1	0.1	0.1	0.0	0.1	1.2
SV	SV	79.3	45.0	38.2	38.4	77.6	38.5	40.0	53.2	77.4	53.4
SV	M	0.0	0.0	0.0	0.0	0.9	0.0	0.0	0.0	0.0	0.0
SV	CE	14.1	39.3	30.0	39.3	13.5	44.6	27.5	25.1	18.6	36.1
SV	O	3.5	12.1	20.8	19.2	7.9	13.9	22.3	17.1	4.0	8.9
M	S4	0.0	4.0	0.0	0.0	0.0	0.0	0.0	0.0	0.0	0.0
M	S2	0.0	0.5	0.0	0.0	0.0	0.0	0.0	0.0	0.0	0.0
M	SV	0.0	0.0	0.0	0.0	0.0	0.5	0.0	0.2	0.0	0.0
M	M	83.3	93.6	86.4	91.0	89.8	91.2	93.5	94.5	85.3	92.7
M	CE	7.1	1.8	5.7	0.0	4.7	4.7	3.2	4.4	10.4	6.6
M	O	9.6	0.0	7.9	9.0	5.4	3.6	3.3	0.9	4.3	0.6
CE	S4	1.3	3.7	4.6	3.4	0.8	1.5	2.3	2.0	0.3	1.1
CE	S2	1.5	2.4	4.0	1.6	0.4	0.6	0.7	0.9	0.4	0.3
CE	SV	0.9	1.6	1.2	1.5	0.7	0.8	0.7	0.7	0.7	0.9
CE	M	0.5	0.1	0.4	0.3	0.2	0.1	0.1	0.0	0.0	0.1
CE	CE	86.7	82.9	73.6	82.9	89.3	88.4	76.9	88.6	93.2	90.0
CE	O	9.1	9.3	16.1	10.3	8.6	8.6	19.3	7.9	5.3	7.6
O	S4	1.0	2.3	10.7	4.3	0.8	1.6	4.1	1.8	0.8	0.9
O	S2	1.3	1.5	2.8	1.4	0.4	0.7	1.5	0.9	0.6	0.3
O	SV	1.8	1.5	2.9	2.0	0.4	0.9	1.3	1.6	1.7	1.3
O	M	0.5	0.7	0.1	0.1	0.1	0.1	0.6	0.1	0.0	0.0
O	CE	24.4	31.9	26.6	31.8	25.5	30.6	27.7	40.0	30.0	28.5
O	O	71.0	62.1	56.9	60.3	72.8	66.1	64.7	55.6	66.9	69.0

The fact that student persistence rates are very low in two-year colleges and vocational-technical schools is not new. Relying on follow-up data for the Class of 1972, Kanouse et al. (1980) reported that, among the freshmen enrolled full-time in four-year colleges in October 1972, 80 percent were still enrolled full-time in October 1973, whereas the corresponding percentages for the two-year colleges and vocational-technical schools were only 60 and 36 percent respectively. Carroll (1989) reported that less than a tenth of the 1980 graduates who entered two-year colleges and vocational-technical schools subsequently attained bachelor's degrees.

Four-year college entrants have substantially higher persistence rates, but their progress toward degree completion is often sporadic and drawn out, and almost half of the four-year college entrants drop out of college before they complete their degrees. Analyzing the progress of 1980 graduates who enrolled full-time in a four-year college directly after graduation, Porter (1989) found that only 55 percent had enrolled continuously for four years, and only 46 percent had earned bachelor's degrees by February 1986. Degree completion rates were somewhat higher in private four-year colleges at 54 percent, as compared with 43 percent in public colleges. And they were higher still for graduates in the highest academic aptitude quartile—55 percent in the public colleges, 63 percent in the independent colleges. But even these higher rates indicate that the pipeline for college graduates suffers from excessive leakage.

The overall 46 percent degree completion rate for four-year college entrants as of *six* years after graduation is well below the *five*-year rates of 60–65 percent reported for four-

Table 25

ESTIMATED SIX-MONTH TRANSITION RATES ACROSS MAIN ACTIVITIES
FOR MEMBERS OF THE CLASS OF 1982: OCTOBER 1982–OCTOBER 1985

Activity		Percent Making Transition During Period					
Start	End	1	2	3	4	5	6
MALES							
S4	S4	95.0	89.1	78.8	87.1	94.7	86.5
S4	S2	0.3	2.2	0.7	0.3	0.4	0.4
S4	SV	0.0	0.7	0.6	0.6	0.1	0.3
S4	M	0.2	0.2	0.6	0.3	0.1	0.0
S4	CE	3.6	6.5	10.5	8.1	3.6	8.5
S4	O	1.0	1.2	8.8	3.7	1.0	4.4
S2	S4	1.3	4.9	3.1	21.7	6.8	18.8
S2	S2	86.8	79.6	53.8	39.3	76.5	46.7
S2	SV	0.5	0.4	0.9	0.8	0.0	0.6
S2	M	0.5	0.7	0.5	0.1	0.4	0.0
S2	CE	8.6	10.3	22.3	30.7	14.2	25.0
S2	O	2.2	4.1	19.4	7.4	2.1	8.9
SV	S4	1.2	2.1	2.4	3.6	0.0	0.0
SV	S2	0.6	1.0	2.1	0.3	1.4	0.1
SV	SV	83.3	69.5	45.4	37.1	69.7	61.5
SV	M	0.3	0.0	0.6	0.0	0.1	0.0
SV	CE	8.1	20.4	30.8	46.6	24.4	31.5
SV	O	6.5	7.0	18.7	12.3	4.3	6.9
M	S4	0.7	0.3	0.4	0.3	0.0	0.9
M	S2	0.0	0.6	0.0	0.4	0.0	0.5
M	SV	0.0	0.0	0.0	0.0	0.0	0.5
M	M	93.8	93.6	90.0	94.6	96.6	80.9
M	CE	2.3	2.3	7.4	3.7	2.2	13.8
M	O	3.3	3.2	2.2	0.9	1.2	3.4
CE	S4	1.2	2.2	1.9	4.2	0.8	1.9
CE	S2	2.4	3.0	1.5	2.3	0.4	0.8
CE	SV	1.5	2.3	1.2	1.5	0.5	1.2
CE	M	3.5	1.9	1.9	1.2	0.9	0.2
CE	CE	83.2	82.7	76.9	82.3	92.5	90.1
CE	O	8.3	8.0	16.7	8.5	4.8	5.8
O	S4	1.0	3.5	4.6	10.5	1.9	4.7
O	S2	1.7	4.5	2.6	3.0	0.7	0.5
O	SV	1.4	2.2	2.5	1.8	2.5	1.7
O	M	6.8	2.4	3.6	1.5	1.5	0.5
O	CE	23.1	36.8	37.0	38.2	32.5	36.2
O	O	66.1	50.6	49.8	45.0	61.0	56.4
FEMALES							
S4	S4	93.4	88.5	79.5	86.8	94.7	84.1
S4	S2	0.8	1.3	0.8	0.4	0.0	0.4
S4	SV	0.3	0.9	0.7	0.4	0.1	0.6
S4	M	0.0	0.0	0.0	0.1	0.0	0.0
S4	CE	3.7	7.0	9.0	8.5	3.3	11.1
S4	O	1.8	2.3	9.9	3.9	1.8	3.7
S2	S4	0.9	5.7	2.7	17.1	4.0	15.0
S2	S2	86.1	74.2	52.9	42.9	77.3	48.7
S2	SV	1.1	2.5	1.8	2.9	1.7	0.0
S2	M	0.4	0.2	0.0	0.0	0.0	0.0
S2	CE	7.4	11.8	24.0	28.4	13.4	29.6
S2	O	4.2	5.5	18.5	8.6	3.7	6.8

Table 25—continued

Activity		Percent Making Transition During Period					
Start	End	1	2	3	4	5	6
SV	S4	0.2	0.6	2.6	5.0	0.0	3.5
SV	S2	1.1	1.2	1.4	2.4	0.0	1.2
SV	SV	78.7	52.2	39.6	39.2	64.6	41.9
SV	M	0.0	0.2	0.0	0.0	0.0	0.0
SV	CE	14.0	32.9	35.3	43.5	25.5	41.6
SV	O	5.9	12.8	21.1	10.0	9.8	11.8
M	S4	0.0	0.0	0.0	3.4	0.0	0.0
M	S2	0.0	0.0	0.0	0.0	0.0	0.0
M	SV	0.0	0.0	0.0	2.6	0.0	0.0
M	M	80.5	96.5	87.6	82.6	94.9	79.1
M	CE	9.1	2.8	3.5	11.3	0.6	19.5
M	O	10.4	0.7	8.9	0.0	4.5	1.4
CE	S4	1.1	3.0	4.2	2.9	0.7	1.6
CE	S2	2.2	1.7	2.2	1.9	0.7	0.4
CE	SV	1.5	2.0	1.5	1.7	1.2	1.1
CE	M	0.6	0.2	0.2	0.1	0.2	0.0
CE	CE	83.5	81.9	72.5	82.4	88.9	89.0
CE	O	11.2	11.2	19.3	10.9	8.2	7.9
O	S4	1.1	1.8	5.8	6.0	0.9	1.2
O	S2	1.6	2.1	2.2	1.8	0.5	1.2
O	SV	2.3	3.2	1.4	2.0	0.8	1.3
O	M	0.4	0.2	0.1	0.5	0.0	0.0
O	CE	28.1	28.7	28.1	36.8	26.2	29.1
O	O	66.6	63.9	62.4	52.7	71.6	67.1

year college entrants in the early 1960s (Folger, Astin, and Bayer, 1970), but it is in line with estimates derived by taking the ratio of the number of bachelor's degrees earned in any year to the number of entering freshmen four years earlier. No matter which estimates are used, it is clear from the overall pattern of student persistence and degree completion rates in the early 1980s that student flows through higher education are impeded by lengthy delays and high dropout rates.

SOURCES OF NEW ENTRANTS

While transition rates provide a convenient means for quantifying the flows *out* of main activities, for some purposes it is of greater interest to examine the flows *into* activities to see where the track entrants are coming from. This is especially true for military service. Although the postservice activities of veterans merit special attention because of the importance of their educational and vocational pursuits to the nation's human resources, the preservice activities of enlistees are of more direct interest for examining the enlistment process among college-age youth. Information about enlistees' main activities between high school graduation and service entry illuminates the pathways into military service and helps guide youth policies bearing on postsecondary education, student aid, military recruitment, and national service.

The precollege activities of late entrants into four-year colleges are also of considerable interest, because this group and the college entrants who "stop out" of college for a year or more before completing their degrees constitute a sizable proportion, if not the majority, of college graduates, and there is some evidence that time lags between high school graduation and college completion are getting longer. Among the members of the Class of 1972 who received bachelor's degrees before 1986, almost half took more than four years to complete their degrees, and 15 percent took more than six years (NCES, 1989a). Among college seniors of age 16–34 in October 1986, 70 percent graduated from high school more than four years earlier, and 45 percent graduated more than five years earlier (U.S. Bureau of the Census, 1988b). As more and more veterans return to college under the Montgomery G.I. Bill, they will add to the growing numbers of students who either delay college entrance or stop out for long periods of time.

To provide a closer look at transition rates *into* military service and other main activities, Tables 26 and 27 present "backward transition rates" analogous to the (forward) transition rates in Tables 24 and 25. Considering the first block of entries for transitions into four-year colleges, we see that, throughout the five-year period covered by Table 26, most of the late four-year college entrants of both sexes came from civilian employment. Since civilian employment is the most common main activity among recent high school graduates, this finding might be dismissed as a natural consequence of the large numbers of graduates pursuing this activity.

However, that is only part of the story. As Tables 24 and 25 show, the transition rates *out* of civilian employment ran about 20 percent per period over the first two years after graduation. Considering that the transitions included in these rates are changes from civilian employment to some other main activity (as distinguished from job-switching from one employer to another), one sees that these transitions represent only a small part of the turbulence in the youth labor market in the five years following high school graduation. The fact that transition rates out of civilian employment run much higher than the rates for military service and four-year college attendance indicates that episodes of employment are of shorter duration than periods of schooling or tours of military duty. Moreover, most transitions out of civilian employment are into the "Other" category and *vice versa*, signifying movements of *nonstudents* into and out of employment. Hence, much of the turbulence in postsecondary activities among recent high school graduates is linked to stints of employment and unemployment rather than to movements in and out of full-time student status or military service.

PRESERVICE ACTIVITIES OF ENLISTEES

It is clear from the backward transition rates in Tables 26 and 27 that most of the late entrants into military service from the Classes of 1980 and 1982 did not come out of full-time student status but from civilian employment and the "Other" (not employed) category. There was a minor departure from this pattern for 1980 male graduates at the four-year point (t = 8) due to the increased flow from the four-year colleges as newly graduated ROTC officers entered the service after completing their bachelor's degrees.

With that exception, the transition rates into military service indicate that few enlistees enter the military directly from full-time student status. Most enlistees who attended colleges or vocational-technical schools after graduation had a break between student status and service entrance in which they either remained unemployed or held one or more jobs in the civilian sector. The overall pattern of the rates, in conjunction with our earlier finding that only two percent of the seniors in 1980 planned to enter the military following

Table 26

ESTIMATED SIX-MONTH BACKWARD TRANSITION RATES FOR MEMBERS OF THE CLASS OF 1980: OCTOBER 1980–OCTOBER 1985

Activity		Percent Making Transition During Period									
Start	End	1	2	3	4	5	6	7	8	9	10
						MALES					
S4	S4	97.6	88.3	84.8	83.2	96.4	92.1	90.4	83.6	94.8	89.6
S4	S2	0.4	2.4	1.6	5.9	1.1	3.6	0.4	1.8	0.6	0.8
S4	SV	0.0	0.4	1.4	0.6	0.1	0.2	0.7	0.2	0.2	0.3
S4	M	0.0	0.1	0.0	0.0	0.1	0.0	0.2	0.2	0.0	1.7
S4	CE	1.6	5.6	7.6	6.3	2.1	3.0	6.0	7.2	3.1	6.5
S4	O	0.4	3.2	4.5	4.0	0.2	1.1	2.3	6.9	1.3	1.2
S2	S4	1.9	6.6	1.9	4.2	2.1	3.3	1.6	0.8	0.0	0.0
S2	S2	90.7	80.4	74.9	71.2	89.0	83.8	72.4	61.9	85.4	80.3
S2	SV	0.1	0.0	2.1	0.5	0.0	0.0	1.5	0.0	0.0	0.0
S2	M	0.1	0.0	0.0	0.0	0.0	0.5	0.0	8.1	0.0	0.0
S2	CE	5.5	9.5	14.0	14.2	5.4	10.2	19.9	21.8	6.9	19.7
S2	O	1.6	3.4	7.2	9.9	3.5	2.1	4.6	7.3	7.6	0.0
SV	S4	0.9	2.2	7.1	5.7	0.6	5.1	6.3	35.3	3.6	5.6
SV	S2	0.1	2.6	0.7	3.5	0.1	5.5	3.1	0.0	0.0	0.4
SV	SV	85.1	70.0	70.6	60.9	84.0	69.8	61.0	40.8	71.6	51.9
SV	M	0.0	0.0	0.0	0.0	1.8	0.0	1.1	0.7	0.0	0.0
SV	CE	10.5	17.8	16.1	16.9	9.7	13.9	23.6	12.9	21.4	35.0
SV	O	3.4	7.4	5.6	13.0	3.9	5.6	5.0	10.3	3.5	7.0
M	S4	1.2	1.4	1.7	0.7	0.3	2.1	0.6	4.2	1.0	1.1
M	S2	1.2	0.8	1.2	0.4	0.1	0.5	0.2	0.5	0.0	0.0
M	SV	0.7	0.1	0.0	0.0	0.3	0.1	0.0	0.5	0.0	0.0
M	M	69.8	86.6	84.8	90.8	90.1	92.4	94.5	87.7	93.1	93.9
M	CE	21.6	8.0	9.7	4.9	5.4	2.1	3.4	3.7	4.2	3.5
M	O	5.6	3.1	2.5	3.3	3.7	2.9	1.4	3.4	1.7	1.4
CE	S4	3.1	4.1	5.2	3.6	2.0	2.2	6.8	11.1	4.2	5.6
CE	S2	1.9	3.1	4.8	5.1	0.9	2.3	2.1	1.2	0.2	0.5
CE	SV	1.5	3.1	2.6	3.0	0.7	2.0	1.3	1.1	0.3	0.9
CE	M	0.4	0.4	0.3	0.7	0.6	1.2	1.9	1.3	0.6	1.3
CE	CE	84.7	80.2	78.8	75.5	88.1	85.1	80.8	71.4	86.9	86.0
CE	O	8.3	9.1	8.2	12.1	7.7	7.2	7.2	14.0	7.8	5.7
O	S4	4.0	5.9	15.9	7.5	2.0	1.6	27.8	12.9	4.3	6.5
O	S2	3.0	4.2	9.2	4.3	2.6	4.3	3.3	1.1	0.5	1.1
O	SV	0.7	2.3	5.2	3.8	0.5	1.3	3.2	0.9	0.7	1.9
O	M	0.4	0.5	0.2	1.0	1.4	4.1	1.4	1.9	1.7	1.5
O	CE	23.8	27.6	39.4	32.1	22.1	28.5	37.1	27.4	21.9	33.5
O	O	68.2	59.5	30.0	51.2	71.4	60.3	27.2	55.7	70.8	55.5
						FEMALES					
S4	S4	97.4	91.4	84.3	87.7	97.7	93.8	88.5	84.3	95.9	80.7
S4	S2	0.1	1.8	1.1	3.6	0.4	2.2	0.5	2.1	0.0	1.9
S4	SV	0.4	0.3	1.0	0.3	0.0	0.3	1.0	0.6	0.0	0.2
S4	M	0.0	0.1	0.0	0.0	0.0	0.0	0.0	0.0	0.0	0.0
S4	CE	1.5	5.0	7.3	5.2	1.3	2.7	6.3	8.7	2.2	14.2
S4	O	0.6	1.3	6.3	3.3	0.5	1.1	3.7	4.3	1.9	3.0
S2	S4	2.6	5.6	1.5	2.5	1.1	2.7	15.7	2.5	2.0	0.0
S2	S2	89.7	81.1	69.8	78.8	92.7	82.6	53.7	54.8	73.2	75.9
S2	SV	0.5	1.1	1.9	0.1	0.1	0.0	0.1	0.0	0.1	2.9
S2	M	0.0	0.0	0.0	0.0	0.0	0.0	0.0	0.0	0.0	0.0
S2	CE	4.9	9.5	21.3	12.8	4.5	9.9	17.7	27.3	17.1	16.2
S2	O	2.3	2.7	5.5	5.8	1.7	4.7	12.7	15.3	7.7	5.0

Table 26—continued

| Activity | | Percent Making Transition During Period | | | | | | | | | |
Start	End	1	2	3	4	5	6	7	8	9	10
SV	S4	2.7	8.5	5.7	10.1	1.4	10.3	11.5	23.7	0.5	2.9
SV	S2	1.6	6.2	5.3	6.9	2.6	8.6	2.4	6.6	0.0	0.0
SV	SV	83.6	62.6	53.9	42.0	79.9	50.3	48.0	35.7	69.2	59.5
SV	M	0.0	0.0	0.0	0.0	0.0	0.3	0.0	0.1	0.0	0.0
SV	CE	6.1	16.3	18.5	24.9	12.9	21.2	23.3	14.9	16.3	27.0
SV	O	5.9	6.4	16.5	16.2	3.2	9.4	14.9	19.0	14.0	10.7
M	S4	4.1	6.0	3.7	0.0	0.0	0.0	0.5	0.6	0.0	0.0
M	S2	0.1	0.0	0.1	0.6	0.0	0.0	1.8	0.0	0.0	0.2
M	SV	0.0	0.0	0.1	0.0	1.8	0.0	0.0	0.0	0.0	0.1
M	M	64.9	80.1	78.0	88.5	89.3	96.3	85.0	96.6	98.1	92.6
M	CE	20.6	2.0	16.1	9.2	6.8	2.9	4.1	0.2	1.8	6.5
M	O	10.3	11.8	2.0	1.7	2.1	0.8	8.5	2.6	0.1	0.6
CE	S4	3.1	4.7	6.5	3.6	1.8	2.9	8.0	11.6	3.0	5.1
CE	S2	3.4	3.4	4.9	4.8	0.8	2.2	2.2	0.8	0.4	0.6
CE	SV	2.1	5.0	2.8	2.3	0.7	2.1	1.0	0.6	0.6	1.3
CE	M	0.1	0.0	0.1	0.0	0.1	0.1	0.1	0.1	0.2	0.1
CE	CE	80.1	74.4	75.5	74.9	86.5	81.6	79.1	69.8	86.4	85.5
CE	O	11.1	12.5	10.2	14.3	10.1	11.0	9.6	17.1	9.4	7.3
O	S4	2.3	4.8	12.1	3.7	1.4	2.2	18.7	8.3	3.2	4.5
O	S2	2.5	3.5	6.7	3.6	1.7	2.0	1.8	1.1	0.9	1.1
O	SV	1.2	4.1	3.9	2.8	1.1	1.9	1.5	1.2	0.5	1.2
O	M	0.4	0.0	0.4	0.6	0.4	0.3	0.1	0.1	0.3	0.0
O	CE	19.3	22.4	33.2	22.7	21.5	23.5	36.4	18.4	18.3	26.9
O	O	74.3	65.2	43.7	66.6	73.9	70.2	41.4	70.9	76.9	66.2

graduation, is consistent with the view that military service was a second or third choice for many enlistees until they had pursued other educational and vocational activities first.

According to our estimates reported in Tables 14 and 15, only 77,800 (2.6 percent) of the 1980 graduates and 69,800 (2.3 percent) of the 1982 graduates had entered military service by October following graduation. These "early entrants" constituted about a third of the graduates from these classes who entered military service before February 1986. Based on the weighted HS&B data for the military entrants, we estimate that 239,000 members of the Class of 1980 and 226,000 of the Class of 1982 served some time on active duty before February 1986.[5]

Tables 28 and 29 show the distribution of main activities for the military entrants in the Classes of 1980 and 1982 at six-month intervals beginning with October in the year of graduation. A comparison of these tables with Tables 21 and 22 for the Classes of 1980 and 1982 shows that the pattern of preservice activities for the enlistees was similar to the pattern of the entire class, except for the fact that the military entrants were less likely to be enrolled as full-time students. In particular, the percentages of military entrants in the "Other" category ran about the same or lower than the percentages for the entire class, contradicting the view that military entrants experience high rates of joblessness before they enlist.

A surprising finding for the Class of 1980 is that over 25 percent of the military entrants were enrolled as full-time students in October 1980, and over 20 percent were

---

[5]These estimates are in line with the reported annual numbers of accessions with high school diplomas during 1980–1985, which ranged from 242,000 in 1980 to 284,000 in 1984. See Table 7.

Table 27

ESTIMATED SIX-MONTH BACKWARD TRANSITION RATES FOR MEMBERS
OF THE CLASS OF 1982: OCTOBER 1982–OCTOBER 1985

Activity		Percent Making Transition During Period					
Start	End	1	2	3	4	5	6
MALES							
S4	S4	97.1	92.7	92.2	79.1	96.3	90.5
S4	S2	0.5	1.9	1.5	6.0	1.2	3.0
S4	SV	0.2	0.3	0.4	0.4	0.0	0.0
S4	M	0.1	0.1	0.1	0.1	0.0	0.3
S4	CE	1.6	3.0	3.3	6.9	1.5	4.0
S4	O	0.6	2.0	2.4	7.5	1.0	2.2
S2	S4	0.7	5.8	2.7	1.7	2.9	3.8
S2	S2	88.1	77.0	83.3	62.7	88.7	74.1
S2	SV	0.2	0.4	1.3	0.2	0.8	0.1
S2	M	0.0	0.4	0.0	0.8	0.0	1.9
S2	CE	8.1	10.0	8.3	22.1	5.2	17.8
S2	O	2.8	6.5	4.5	12.5	2.3	2.2
SV	S4	0.2	4.4	5.8	5.7	1.2	3.1
SV	S2	1.4	0.9	3.2	2.5	0.0	1.0
SV	SV	79.0	66.5	65.0	49.0	72.0	58.5
SV	M	0.0	0.0	0.0	0.0	0.0	1.8
SV	CE	13.0	20.0	15.7	28.4	11.3	27.1
SV	O	6.3	8.2	10.3	14.4	15.5	8.4
M	S4	0.8	0.9	1.9	0.8	0.4	0.0
M	S2	0.8	1.0	0.7	0.1	0.2	0.0
M	SV	0.2	0.0	0.3	0.0	0.0	0.0
M	M	60.6	83.7	82.3	89.8	92.1	97.9
M	CE	19.2	9.3	9.4	6.1	4.9	1.3
M	O	18.4	5.1	5.4	3.2	2.3	0.7
CE	S4	2.8	4.6	6.7	3.9	1.8	3.9
CE	S2	2.5	2.7	5.7	4.5	1.2	1.7
CE	SV	0.8	2.1	3.1	2.9	1.1	1.2
CE	M	0.3	0.4	1.3	0.6	0.4	2.3
CE	CE	82.3	75.8	72.6	73.4	86.8	83.5
CE	O	11.3	14.5	10.6	14.6	8.7	7.4
O	S4	1.7	2.9	13.1	6.2	2.3	9.8
O	S2	1.5	3.6	11.6	3.8	0.8	3.0
O	SV	1.6	2.3	4.4	2.7	0.9	1.3
O	M	0.9	1.8	0.9	0.6	0.9	2.8
O	CE	19.0	24.1	36.7	26.6	20.7	26.3
O	O	75.3	65.4	33.4	60.2	74.4	56.7
FEMALES							
S4	S4	97.4	91.9	87.2	83.9	97.2	92.4
S4	S2	0.4	2.5	1.1	4.8	0.7	2.6
S4	SV	0.0	0.1	0.5	0.6	0.0	0.4
S4	M	0.0	0.0	0.0	0.1	0.0	0.0
S4	CE	1.3	4.1	6.9	4.7	1.4	3.6
S4	O	0.8	1.3	4.3	5.9	0.7	1.0
S2	S4	1.8	3.4	3.2	2.4	0.1	4.4
S2	S2	88.8	86.1	77.4	68.0	88.3	76.8
S2	SV	0.5	0.7	1.0	1.7	0.0	1.2
S2	M	0.0	0.0	0.0	0.0	0.0	0.0
S2	CE	6.0	5.8	12.7	17.6	9.2	8.0
S2	O	2.8	4.0	5.7	10.3	2.4	9.5

Table 27—continued

| Activity | | Percent Making Transition During Period | | | | | |
Start	End	1	2	3	4	5	6
SV	S4	1.5	5.5	6.3	3.2	1.3	7.7
SV	S2	2.3	6.2	5.9	7.4	2.9	0.0
SV	SV	79.0	60.8	60.1	44.9	67.8	54.1
SV	M	0.0	0.0	0.0	0.8	0.0	0.0
SV	CE	8.6	14.9	19.3	25.4	21.8	26.3
SV	O	8.6	12.6	8.4	18.3	6.2	11.9
M	S4	1.5	0.0	0.0	1.4	1.3	0.0
M	S2	6.3	3.4	0.0	0.0	0.0	0.0
M	SV	0.0	1.5	0.0	0.0	0.1	0.0
M	M	55.6	82.8	87.7	77.9	87.1	96.9
M	CE	26.6	8.0	10.8	6.3	10.8	3.0
M	O	10.0	4.3	1.5	14.3	0.9	0.1
CE	S4	3.0	4.9	5.9	4.3	1.7	5.0
CE	S2	2.5	3.5	6.1	4.1	1.2	2.1
CE	SV	2.2	4.6	4.1	2.8	1.4	2.0
CE	M	0.1	0.1	0.1	0.2	0.0	0.4
CE	CE	75.6	73.3	71.3	69.6	85.6	80.7
CE	O	16.5	13.7	12.6	18.9	10.1	9.9
O	S4	2.7	3.4	10.7	4.9	2.4	5.1
O	S2	2.7	3.6	7.7	3.1	0.9	1.5
O	SV	1.7	3.9	4.1	1.6	1.4	1.7
O	M	0.3	0.0	0.3	0.0	0.2	0.1
O	CE	19.0	22.1	31.2	23.0	21.2	22.0
O	O	73.5	66.9	46.0	67.3	73.9	69.7

enrolled full-time in October 1981. These percentages are substantially higher than the October 1982 and October 1983 rates for the Class of 1982—17 and 14 percent. A partial explanation for the difference between classes is that both sets of figures pertain to military service prior to February 1986, which is more than five years beyond the normal graduation date for the Class of 1980 but less than four years for the Class of 1982. Hence, officers from the Class of 1982 who completed four years of college before entering the service were excluded by virtue of the February 1986 cutoff date, whereas those from the Class of 1980 were included.

TIMING OF SERVICE ENTRY

Our data on the preservice activities of enlistees from the Classes of 1980 and 1982 come from the HS&B/DMDC records for 1,025 members of the senior cohort and 1,042 members of the sophomore cohort who were identified as having served some time on active duty through February 1986. Both samples included a small number of enlistees who did not graduate from high school—24 seniors and 163 sophomores. There were 42 officers in the senior sample, none in the sophomore sample.

In addition to having the data on military service that the HS&B participants reported on the follow-up surveys, we had access to more detailed and more reliable information for a subset of 752 seniors and 761 sophomores whose military service was verified by matches of social security numbers and dates of birth on DMDC military personnel files. See Appendix

68

Table 28

DISTRIBUTION OF MILITARY ENTRANTS FROM CLASS OF 1980 ACROSS
MAIN ACTIVITIES: OCTOBER 1980–OCTOBER 1985

| | Percentage in Main Activity | | | | | |
| | Student | | | Military | Civilian | |
Month	4-year	2-year	Voc-tech	Service	Employment	Other
			MALES			
Oct 1980	16.5	6.2	2.9	33.2	32.1	9.1
Apr 1981	15.2	4.9	2.5	45.3	24.5	7.8
Oct 1981	13.0	4.6	2.7	50.2	23.9	5.5
Apr 1982	10.5	2.5	2.3	57.8	17.5	9.4
Oct 1982	12.5	1.5	1.4	60.1	17.1	7.4
Apr 1983	11.5	1.7	1.5	62.7	15.3	7.4
Oct 1983	10.5	0.9	2.1	59.9	20.1	6.6
Apr 1984	8.2	0.7	1.4	53.7	23.5	12.6
Oct 1984	4.5	1.1	0.8	51.3	31.4	10.9
Apr 1985	3.7	1.2	1.1	50.3	34.0	9.7
Oct 1985	2.7	0.7	1.4	44.1	41.8	9.3
			FEMALES			
Oct 1980	14.6	7.4	3.3	28.3	27.3	19.0
Apr 1981	13.7	6.2	2.5	36.4	26.7	14.6
Oct 1981	11.6	5.5	4.5	42.5	27.1	8.7
Apr 1982	8.6	1.0	0.4	47.1	29.3	13.6
Oct 1982	9.4	2.8	1.2	48.5	23.1	15.0
Apr 1983	9.3	2.0	0.0	48.8	21.3	18.7
Oct 1983	11.5	1.8	1.5	46.2	23.2	15.8
Apr 1984	4.9	3.0	1.7	50.8	19.9	19.6
Oct 1984	4.8	3.0	1.4	49.7	29.1	11.9
Apr 1985	3.5	5.0	1.4	43.2	34.2	12.6
Oct 1985	2.3	3.7	0.1	43.3	39.2	11.5
			BOTH SEXES			
Oct 1980	16.2	6.4	2.9	32.5	31.4	10.6
Apr 1981	14.9	5.1	2.5	43.9	24.9	8.8
Oct 1981	12.8	4.8	3.0	49.0	24.4	6.0
Apr 1982	10.2	2.3	2.0	56.1	19.3	10.1
Oct 1982	12.0	1.7	1.4	58.3	18.1	8.6
Apr 1983	11.1	1.7	1.3	60.5	16.2	9.1
Oct 1983	10.6	1.0	2.0	57.8	20.6	8.0
Apr 1984	7.6	1.0	1.5	53.3	22.9	13.7
Oct 1984	4.5	1.4	0.9	51.1	31.1	11.1
Apr 1985	3.7	1.8	1.2	49.2	34.0	10.1
Oct 1985	2.6	1.2	1.2	44.0	41.4	9.7

B. Although we found good agreement between the service-related items on the HS&B files and those on DMDC records, we relied on the "official" DMDC data for key service information, including the date of entry into active duty.

Figure 4 shows how many of the 752 seniors with DMDC-validated service dates entered the service as of the end of each month through September 1985. Less than half

Table 29

DISTRIBUTION OF MILITARY ENTRANTS FROM CLASS OF 1982 ACROSS
MAIN ACTIVITIES: OCTOBER 1982–OCTOBER 1985

| | Percentage in Main Activity | | | | | |
| | Student | | | | | |
Month	4-year	2-year	Voc-tech	Military Service	Civilian Employment	Other
			MALES			
Oct 1982	8.7	4.3	2.4	31.9	30.6	22.1
Apr 1983	7.6	3.0	2.3	49.3	24.2	13.6
Oct 1983	7.2	4.6	1.6	55.1	21.7	9.8
Apr 1984	5.1	1.3	1.1	60.3	22.1	10.1
Oct 1984	4.8	1.0	0.6	63.5	23.8	6.3
Apr 1985	3.9	0.9	0.5	66.6	22.6	5.6
Oct 1985	4.6	0.7	0.5	55.0	32.6	6.6
			FEMALES			
Oct 1982	10.0	9.9	5.9	24.5	33.5	16.2
Apr 1983	8.9	7.2	5.8	35.4	24.7	18.0
Oct 1983	8.2	6.7	3.3	41.3	32.1	8.4
Apr 1984	7.7	5.0	0.8	41.3	25.1	20.2
Oct 1984	5.1	0.0	1.9	43.7	31.8	17.4
Apr 1985	5.0	0.0	2.2	47.7	21.7	23.4
Oct 1985	10.2	0.0	2.2	38.9	30.1	18.6
			BOTH SEXES			
Oct 1982	8.9	5.1	2.9	30.9	31.0	21.3
Apr 1983	7.8	3.6	2.8	47.4	24.3	14.2
Oct 1983	7.3	4.9	1.8	53.2	23.2	9.6
Apr 1984	5.5	1.8	1.0	57.7	22.5	11.5
Oct 1984	4.8	0.9	0.8	60.8	24.9	7.8
Apr 1985	4.1	0.7	0.7	64.0	22.4	8.1
Oct 1985	5.4	0.6	0.7	52.8	32.3	8.3

(355) went on active duty before April 1981—nine months after the normal graduation date for most members of the Class of 1980. And one of every four of these seniors entered the service after January 1983, more than 2-1/2 years after graduation. As the figure shows, the pattern of service entrances was relatively steady over the five-year period after graduation, with a continual flow into the military even after the three-year point following graduation, when most entrants would be 20–22 years of age.

Figure 5 shows the breakdowns into student and employment activities of the same 752 seniors as a function of months before enlistment. With the inverted time scale used here, the last bar on the right depicts the activity breakdown during the month before service entry. It confirms that few enlistees entered the service directly from full-time student status, but the pattern for earlier months indicates that many of the later entrants had attended college and vocational-technical schools previously. Although almost half of the enlistees were in the "Not employed" category during the month preceding service entry, the pattern for earlier months suggests that many of the enlistees took a one- or two-month break from full-time student and employment activities before they entered the service.

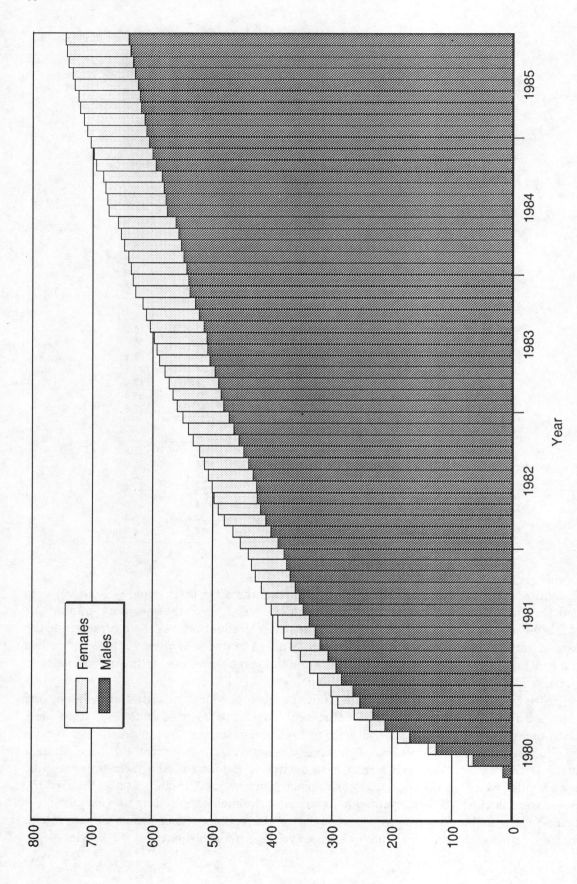

Fig. 4—Timing of service entry for HS&B participants in Class of 1980

71

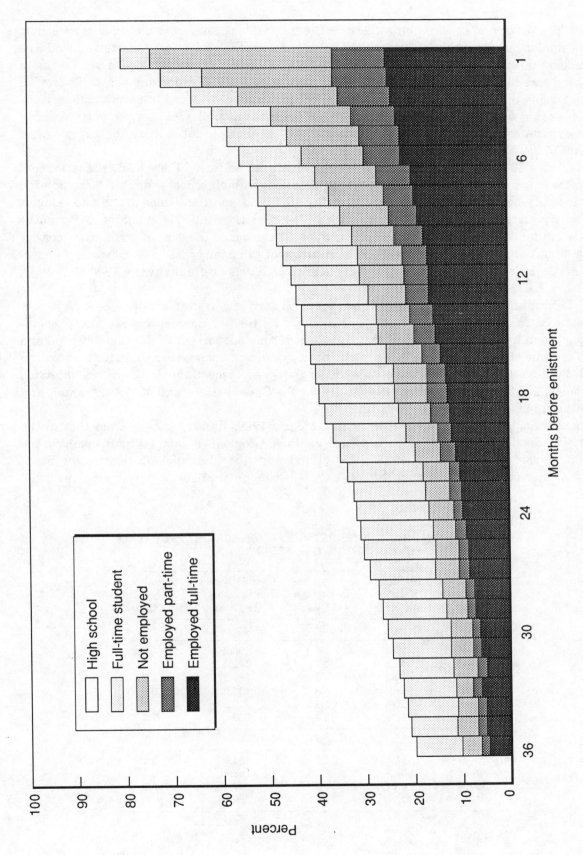

Fig. 5—Preservice main activities among military entrants in Class of 1980

The pattern of service entry dates for the military entrants from the sophomore cohort was similar but somewhat more variable, partly because the sophomore cohort included large numbers of school dropouts, early graduates, and students who graduated a year or more behind schedule, leading to a wider range of graduation and school-leaving dates. To provide comparable distributions of service entry times for both cohorts and to permit comparisons with analogous data for the Class of 1972, we rescaled the individual service entry dates of the graduates relative to their graduation dates, so that all dates would be expressed in terms of months since graduation.

Table 30 shows the distribution of these "lag times" between high school graduation and service entry based on the weighted HS&B data for the high school graduates who entered active duty between June 1980 and December 1985. For most enlistees in the two samples (who graduated in June 1980 or June 1982), the first time interval spanning 0–6 months after graduation corresponds to the period June–December in the year of graduation, so that the later 12-month periods correspond to subsequent calendar years. The bases for the percentages in Table 30 are the total numbers of high school graduates in 1980 and 1982, namely, 3,021,000 and 2,984,000.

Except for the fact that the estimated rates of service entry ran about 10 percent higher for the Class of 1982, the distributions of lag times for the two classes were remarkably similar through 3-1/2 years after graduation, by which time 6.8 percent of the Class of 1980 and 7.6 percent of the Class of 1982 had entered active duty. Among those who entered within 3-1/2 years after graduation, the estimated percentages in each of the first four time intervals were 44, 25, 18, and 13 percent respectively for the Class of 1980, and 43, 29, 19, and 8 percent for the Class of 1982.

Although the recruitment climate in the early 1980s differed greatly from that in the early 1970s during the transition to an All-Volunteer Force, it is interesting to compare the percentages in these time intervals with estimates for the Class of 1972 reported by Black and Fraker (1984). Of the members of that class who entered active duty before 1976, the

Table 30

DISTRIBUTION OF LAG TIMES BETWEEN HIGH SCHOOL GRADUATION
AND SERVICE ENTRY: CLASSES OF 1980 AND 1982

Months from Graduation to Service Entry	Number of Enlistees (in 1000s)	Percentage of Class	Cumulative No. of Enlistees (in 1000s)	Cumulative Percentage of Class
CLASS OF 1980				
0–6	90.3	3.0	90.3	3.0
7–18	51.8	1.7	142.0	4.7
19–30	38.2	1.3	180.2	6.0
31–42	26.7	0.9	207.0	6.8
43–54	20.9	0.7	227.8	7.5
55–66	11.6	0.4	239.4	7.9
CLASS OF 1982				
0–6	98.0	3.3	98.0	3.3
7–18	65.5	2.2	163.5	5.5
19–30	43.7	1.5	207.3	6.9
31–42	18.6	0.6	225.8	7.6

percentages who enlisted in 1972, 1973, 1974, and 1975 were 53, 24, 12, and 11 percent respectively. Hence, except for a tighter clustering of entrances during the first six months after graduation (perhaps linked to inductions and draft-induced enlistments in the latter half of 1972), the pattern of service entry rates for the Class of 1972 was similar to the patterns for the Classes of 1982 and 1984.

CHARACTERISTICS OF MILITARY ENTRANTS

Our regression analyses of enlistment status as of October in the year of graduation identified socioeconomic status (SES) and minority group membership as factors that tended to distinguish military entrants from their classmates. The SES scores of the HS&B participants who entered the military before February 1986 averaged about one-fourth of a standard deviation below the class averages. See Table B.3.

In terms of their academic aptitude (TEST) scores, the military entrants differed little from their classmates, except that the dropouts from the sophomore cohort who entered the military had TEST scores that averaged 37 points above the mean for all sophomore dropouts and 33 points above the mean for senior dropouts who entered the military. The apparent reason for this change is that, effective October 1, 1981, the services curtailed enlistments among high school dropouts whose Armed Forces Qualification Test (AFQT) scores fell below the 31st percentile.[6]

Just as there is no such thing as a typical high school graduate, there is no such thing as a typical enlistee or a characteristic pattern of preservice activities. As the preceding discussion has shown, there was a remarkable lack of uniformity in the service entry times of the military entrants. Except for the graduates who went on active duty within a month or two after leaving school, the preservice activities of military enlistees appear to be more variable than their classmates, but they were similar in other respects. Although late military entrants were less likely to enter college, about a fourth of the enlistees from the Class of 1980 were full-time students in colleges and vocational-technical schools in October 1980. Like many of their classmates, the late military entrants evidenced considerable mobility into and out of the civilian work force before they enlisted.

Table 31 presents summary statistics that permit contrasting the characteristics of early and late military entrants. There are notable differences between the two cohorts. The enlistees from the Class of 1980 who entered within six months of graduation averaged about 25 points lower on TEST and 10 points lower on SES than those who entered later, and a higher proportion of the early entrants came from minority groups. While the latter was also true for the early entrants from the Class of 1982, the mean TEST and SES scores were almost exactly the same across service entry time categories.

There were two factors affecting enlistment behavior in the early 1980s that would explain the differences between the cohorts. One was the 1981–1982 recession. It seems plausible that many of the 1980 graduates with above average TEST and SES scores, especially those who entered college or vocational-technical training after graduation, experienced greater difficulties when they tried to shift into civilian employment from other main activities in 1981 and 1982. Because their mobility into civilian jobs was restricted, military service became a more attractive option.

---

[6]AFQT scores are reported as percentiles. Enlistees with AFQT scores between 10 and 30 are classified as belonging to AFQT Category IV. In addition to proscribing enlistments of high school dropouts in Category IV, the services also limited the total number of Category IV enlistments among high school graduates to not more than 20 percent of the total number of accessions in any one fiscal year (Office of the Assistant Secretary of Defense, 1988).

Table 31

SUMMARY STATISTICS FOR MILITARY ENTRANTS BY TIMING OF
SERVICE ENTRY: CLASSES OF 1980 AND 1982

Months from Graduation to Service Entry	Number of Enlistees (in 1000s)	Mean TEST	Mean SES	Percent Minority		Percent Female
				Black	Other	
CLASS OF 1980						
0–6	90.3	489	470	20.8	10.0	15.2
7–18	51.8	510	471	13.7	7.9	16.7
19–30	38.2	514	485	10.6	6.0	16.4
31–42	26.7	499	484	17.7	5.0	19.3
43–66	32.4	553	508	14.2	6.5	17.3
Total	239.4	507	479	16.4	7.8	15.7
CLASS OF 1982						
0–6	98.0	517	475	14.6	9.5	13.5
7–18	65.5	518	479	10.5	11.0	11.8
19–30	43.7	518	480	10.4	7.3	14.9
31–42	18.6	507	476	12.5	9.9	19.7
Total	225.8	517	478	12.4	9.5	13.8

Another explanation is that the military services tightened their enlistment standards considerably between 1980 and 1982. Whereas only 65 percent of the nonprior service enlistees in Fiscal Year 1980 had AFQT scores above the 30th percentile (AFQT Categories I–III), the analogous percentages for 1981 and 1982 were 79 and 85 percent, and the percentage continued to rise, reaching 96 percent in FY 1986 (Office of the Assistant Secretary of Defense, 1988, p. II-21). While restricting enlistments among applicants with low AFQT scores would only seem to affect the mean TEST scores, not the SES scores, the two scores are positively correlated. The sample correlation coefficients were .32 for the senior cohort, .38 for the sophomores.

The sharp drop in the percentage of minorities between 1980 and 1982 is consistent with national recruitment data. Whereas 36 percent of the nonprior service accessions in FY 1980 were from minority groups, the percentage dropped to 25 in FY 1982 (*Ibid.*, p. II-33). These percentages are much higher than the figures listed in Table 31, because the latter pertain to high school graduates. But both sets of figures indicate that minority groups— especially blacks—were overrepresented among military entrants. According to our estimates (see Tables B.1 and B.2), blacks accounted for 11.3 percent of the graduates in the Class of 1980 and 11.5 percent in 1982, and other minorities accounted for 7.1 and 7.3 percent of the graduates in those classes. Hence, the extent to which minorities were overrepresented among recruits with high school diplomas dropped considerably between 1980 and 1982.

The marked changes in the characteristics of recruits between 1980 and 1982 indicate that recruitment policies play an important role in the sorting-out process. Because so many young people move into and out of educational activities and short-term employment during the first few years after leaving school, they constitute a highly mobile population that would seem to be especially amenable to changes in economic policies and youth policies, such as the implementation of the Montgomery G.I. Bill in 1985. Nevertheless, summary statistics on the characteristics of nonprior service accessions have remained surprisingly stable since 1982. It is noteworthy that the median age of military entrants in FY 1987 was 19.9 years (*Ibid.*, p. II-37), which is about two years above the median age of high school graduates. This suggests that, like the enlistees from the Classes of 1980 and 1982, a substantial proportion of the military entrants from the Classes of 1983 to 1987 spent a year or more in other activities before they entered the service.

V. CONCLUSIONS

During the 1980s, 28 million American youth completed high school and embarked on career paths, some taking entry-level civilian jobs or entering military service, others continuing in the educational pipeline to become tomorrow's professional and technical workers. Despite this huge influx of high school graduates into the educational pipeline and the labor market during the 1980s, the demand for college-trained workers, technicians, skilled craftsmen, and administrative personnel outpaced the supply of entry-level workers in these areas, eroding the labor surpluses that existed in the late 1970s and early 1980s. As a consequence, there are mounting concerns about the adequacy of America's human resources to satisfy manpower requirements in the 1990s.

It has become a cliche to say that America's future depends on its youth. The educational and vocational activities that young people enter in the first few years after leaving high school are critical in assessing the extent to which they will contribute to the nation's human resources. Yet, the postsecondary pursuits of young people have been poorly tracked. Nationally published statistics provide at best only crude indicators of the flows of young people into postsecondary education, military service, and civilian employment activities. To augment the existing data and thus provide the needed information, we examined patterns of college enrollment, military service, and civilian labor force participation among recent high school graduates and dropouts.

In carrying out this work, we relied extensively on data from HS&B, a panel study of 26,000 high school sophomores and seniors in 1980 who participated in follow-up surveys in 1982, 1984, and 1986, and on supplemental data for a subset of HS&B participants who entered military service before 1986. These data are well-suited for examining the postsecondary sorting-out process among members of the Classes of 1980 and 1982. However, being restricted to two classes in the early 1980s, these data could not provide a complete picture of activity patterns in the 1980s that would take into account demographic trends, changes in economic conditions, and other developments that have affected young people's activities since 1982, such as the Montgomery G.I. Bill. For those purposes, it was necessary to link HS&B to other national data sources.

In particular, we needed more detailed information about the demographics of high school graduation classes in the 1980s. Building on existing data from several sources and relying heavily on Census Bureau estimates and projections of age group sizes, we derived the estimates and projections of numbers of high school graduates by state, sex, race, and Hispanic origin for the years 1980–2000 that are reported in Appendix A. The near-term projections point to a 15 percent decline in the number of graduates between 1989 and 1992. Although the decline will be followed by steady increases over the remainder of the 1990s, the projected total number of graduates during the 1990s will be 10 percent below the total for the 1980s.

While reductions in the numbers of high school graduates do not imply commensurate reductions in the educational pipeline or in the numbers of new entrants into the labor force, our study of the postsecondary activities of recent high school graduates and dropouts led us to conclude that the postsecondary sorting-out process has remained remarkably stable during the last 20 years. High school graduation rates, college entrance rates, and student persistence rates have changed little during that period, except for the closing of the gender gap in student flows through higher education.

According to our estimates, in 1986, the last year for which state estimates were available for both public and private schools, the high school graduation rate was 73 percent (71 percent for males, 76 for females), implying that 27 percent of the 18-year-olds in 1986 had either already dropped out of school or would do so before graduation. The dropout rates were substantially higher for blacks and Hispanics at 40 and 48 percent respectively. Although dropout rates have moved up and down by a few percentage points over the last 25 years, the dropout rate in 1986 was almost exactly the same as it was in 1976 and 1965. During the 1980s, 10 million young people dropped out of school before graduation, a fact that points to a large waste of human resources in the secondary schools.

The statistics measuring educational progress beyond high school indicate that postsecondary educational institutions have not performed much better. Only 40 percent of the graduates in the Classes of 1980 and 1982 were enrolled full-time in college as of October in the year of graduation. Adding part-time college enrollments (8 percent in 1980, 7 percent in 1982) brings the rates nearer to 50 percent. Assuming that other members of those classes will enter college later, we estimate that the (cumulative) college entrance rate among high school graduates in the early 1980s was about 60 percent. Based on earned degrees data and student persistence patterns for the Classes of 1980 and 1982, we estimate that about half of the college entrants from these classes will eventually complete a college degree, a figure that has apparently prevailed since the early 1900s except during wartime periods.

Our analyses indicate that academic aptitude is the main factor affecting individual college enrollment decisions after high school. However, only 63 percent of the 1980 graduates in the top academic aptitude quartile were enrolled full-time in college in October following graduation. Although the analogous figure for the Class of 1982 was somewhat higher at 70 percent, both figures are surprisingly low for a nation that, in the past, has prided itself on the way that it develops its human resources.

Among the 30 percent of high school graduates who eventually complete college, progress toward degree completion is often sporadic and drawn out. Only about one of every ten two-year college students eventually earns a bachelor's degree. Among the 1980 graduates who enrolled full-time in a four-year college directly after graduation, only 46 percent had earned bachelor's degrees through February 1986. The obvious conclusion is that student flows through higher education are impeded by lengthy delays and high dropout rates, signaling more talent loss.

College students are not the only ones whose postsecondary activities are prone to false steps and backtracking. Our examination of six-month transition rates across main activities indicates a substantial amount of activity switching, both among students and nonstudents. Most of these transitions are either into or out of civilian employment, indicating that a large part of the turbulence in postsecondary activities is linked to brief episodes of employment and unemployment.

For the most part, the graduates in the Classes of 1980 and 1982 who joined the military also spent considerable time in other activities before they entered the service. According to our estimates, only 3.0 percent of the Class of 1980 and 3.3 percent of the Class of 1982 entered the service within six months after graduation, whereas the cumulative percentages of military entrants through 1985 were 7.9 and 7.6 percent for the two classes.

Patterns of preservice activities among late military entrants were similar to those of their classmates, although the enlistees were less likely to enter college after graduation. Except for the fact that the military entrants were mostly male, they differed only slightly from their classmates in terms of demographic characteristics. A somewhat higher proportion of them came from lower socioeconomic status families and from minority groups. In terms of academic aptitude, the military entrants were on a par with their classmates.

Our finding that about half of the high school graduates were not pursuing the same activities in October following graduation that they planned to follow in the spring indicates that many, if not most, high school seniors do not know where they are headed or how they will get there. Our examination of postsecondary activities indicates that this lack of direction persists beyond high school. A substantial proportion of the military enlistees enter the service only after having tried other alternatives, and only one-sixth of the graduates who enter four-year colleges after graduation enroll continuously until they complete bachelor's degrees. The prevalence of lengthy delays in completing degree programs and high college dropout rates, even among four-year college students, show that most high school graduates follow indirect courses in pursuing their educational objectives, and a surprisingly large proportion of them fail to achieve their objectives. As a result, the nation's supply of college-trained personnel will be severely tested over the next decade.

Appendix A

ESTIMATING NUMBERS OF HIGH SCHOOL GRADUATES

This study relies heavily on the High School and Beyond surveys of the Classes of 1980 and 1982 for the purposes of examining how high school graduates and dropouts sort themselves into postsecondary paths. The longitudinal data base derived from HS&B raises numerous analytic problems for reasons that are outlined in Appendix B. To profile the Classes of 1980 and 1982 accurately and to derive the case weights needed to compensate for the nonrepresentativeness of the HS&B school and student samples, counts of the numbers of high school graduates by state, sex, race, and school affiliation are required. Given the nonexistence of these counts, we sought ways to provide estimates that would accord with the more reliable published estimates.

Because counts of *public* high school graduates by state are regularly published in the *Digest of Education Statistics* (NCES, 1988), the main problem in deriving the estimates for 1980 and 1982 was to devise a means for estimating numbers of *private* (nonpublic) school graduates. For that purpose, we made use of state-level data for the years 1980–1986 compiled by the Western Interstate Commission on Higher Education (WICHE, 1988). Although the WICHE state data are incomplete except for 1986, they provide complete time series on most states that have large numbers of private school graduates. Exploiting patterns in the private/public ratios in the states having no missing values, we extended WICHE's estimates to provide a complete set of state estimates for 1980–1986. To provide further breakdowns of the state totals by sex, race, and Hispanic origin, we derived a second set of state estimates by applying high school completion rates by sex and race to Census Bureau estimates of age group sizes; the resulting detailed estimates were then adjusted to agree with the state totals.

The state high school graduation rates derived from the 1980–1986 estimates were listed in Table 5. The rates are defined by dividing the estimated number of high school graduates in any year by the number of 17-year-olds as of July 1 in the previous year. The analogous census division and regional rates for 1980–1986 evidence the same overall pattern as the U.S. rates in Table 5, including the stable pattern over the years 1984–1986. This apparent leveling off of the graduation rates was confirmed by the 1987 state data for public high school graduates, which showed a very slight decrease of 0.1 percent in the public high school graduation rate.

Adopting the assumption that the state graduation rates remained stable through the 1980s and applying the estimated 1987 graduation rates to Census Bureau age group sizes by state, sex, and race, we extended our state estimates through 1989. Since the scheme could be readily extended to future years by applying the estimated graduation rates to the Census Bureau projections of age group sizes, we have also provided "projections" of high school graduates by state, sex, race, and control (public or private) for the years 1990–2000. The remainder of this appendix is devoted to presenting the estimates and projections, and documenting the estimation process that led to them.

THE ESTIMATES AND PROJECTIONS

Table A.1 summarizes the state estimates by sex, control of school, and race/Hispanic category for the years 1980–1989. Table A.2 provides the corresponding projections for 1990–2000. Although all estimates and projections are listed to the nearest unit for the convenience of potential users, this belies the precision of the estimates, not only for the years after 1987 but for most of the entries before 1987. The only estimates in the tables that accord with published state-level counts are the 1980–1987 entries for public high school graduates and a subset of the 1980–1986 entries for private high school graduates.

The 1980–1987 state data on public high school graduates are taken from the *Digest of Education Statistics* (NCES, 1988, p. 100). These data, which pertain to graduates from regular public day schools and exclude persons receiving high school equivalency certificates, come from NCES's Common Core of Data. In theory, the NCES counts result from annual censuses of the public school systems in all states, but the published counts may not be totally reliable, and we have filled in a few missing values.

There is no analogous source of counts of private high school graduates, because NCES has no systematic means for gathering complete data from the private schools. In the past, NCES has published tables displaying state-by-state estimates for the private schools, but those estimates were derived from school surveys that relied on incomplete, out-of-date sampling frames and were not designed to provide accurate state estimates.

THE WICHE DATA

In a notable effort to fill the information gap on private high school graduates, WICHE elicited the cooperation of state educational agencies in compiling a data base on school enrollments by grade level and numbers of graduates, both public and private, for the academic years 1978–79 through 1985–86. Although some states were unable to provide time series of counts of private school graduates, WICHE published the time series that were available as well as their best estimates for 1986. Using their more complete data on enrollments by grade level in both public and private schools, they applied a cohort survival method to generate projections of numbers of high school graduates for the years 1987–2004. The accordance of the WICHE projections with those generated in this study will be examined at the end of this appendix.

WICHE provides no 1980–1985 estimates of private high school graduates for 20 states and the District of Columbia, and a few other states have isolated missing values. However, the WICHE data are complete for most states with large numbers of private high school graduates, including California where their estimates agree with those reported by the California State Department of Education. In fact, the states with complete time series accounted for 70 percent of the nation's private high school graduates in 1986.

Restricting attention to the WICHE state estimates for the states with no missing values, we found that there were small, relatively uniform increases in the private/public ratios in all census divisions from 1980 to 1986. For the states having no missing values, the overall private/public ratio rose steadily from .109 in 1980 to .124 in 1985 and then dipped slightly to .122 in 1986. Led by the consistency of this pattern both within and across regions, we estimated the missing values in the WICHE time series for 1980–1985 by using their 1986 private school estimates and imposing the assumption that the private/public ratios for 1980–1986 in the "missing states" were proportional to the overall ratios for the

Table A.1

ESTIMATED NUMBERS OF HIGH SCHOOL GRADUATES
BY STATE AND CATEGORY: 1980–1989

Category: All

State	1980	1981	1982	1983	1984	1985	1986	1987	1988	1989
Alabama	48643	48247	48876	47651	45242	43177	42855	45930	45976	47739
Alaska	5312	5435	5582	5736	5573	5297	5574	5807	6110	6226
Arizona	29196	29196	28904	27386	29284	28836	28408	30495	31280	32726
Arkansas	29959	30529	30679	29291	27908	27182	27032	28060	28211	29242
California	271526	263389	265924	261994	257633	251143	252150	262921	274707	278802
Colorado	39174	38234	38060	37543	35580	34887	35079	37049	37758	38533
Connecticut	45106	45884	45236	43994	41218	39610	40912	39485	40720	39746
Delaware	9054	9003	8798	8559	8072	7502	7399	7532	7626	7774
D. of Columbia	6141	5977	6031	6048	5046	4915	4862	4821	4864	5111
Florida	96681	98052	100451	95934	95142	90171	92536	91114	96515	100561
Georgia	65710	67048	68765	67382	64760	62697	63272	64014	67923	71184
Hawaii	14013	13994	13948	13251	12948	12516	12468	13135	12854	12981
Idaho	13419	12916	12788	12349	11995	12391	12277	12485	12478	12991
Illinois	154716	156598	156802	148861	141935	136054	132770	134809	135960	137724
Indiana	77346	78607	78202	75108	69348	67605	63846	65868	66996	69545
Iowa	46593	45866	44616	42645	40205	39061	37074	37496	37713	37741
Kansas	32507	30975	29860	30048	28310	27560	27195	28165	28067	28799
Kentucky	45447	45872	46713	44602	43536	41713	40896	40787	41873	43640
Louisiana	54931	54571	47999	46663	46910	47558	48322	47748	48687	49143
Maine	17261	17395	16591	16440	15805	15721	14773	15552	15464	15699
Maryland	61146	60893	61578	59353	57440	55175	53438	52770	53356	53420
Massachusetts	85674	87141	85715	83492	77496	75012	71522	71095	70906	70452
Michigan	136104	136129	132644	123410	119826	117253	111784	111738	115399	117461
Minnesota	69204	68443	66429	63113	59593	57530	56149	57890	56740	56996
Mississippi	29937	30422	30409	29533	28574	27556	27423	28587	29336	30043
Missouri	68080	66868	65838	62799	59388	57427	54867	56691	57288	58643
Montana	12569	12096	11616	11080	10546	10370	10079	10497	10424	10653
Nebraska	24794	23718	23404	22173	20871	20079	19798	20113	19859	20176
Nevada	8773	9375	9599	9349	9096	8955	9175	9182	9991	10290
New Hampshire	13302	13144	13307	13126	13173	12746	12298	12601	13167	13779
New Jersey	111206	109936	110937	107025	102067	97870	94720	95284	95397	94356
New Mexico	19133	19097	18726	17765	17304	16930	16885	17139	17512	17881
New York	235937	230237	226856	216082	205901	197595	192593	193941	194629	193538
North Carolina	73694	72106	74053	71459	69481	70036	68678	68866	72458	75331
North Dakota	10731	10635	10226	9601	9270	8732	8149	8375	8382	8257
Ohio	159169	158043	154597	148124	142377	135973	132805	134538	137376	141149
Oklahoma	39941	39490	38967	37379	35826	35208	35048	36128	36879	38088
Oregon	31310	30228	30235	29565	28804	28373	27746	28674	29001	28838
Pennsylvania	170646	169202	167541	160329	154744	149666	145005	144862	145063	146945
Rhode Island	12671	12542	12372	12410	11411	11060	10510	10542	10733	10938
South Carolina	41043	40619	40988	39784	39038	36672	36735	36644	38231	40011
South Dakota	11444	11131	10550	9904	9304	8949	8382	8599	8307	8559
Tennessee	52970	53753	54670	49555	47523	46113	46162	46779	49271	51040
Texas	180454	180479	181115	177533	170093	167921	170194	177883	189213	196314
Utah	20282	20120	19667	19583	19874	20189	20073	21246	22068	23721
Vermont	7725	7392	7513	6960	6971	6736	6776	6950	7089	7266
Virginia	70552	70998	71807	69338	65858	64696	67093	69819	68955	70722
Washington	52928	52638	52772	48588	47740	48368	48742	51344	51486	51687
West Virginia	24376	24300	24352	24296	23309	22913	22546	23093	23419	24068
Wisconsin	76233	75692	74246	71037	68541	65165	64522	62898	63939	64213
Wyoming	6230	6323	6175	6092	5950	5875	5758	6115	6189	6365
United States	3021207	3000978	2983729	2871325	2763839	2682739	2645375	2694156	2752981	2807407

Table A.1—continued

Category: Public

State	1980	1981	1982	1983	1984	1985	1986	1987	1988	1989
Alabama	45190	44894	45409	44352	42021	40002	39620	42463	42506	44135
Alaska	5223	5343	5477	5622	5457	5184	5464	5692	5989	6103
Arizona	28633	28416	28049	26530	28332	27877	27533	29556	30317	31718
Arkansas	29052	29577	29710	28447	27049	26342	26227	27224	27371	28371
California	249217	242172	241343	236897	232199	225448	229026	237414	249518	253238
Colorado	36804	35897	35494	34875	32954	32255	32621	34453	35112	35833
Connecticut	37683	38369	37706	36204	33679	32126	33571	32400	33413	32614
Delaware	7582	7349	7144	6924	6410	5893	5791	5895	5969	6084
D. of Columbia	4959	4848	4871	4909	4073	3940	3875	3842	3876	4073
Florida	87324	88755	90736	86871	85908	81140	83029	81753	86599	90229
Georgia	61621	62963	64489	63293	60718	58654	59082	59775	63425	66470
Hawaii	11493	11472	11563	10757	10454	10092	9958	10491	10267	10368
Idaho	13187	12679	12560	12126	11732	12148	12059	12243	12236	12739
Illinois	135579	136795	136534	128814	122051	117027	114319	116075	116322	118585
Indiana	73143	73381	73984	70549	65710	63308	59817	61711	62768	65156
Iowa	43445	42635	41509	39569	37248	36087	34279	34669	34870	34896
Kansas	30890	29397	28298	28316	26730	25983	25587	26500	26408	27097
Kentucky	41203	41714	42531	40478	39645	37999	37288	37189	38179	39790
Louisiana	46297	46199	39895	39539	39400	39742	39965	39490	40267	40644
Maine	15445	15554	14764	14600	13935	13924	13006	13692	13615	13821
Maryland	54270	54050	54621	52446	50684	48299	46700	46116	46628	46684
Massachusetts	73802	74831	73414	71219	65885	63411	60360	60000	59840	59457
Michigan	124316	124372	121030	112950	108926	105908	101042	101000	104309	106173
Minnesota	64908	64166	62145	59015	55376	53352	51988	53600	52535	52772
Mississippi	27586	28083	28023	27271	26324	25315	25134	26201	26887	27535
Missouri	62265	60359	59872	56420	53388	51290	49204	50840	51375	52591
Montana	12135	11634	11162	10689	10224	10016	9761	10166	10095	10317
Nebraska	22410	21411	21027	19986	18674	18036	17845	18129	17900	18456
Nevada	8473	9069	9240	8979	8726	8572	8784	8791	9566	9852
New Hampshire	11722	11552	11669	11470	11478	11052	10648	10910	11400	11930
New Jersey	94564	93168	93750	90048	85569	81547	78781	79250	79344	78478
New Mexico	18424	17915	17635	16530	15914	15622	15468	15701	16043	16381
New York	204064	198465	194605	184022	174762	166752	162165	163300	163879	162961
North Carolina	70862	69395	71210	68783	66803	67245	65865	66045	69490	72245
North Dakota	9928	9924	9504	8886	8560	8146	7610	7821	7828	7711
Ohio	144169	143503	139899	133524	127837	122281	119561	121121	123676	127073
Oklahoma	39305	38875	38347	36799	35254	34626	34452	35514	36252	37441
Oregon	29939	28729	28780	28099	27214	26870	26286	27165	27475	27320
Pennsylvania	146458	144645	143356	137494	132412	127226	122871	122750	122920	124515
Rhode Island	10864	10719	10545	10533	9652	9201	8749	8776	8935	9106
South Carolina	38697	38347	38697	37570	36800	34500	34500	34415	35905	37577
South Dakota	10689	10385	9864	9206	8638	8206	7870	8074	7800	8036
Tennessee	49845	50648	51447	46704	44711	43293	43263	43841	46176	47834
Texas	171449	171665	172085	168897	161580	159234	161150	168430	179158	185882
Utah	20035	19886	19400	19350	19606	19890	19774	20930	21740	23368
Vermont	6733	6424	6513	6011	6002	5769	5794	5943	6062	6213
Virginia	66621	67126	67809	65571	62177	60959	63113	65677	64864	66526
Washington	50402	50046	50148	45809	44919	45431	45805	48250	48383	48572
West Virginia	23369	23580	23589	23561	22613	22262	21870	22401	22717	23347
Wisconsin	69332	67743	67357	64321	62189	58851	58340	56872	57813	58061
Wyoming	6072	6161	5999	5909	5764	5687	5587	5933	6005	6176
United States	2747678	2725285	2704758	2597744	2494885	2414020	2382457	2426489	2482027	2532554

82

Category: Private

Table A.1—continued

State	1980	1981	1982	1983	1984	1985	1986	1987	1988	1989
Alabama	3453	3353	3467	3299	3221	3175	3235	3467	3470	3604
Alaska	89	92	105	114	116	113	110	115	121	123
Arizona	777	780	855	856	952	959	875	939	963	1008
Arkansas	907	952	969	844	859	840	805	836	840	871
California	22309	21217	24581	25097	25434	25695	23124	25507	25189	25564
Colorado	2370	2337	2566	2668	2626	2632	2458	2596	2646	2700
Connecticut	7423	7515	7530	7790	7539	7484	7341	7085	7307	7132
Delaware	1472	1654	1654	1635	1662	1609	1608	1637	1657	1690
D. of Columbia	1182	1129	1160	1139	973	975	987	979	988	1038
Florida	9357	9297	9715	9063	9234	9031	9507	9361	9916	10332
Georgia	4089	4085	4276	4089	4042	4043	4190	4239	4498	4714
Hawaii	2520	2522	2385	2494	2494	2424	2510	2644	2587	2613
Idaho	232	237	228	223	263	243	238	242	242	252
Illinois	19137	19803	20268	20047	19374	19027	18451	18734	18774	19139
Indiana	4203	5226	4218	4559	3638	4297	4029	4157	4228	4389
Iowa	3148	3231	3107	3076	2957	2974	2795	2827	2843	2845
Kansas	1617	1578	1562	1732	1580	1577	1608	1665	1659	1702
Kentucky	4244	4158	4182	4124	3891	3714	3608	3598	3694	3850
Louisiana	8634	8372	8104	7124	7510	7816	8357	8258	8420	8499
Maine	1816	1841	1827	1840	1870	1797	1767	1860	1849	1878
Maryland	6876	6843	6957	6907	6756	6876	6738	6654	6728	6736
Massachusetts	11878	12301	12301	12273	11611	11601	11162	11095	11066	10995
Michigan	11788	11757	11614	10460	10900	11345	10742	10738	11090	11288
Minnesota	4296	4277	4284	4098	4217	4178	4161	4290	4205	4224
Mississippi	2351	2339	2386	2262	2250	2241	2289	2386	2449	2508
Missouri	5815	6509	5966	6379	6000	6137	5663	5851	5913	6052
Montana	434	462	454	391	322	354	318	331	329	336
Nebraska	2384	2307	2377	2187	2197	2043	1953	1984	1959	2020
Nevada	300	306	359	370	370	383	391	391	425	438
New Hampshire	1580	1592	1638	1656	1695	1694	1650	1691	1767	1849
New Jersey	16642	16768	17187	16977	16498	16323	15939	16034	16053	15878
New Mexico	709	1182	1091	1235	1390	1308	1417	1438	1469	1500
New York	31873	31772	32251	32060	31139	30843	30428	30641	30750	30577
North Carolina	2832	2711	2843	2676	2678	2791	2813	2821	2968	3086
North Dakota	803	711	722	715	701	586	539	554	554	546
Ohio	15000	14540	14698	14600	14540	13692	13244	13417	13700	14076
Oklahoma	636	615	620	580	572	582	596	614	627	647
Oregon	1371	1499	1455	1466	1590	1503	1460	1509	1526	1518
Pennsylvania	24188	24557	24185	22835	22332	22440	22134	22112	22143	22430
Rhode Island	1807	1823	1827	1877	1759	1859	1761	1766	1798	1832
South Carolina	2346	2272	2341	2217	2238	2172	2235	2229	2326	2434
South Dakota	755	746	686	698	666	743	512	525	507	523
Tennessee	3125	3105	3223	2851	2812	2820	2899	2938	3095	3206
Texas	9005	8814	9030	8636	8513	8687	9044	9453	10055	10432
Utah	247	234	267	233	268	299	299	316	328	353
Vermont	992	968	1000	949	969	967	982	1007	1027	1053
Virginia	3931	3872	3998	3767	3681	3737	3980	4142	4091	4196
Washington	2526	2592	2624	2779	2821	2937	2937	3094	3103	3115
West Virginia	1007	720	763	735	696	651	676	692	702	721
Wisconsin	6901	7949	6889	6716	6352	6314	6182	6026	6126	6152
Wyoming	158	162	176	183	186	188	171	182	184	189
United States	273529	275693	278971	273581	268954	268719	262918	267667	270954	274853

Table A.1—continued

Category: Male

State	1980	1981	1982	1983	1984	1985	1986	1987	1988	1989
Alabama	23348	22995	23446	22834	21874	20899	20714	22232	22322	23072
Alaska	2650	2816	2903	2974	2974	2765	2884	2944	3177	3178
Arizona	14443	14432	14324	13499	14578	14317	14137	15091	15571	16292
Arkansas	15247	14795	14929	14231	13663	13305	13326	13755	13838	14477
California	136718	131361	133167	130918	129376	125567	126720	132464	137844	139454
Colorado	19454	19129	19102	18844	17826	17405	17547	18600	19082	19594
Connecticut	21153	22517	22263	21655	20297	19635	20489	19528	20222	19703
Delaware	4345	4336	4241	4117	3957	3573	3510	3652	3682	3744
D. of Columbia	2737	2668	2699	2693	2274	2181	2151	2207	2196	2279
Florida	46599	46931	48358	46000	45881	43226	44574	43549	46363	48564
Georgia	31447	32602	33558	32602	31329	30282	30417	31235	32747	34382
Hawaii	6925	7036	7032	6655	6459	6247	6234	6492	6502	6579
Idaho	6800	6508	6457	6205	6108	6259	6243	6340	6248	6520
Illinois	75698	77159	77577	73380	70316	67328	65677	67032	67144	68286
Indiana	38115	38521	38483	36938	34042	33297	31711	32465	33253	34537
Iowa	22913	22714	22180	21245	20069	19579	18551	18733	19104	19290
Kansas	16252	15165	14642	14819	13956	13522	13506	13924	13953	14579
Kentucky	22310	22983	23455	22239	21818	20793	20163	20606	20653	21554
Louisiana	25355	25653	22358	21757	22170	22577	23033	22524	23295	23641
Maine	8487	8570	8191	8144	7967	7886	7394	7733	7810	7833
Maryland	29138	29496	30026	28887	27860	26965	26033	25641	26242	26213
Massachusetts	42495	43290	42578	41419	38089	36818	35014	35361	34803	34968
Michigan	67249	66769	65261	60454	59090	57701	55197	54984	57266	58256
Minnesota	34566	34288	33358	31647	29707	28941	28589	29313	28872	28952
Mississippi	14129	14390	14427	13975	13663	13078	13130	13696	13995	14382
Missouri	33913	33165	32717	31111	29340	28349	26847	28286	28469	29309
Montana	6388	6211	5968	5681	5431	5305	5192	5435	5374	5530
Nebraska	12436	11799	11685	11055	10546	10220	10037	10083	10052	10329
Nevada	4406	4745	4868	4739	4546	4508	4595	4704	4993	5257
New Hampshire	6279	6435	6573	6477	6572	6398	6126	6212	6538	6844
New Jersey	55073	54648	55337	53238	50600	48450	46932	47546	47144	46942
New Mexico	9274	9548	9372	8847	8612	8489	8402	8597	8776	8894
New York	116249	111700	110209	104576	99423	95888	93527	94385	94853	94782
North Carolina	35630	34546	35705	34354	33675	33645	33165	33131	34991	36478
North Dakota	5348	5257	5084	4765	4746	4490	4167	4129	4312	4135
Ohio	78683	77999	76538	73213	70975	67878	66491	66812	68865	70262
Oklahoma	20135	19684	19442	18610	18027	17478	17437	18065	18407	19149
Oregon	15430	15087	15165	14839	14324	14379	13945	14467	14681	14690
Pennsylvania	84224	83494	82919	79199	76729	74062	71981	71902	72124	73291
Rhode Island	6042	6036	5983	6015	5567	5332	5165	5092	5221	5283
South Carolina	19952	19792	19997	19309	18853	17657	17833	17885	18390	19301
South Dakota	5784	5582	5276	4918	4658	4432	4132	4317	4143	4238
Tennessee	25448	25893	26489	23759	23017	22268	22441	22583	23849	24520
Texas	89393	87936	88634	86814	83832	82601	83998	87176	93097	96143
Utah	10178	10117	9888	9809	10002	10127	9952	10797	10988	11778
Vermont	3824	3606	3693	3410	3428	3298	3370	3443	3536	3666
Virginia	33160	34397	34994	33677	32021	31523	32998	34101	34012	34592
Washington	26377	26350	26540	24352	24003	24353	24516	25850	26123	26229
West Virginia	12112	11817	11914	11957	11530	11253	11051	11362	11624	12117
Wisconsin	37341	37564	36978	35370	34310	32663	32441	31503	32251	32469
Wyoming	3184	3227	3137	3104	2975	2920	2855	3138	3087	3313
United States	1484836	1473759	1470140	1411492	1363085	1322108	1306540	1331102	1362084	1389870

Table A.1—continued

Category: Female

State	1980	1981	1982	1983	1984	1985	1986	1987	1988	1989
Alabama	25295	25252	25430	24817	23368	22278	22141	23698	23654	24667
Alaska	2662	2619	2679	2762	2599	2532	2690	2863	2933	3048
Arizona	14967	14764	14580	13887	14706	14519	14271	15404	15709	16434
Arkansas	14712	15734	15750	15060	14245	13877	13706	14305	14373	14765
California	134808	132028	132757	131076	128257	125576	125430	130457	136863	139348
Colorado	19720	19105	18958	18699	17754	17482	17532	18449	18676	18939
Connecticut	23953	23367	22973	22339	20921	19975	20423	19957	20498	20043
Delaware	4709	4667	4557	4442	4115	3929	3889	3880	3944	4030
D. of Columbia	3404	3309	3332	3355	2772	2734	2711	2614	2668	2832
Florida	50082	51121	52093	49934	49261	46945	47962	47565	50152	51997
Georgia	34263	34446	35187	34617	33431	32415	32855	32779	35176	36802
Hawaii	7088	6958	6916	6596	6489	6269	6234	6643	6352	6402
Idaho	6619	6408	6331	6144	5887	6132	6054	6145	6230	6471
Illinois	79018	79439	79225	75481	71619	68726	67093	67777	67952	69438
Indiana	39231	40086	39719	38170	35306	34308	32135	33403	33743	35008
Iowa	23680	23152	22436	21400	20136	19482	18523	18763	18609	18451
Kansas	16255	15810	15218	15229	14354	14038	13689	14241	14114	14220
Kentucky	23137	22889	23258	22363	21718	20920	20733	20181	21220	22086
Louisiana	29576	28918	25641	24906	24740	24981	25289	25224	25392	25502
Maine	8774	8825	8400	8296	7838	7835	7379	7819	7654	7866
Maryland	32008	31397	31552	30466	29580	28210	27405	27129	27114	27207
Massachusetts	43179	43851	43137	42073	39407	38194	36508	35734	36103	35484
Michigan	68855	69360	67383	62956	60736	59552	56587	56754	58133	59205
Minnesota	34638	34155	33071	31466	29886	28589	27560	28577	27868	28044
Mississippi	15808	16032	15982	15558	14911	14478	14293	14891	15341	15661
Missouri	34167	33703	33121	31688	30048	29078	28020	28405	28819	29334
Montana	6181	5885	5648	5399	5115	5065	4887	5062	5050	5123
Nebraska	12358	11919	11719	11118	10325	9859	9761	10030	9807	10147
Nevada	4367	4630	4731	4610	4550	4447	4580	4478	4998	5033
New Hampshire	7023	6709	6734	6649	6601	6348	6172	6389	6629	6935
New Jersey	56133	55288	55600	53787	51467	49420	47788	47738	48253	47414
New Mexico	9859	9549	9354	8918	8692	8441	8483	8542	8736	8987
New York	119688	118537	116647	111506	106478	101707	99066	99556	99776	98756
North Carolina	38064	37560	38348	37105	35806	36391	35513	35735	37467	38853
North Dakota	5383	5378	5142	4836	4524	4242	3982	4246	4070	4122
Ohio	80486	80044	78059	74911	71402	68095	66314	67726	68511	70887
Oklahoma	19806	19806	19525	18769	17799	17730	17611	18063	18472	18939
Oregon	15880	15141	15070	14726	14480	13994	13801	14207	14320	14148
Pennsylvania	86422	85708	84622	81130	78015	75604	73024	72960	72939	73654
Rhode Island	6629	6506	6389	6395	5844	5728	5345	5450	5512	5655
South Carolina	21091	20827	20991	20478	20185	19015	18902	18759	19841	20710
South Dakota	5660	5549	5274	4986	4646	4517	4250	4282	4164	4321
Tennessee	27522	27860	28181	25796	24506	23845	23721	24196	25422	26520
Texas	91061	92543	92481	90719	86261	85320	86196	90707	96116	100171
Utah	10104	10003	9779	9774	9872	10062	10121	10449	11080	11943
Vermont	3901	3786	3820	3550	3543	3438	3406	3507	3553	3600
Virginia	37392	36601	36813	35661	33837	33173	34095	35718	34943	36130
Washington	26551	26288	26232	24236	23737	24019	24226	25494	25363	25458
West Virginia	12264	12483	12438	12339	11779	11660	11495	11731	11795	11951
Wisconsin	38892	38128	37268	35667	34231	32502	32081	31395	31688	31744
Wyoming	3046	3096	3038	2988	2975	2955	2903	2977	3102	3052
United States	1536371	1527219	1513589	1459833	1400754	1360631	1338835	1363054	1390897	1417537

Table A.1—continued

Category: White Non-Hispanic

State	1980	1981	1982	1983	1984	1985	1986	1987	1988	1989
Alabama	35325	35067	35257	34028	32309	31088	31025	33210	33833	34632
Alaska	4121	4202	4196	4175	3996	3888	4125	4488	4698	4713
Arizona	22735	22597	22160	20837	21640	21310	21099	23122	23921	25047
Arkansas	24362	24780	24775	23500	22191	21731	21587	22797	23021	23646
California	186977	182201	182391	177267	167674	160897	158234	161878	171963	172877
Colorado	32806	32120	31720	30943	28893	28399	28397	30261	30846	31346
Connecticut	40504	41160	40384	38960	36308	34626	35273	34087	35257	34056
Delaware	7321	7283	7084	6804	6359	5941	5720	5800	5916	5926
D. of Columbia	727	713	725	745	664	835	972	919	1085	1066
Florida	73497	74416	75981	72281	70766	67515	69701	70356	74746	77329
Georgia	47506	48378	49192	47544	45185	44442	45188	46142	49633	51352
Hawaii	3744	3742	3457	3172	2917	2834	2705	2989	2880	2874
Idaho	12710	12256	12115	11664	11295	11469	11750	11750	11698	12149
Illinois	125687	126983	126396	119002	111436	106153	102145	102749	103094	103213
Indiana	71120	72186	71650	68504	63200	61541	57997	59723	60868	62787
Iowa	45350	44666	43383	41388	38868	37677	35716	35967	36158	36122
Kansas	29910	28600	27489	27431	25710	24883	24421	25195	25170	25628
Kentucky	41943	42324	43026	41004	39947	38429	37555	37531	38592	40051
Louisiana	37197	37000	32810	31434	30723	31239	31318	31707	32960	32587
Maine	17092	17223	16407	16248	15625	15521	14591	15352	15278	15491
Maryland	44987	44830	44887	42691	40866	39230	37333	36732	37151	36491
Massachusetts	80426	81693	80128	77642	71949	69409	65988	65394	65229	64440
Michigan	119161	119173	115753	107315	102789	100057	94591	93645	96974	97195
Minnesota	67054	66344	64286	60881	57321	55087	53555	55008	53753	53788
Mississippi	18828	19093	18934	18110	17379	16857	16884	17563	18495	18586
Missouri	60736	59753	58734	55762	52321	50712	48449	50137	50698	51628
Montana	11790	11378	10868	10313	9735	9571	9252	9629	9580	9748
Nebraska	23368	22419	22080	20808	19449	18632	18349	18645	18385	18937
Nevada	7338	7806	7950	7697	7494	7344	7532	7425	8215	8415
New Hampshire	13170	13019	13155	12975	12982	12560	12123	12445	12978	13581
New Jersey	90423	89635	89393	85115	80000	76291	72838	73442	73245	70914
New Mexico	10066	10061	9865	9249	8295	7595	7280	8254	8300	8606
New York	186385	182778	178860	168815	159088	151743	145519	145478	146691	143321
North Carolina	54980	53922	54848	52394	50473	51689	50704	51159	54175	55776
North Dakota	10265	10179	9770	9130	8780	8290	7664	7944	7913	7786
Ohio	143077	142161	138718	132331	126664	121334	118143	118836	121688	124177
Oklahoma	33836	33482	32776	31069	29502	28993	28744	29701	30380	31048
Oregon	29444	28454	28380	27653	26838	26368	25660	26490	26741	26536
Pennsylvania	154102	152948	150972	143893	138426	133988	129480	129305	129728	130590
Rhode Island	12082	11966	11768	11742	10813	10445	9933	9863	10056	10210
South Carolina	27490	27247	27269	26125	25266	24319	24469	24778	26138	26992
South Dakota	10625	10360	9770	9130	8463	8103	7560	7729	7461	7640
Tennessee	44086	44693	45224	40967	39086	38328	38301	38899	41214	42242
Texas	120044	120032	119330	113538	105264	103157	104226	112110	121989	126349
Utah	18745	18602	18107	17952	18225	18429	18341	19383	20145	21669
Vermont	7665	7338	7451	6903	6896	6660	6687	6840	6967	7141
Virginia	55369	55708	55885	53385	50308	49793	51245	53371	53477	54132
Washington	48258	48003	47880	43889	43005	43318	43449	45569	45617	45647
West Virginia	23403	23330	23318	23236	22281	21941	21621	22132	22539	23099
Wisconsin	72023	71547	70004	66799	63976	60749	59419	58022	58861	58766
Wyoming	5823	5906	5756	5634	5440	5332	5189	5540	5608	5770
United States	2465683	2451757	2422717	2310074	2195080	2126891	2079713	2117524	2172002	2194112

Table A.1—continued

Category: Black Non-Hispanic

State	1980	1981	1982	1983	1984	1985	1986	1987	1988	1989
Alabama	12776	12645	13085	13075	12360	11520	11249	12082	11517	12444
Alaska	138	142	145	156	146	131	155	153	157	181
Arizona	962	954	960	927	1002	933	918	997	999	1049
Arkansas	5203	5342	5481	5365	5259	4969	4930	4710	4646	5043
California	24995	24202	24663	24939	25690	24562	24371	25675	26113	27429
Colorado	1475	1437	1475	1516	1436	1349	1386	1464	1456	1636
Connecticut	2973	3054	3116	3208	3095	3018	3281	3179	3180	3388
Delaware	1549	1537	1526	1548	1518	1368	1458	1501	1459	1593
D. of Columbia	5239	5095	5135	5136	4227	3922	3792	3688	3630	3882
Florida	15129	15409	16105	15753	16237	15122	15268	14302	14678	16213
Georgia	17283	17720	18680	18862	18612	17311	17081	16831	17190	18628
Hawaii	112	112	115	106	123	146	117	158	40	174
Idaho	35	34	27	21	32	30	31	36	40	50
Illinois	20798	21209	21850	21363	21484	20852	20811	21339	21032	23225
Indiana	4987	5141	5274	5267	4879	4733	4483	4700	4557	5151
Iowa	625	603	596	609	631	658	604	691	733	762
Kansas	1610	1477	1433	1579	1515	1462	1470	1501	1417	1586
Kentucky	3093	3132	3289	3198	3166	2906	2926	2866	2887	3206
Louisiana	16279	16131	13937	13937	14735	14725	15359	14441	14083	14900
Maine	23	23	23	19	19	21	21	27	24	26
Maryland	14454	14370	14889	14800	14638	13992	14023	13904	13937	14607
Massachusetts	3060	3173	3163	3281	3062	2947	2919	2987	2882	3138
Michigan	13921	13933	13780	13098	13815	13820	13762	14423	14647	16308
Minnesota	721	704	690	697	701	702	743	773	810	876
Mississippi	10723	10936	11083	11009	10747	10508	10077	10508	10367	10960
Missouri	6345	6148	6147	6113	6089	5751	5441	5533	5520	5921
Montana	11	11	17	15	24	22	23	24	31	32
Nebraska	807	736	749	747	739	740	703	726	727	789
Nevada	693	747	773	770	767	777	744	750	798	837
New Hampshire	39	36	37	41	59	55	46	50	56	65
New Jersey	13767	13467	14217	14338	14197	13480	13538	13573	13519	14401
New Mexico	389	389	389	381	387	347	398	361	384	428
New York	29258	28077	28095	27729	26795	25441	25634	26507	26040	27805
North Carolina	17160	16676	17552	17383	17328	16591	16211	15891	16390	17554
North Dakota	21	21	10	13	25	18	15	22	22	34
Ohio	13999	13815	13724	13662	13382	12388	12319	13105	13105	14331
Oklahoma	2856	2811	2802	2794	2756	2600	2521	2578	2558	2870
Oregon	512	490	497	506	537	499	472	481	500	522
Pennsylvania	13939	13696	13899	13721	13316	12669	12254	12138	11903	12689
Rhode Island	334	327	334	364	316	312	279	319	310	344
South Carolina	12986	12813	13164	13105	13209	11805	11681	11304	11536	12421
South Dakota	13	13	10	13	16	15	17	22	24	26
Tennessee	8391	8558	8925	8119	7963	7305	7379	7366	7524	8257
Texas	22587	22589	23127	23407	23105	22374	22305	22285	22785	25065
Utah	235	233	226	218	172	187	173	161	171	176
Vermont	8	7	9	8	17	16	19	22	23	31
Virginia	13541	13640	14166	14150	13677	12889	13494	13893	12906	13892
Washington	1409	1400	1421	1352	1272	1280	1310	1405	1437	1532
West Virginia	818	815	830	871	800	741	681	703	647	728
Wisconsin	2717	2675	2692	2693	2872	2746	3220	3011	3145	3478
Wyoming	47	48	46	50	33	54	43	60	48	60
United States	341045	338753	344378	342031	338985	322576	322155	325245	324701	350743

Category: Other Non-Hispanic

Table A.1—continued

State	1980	1981	1982	1983	1984	1985	1986	1987	1988	1989
Alabama	170	168	188	195	218	205	235	268	284	299
Alaska	964	997	1143	1303	1322	1186	1182	1070	1139	1206
Arizona	1746	1726	1896	1876	2118	2115	2065	2046	2043	2192
Arkansas	184	189	217	224	241	252	286	309	311	321
California	17170	16716	18619	19377	20383	20972	22683	24751	26163	27667
Colorado	598	582	670	700	725	713	761	853	889	962
Connecticut	260	265	290	313	309	389	455	467	545	552
Delaware	48	48	55	64	68	61	81	86	99	101
D. of Columbia	59	57	64	65	74	60	56	54	55	60
Florida	663	675	784	801	870	960	1141	1190	1310	1447
Georgia	286	293	333	345	355	365	422	473	540	600
Hawaii	9163	9154	9490	9235	9053	8588	8645	8884	8697	8805
Idaho	208	196	220	238	234	267	263	261	256	289
Illinois	1643	1666	1881	1910	1986	2099	2350	2725	2869	3048
Indiana	298	306	344	365	323	391	421	485	563	573
Iowa	286	279	298	311	347	345	370	448	424	460
Kansas	317	294	321	379	379	493	544	654	647	699
Kentucky	122	123	146	144	140	124	164	140	129	140
Louisiana	390	387	384	408	460	558	583	626	662	700
Maine	100	102	108	118	106	112	112	114	112	120
Maryland	901	895	1009	1022	1126	1101	1281	1345	1505	1523
Massachusetts	695	711	784	818	832	907	972	1021	1062	1130
Michigan	1106	1106	1194	1172	1268	1323	1422	1486	1637	1719
Minnesota	998	977	1051	1101	1127	1242	1333	1562	1609	1749
Mississippi	137	138	157	167	176	157	188	231	219	238
Missouri	390	381	418	428	425	427	464	505	531	554
Montana	620	571	597	627	642	621	657	675	654	705
Nebraska	218	202	227	243	267	300	328	293	294	304
Nevada	299	324	373	390	348	361	380	442	457	492
New Hampshire	51	48	56	54	70	73	69	67	75	80
New Jersey	1086	1073	1211	1274	1448	1571	1838	2213	2290	2536
New Mexico	1625	1618	1747	1735	1782	1775	1864	1886	1917	1997
New York	3894	3784	4179	4207	4355	4531	4962	5462	5587	6000
North Carolina	1006	978	1131	1142	1144	1193	1209	1274	1368	1444
North Dakota	392	384	404	407	409	372	418	365	394	386
Ohio	627	622	688	700	779	794	862	956	1005	1044
Oklahoma	2524	2485	2740	2844	2851	2866	3027	3159	3158	3385
Oregon	723	692	782	826	826	873	920	1009	1058	1073
Pennsylvania	876	867	955	982	1065	1087	1262	1443	1514	1657
Rhode Island	105	102	116	130	132	138	148	194	206	221
South Carolina	165	163	182	194	180	181	222	208	228	255
South Dakota	747	702	709	714	775	775	743	803	759	830
Tennessee	163	165	195	186	177	207	214	239	254	272
Texas	1656	1656	1847	1909	2119	2290	2526	2907	3076	3314
Utah	599	593	643	706	689	740	761	843	895	959
Vermont	21	20	27	28	33	34	42	54	68	66
Virginia	823	825	936	969	1023	1144	1391	1585	1632	1745
Washington	2048	2034	2292	2247	2265	2456	2579	2895	2948	3032
West Virginia	44	45	53	56	71	88	84	113	107	115
Wisconsin	685	675	734	766	829	813	895	896	942	964
Wyoming	102	104	115	124	155	149	164	161	157	180
United States	60001	59163	65003	66539	69099	70850	76044	82196	85343	90210

Table A.1—continued

Category: Hispanic

State	1980	1981	1982	1983	1984	1985	1986	1987	1988	1989
Alabama	372	367	346	353	355	364	346	370	342	364
Alaska	89	94	98	102	109	92	112	96	116	126
Arizona	3967	3919	3888	3746	4524	4478	4326	4330	4317	4438
Arkansas	210	218	206	202	217	230	229	244	233	232
California	42384	40270	40251	40411	43886	44712	46862	50617	50468	50829
Colorado	4295	4095	4195	4384	4526	4426	4535	4471	4567	4589
Connecticut	1369	1405	1446	1513	1506	1577	1903	1752	1738	1750
Delaware	136	135	133	143	127	132	140	145	152	154
D. of Columbia	116	112	107	102	81	98	95	107	94	103
Florida	7392	7552	7581	7099	7269	6574	6426	5266	5781	5572
Georgia	635	657	560	631	608	579	581	568	560	604
Hawaii	994	986	886	738	855	948	1001	1104	1126	1128
Idaho	466	430	426	426	434	476	534	438	484	503
Illinois	6588	6740	6675	6586	7029	6950	7464	7996	8101	8238
Indiana	941	974	934	972	946	940	945	960	1008	1034
Iowa	332	318	339	337	359	381	384	390	398	397
Kansas	670	604	617	659	706	722	760	815	833	886
Kentucky	289	293	252	256	283	254	251	250	265	243
Louisiana	1065	1053	868	884	992	1036	1062	974	982	956
Maine	46	47	53	55	55	61	49	59	50	62
Maryland	804	798	793	840	810	852	801	789	763	799
Massachusetts	1493	1564	1640	1751	1653	1749	1643	1693	1733	1744
Michigan	1916	1917	1917	1825	1954	2053	2009	2184	2141	2239
Minnesota	431	418	402	434	444	499	518	547	568	583
Mississippi	249	255	235	247	272	267	274	285	255	259
Missouri	609	586	539	496	553	537	513	516	539	540
Montana	148	136	134	125	145	156	147	169	159	168
Nebraska	401	361	348	375	416	407	418	449	453	446
Nevada	443	498	503	492	487	473	519	565	521	546
New Hampshire	42	41	59	56	62	58	60	59	58	53
New Jersey	5930	5761	6116	6298	6422	6528	6506	6056	6343	6505
New Mexico	7053	7029	6725	6400	6840	7213	7343	6638	6911	6850
New York	16400	15598	15722	15331	15663	15880	16478	16494	16311	16412
North Carolina	548	530	522	540	536	563	554	542	525	557
North Dakota	53	51	42	51	56	56	53	44	53	51
Ohio	1466	1445	1467	1431	1552	1457	1481	1617	1578	1597
Oklahoma	725	712	649	672	717	749	756	690	783	785
Oregon	631	592	576	580	603	633	694	694	702	707
Pennsylvania	1729	1691	1715	1733	1934	1922	2009	1976	1918	2009
Rhode Island	150	147	154	174	150	165	150	166	161	163
South Carolina	402	396	373	363	383	367	363	354	329	343
South Dakota	59	56	61	48	56	56	62	63	63	63
Tennessee	330	337	326	283	297	273	268	275	279	269
Texas	36167	36202	36811	38679	39605	40100	41137	40581	41363	41586
Utah	703	692	691	707	788	833	798	859	857	917
Vermont	31	27	26	21	25	26	28	34	31	28
Virginia	819	825	820	834	850	870	963	970	946	953
Washington	1213	1201	1179	1100	1198	1314	1404	1475	1484	1476
West Virginia	111	110	151	133	157	143	160	145	126	126
Wisconsin	808	795	816	779	864	857	988	969	991	1005
Wyoming	258	265	258	284	322	340	362	354	376	355
United States	154478	151305	151631	152681	160675	162422	167463	169191	170935	172342

Table A.2

PROJECTED NUMBERS OF HIGH SCHOOL GRADUATES
BY STATE AND CATEGORY: 1990–2000

Category: All

State	1990	1991	1992	1993	1994	1995	1996	1997	1998	1999	2000
Alabama	45010	43028	41866	42031	40907	42748	42960	43979	45304	45321	45133
Alaska	5825	5647	5591	5818	5876	6188	6383	6782	7118	7500	7836
Arizona	30868	30199	30127	31628	31661	33721	34454	36303	38744	40655	41768
Arkansas	27538	26443	26122	26726	26096	27180	27172	27863	28823	28576	28469
California	257646	249112	247643	257940	257744	271572	274567	287286	303502	320683	328120
Colorado	35379	33636	33259	34553	34351	36417	36977	38635	40580	42038	43190
Connecticut	35058	32146	30981	31554	30809	31827	32125	32966	33991	34475	35481
Delaware	7122	6626	6380	6606	6499	6824	6995	7242	7404	7384	7497
D. of Columbia	4693	4296	4078	4093	3979	4181	4206	4319	4539	4899	4997
Florida	94916	90464	88611	91022	89885	95194	97005	101205	106839	111663	114945
Georgia	67379	65018	63740	64244	62797	66275	67648	70434	73576	74960	75628
Hawaii	12285	11879	11973	12383	12588	13227	13349	14276	15096	15560	15947
Idaho	12076	11796	11887	12448	12476	13345	13349	13886	14059	13846	13717
Illinois	126101	117856	113642	116295	114359	118514	118175	121472	126839	127190	126086
Indiana	64176	60256	58395	59253	57561	59565	59358	60443	61614	60343	59662
Iowa	34105	31489	31022	32311	31922	33470	33602	34132	34804	33796	32902
Kansas	26410	25513	25246	26373	26171	27393	27512	28323	29345	29754	29784
Kentucky	40922	38494	37310	37886	37133	38577	38246	38889	39284	38537	37920
Louisiana	46239	44022	43246	43938	43622	45784	45716	46919	48770	48981	49239
Maine	14587	13616	13194	13131	12877	13446	13572	13832	14174	14256	14449
Maryland	48629	44599	42761	43909	43457	45762	46852	48431	50635	52429	54405
Massachusetts	63132	58432	55719	55979	54188	55891	56645	58047	59532	60767	62708
Michigan	106209	99089	95753	96093	93487	96678	97841	100175	101846	100090	99307
Minnesota	50913	47634	47218	49220	48792	51253	52818	55227	56452	57169	57818
Mississippi	28569	27459	26748	27255	26748	28000	28162	28991	30004	30155	29924
Missouri	54227	51210	49835	51437	50686	53342	54098	55803	57801	58240	58345
Montana	9640	9113	9123	9512	9437	9858	9925	10348	10541	10537	10582
Nebraska	18912	17860	17653	18356	17904	18640	18682	19144	19827	19955	19956
Nevada	9618	9219	9084	9446	9600	10277	10463	11172	11841	12269	12474
New Hampshire	12688	11888	11588	11855	11627	12283	12590	13002	13487	13868	14244
New Jersey	84278	78876	76764	77937	76424	79404	79910	81988	84622	85411	87685
New Mexico	16855	16445	16317	17040	17211	18273	18644	19928	21376	22024	22675
New York	171764	161527	157212	160913	158347	164287	163916	165610	169431	169348	172250
North Carolina	70311	66707	64794	65355	63057	66138	67018	68456	70214	70543	71718
North Dakota	7778	7531	7394	7708	7751	8141	8346	8563	8755	8796	8889
Ohio	128215	118779	114547	116417	112756	116344	116687	119842	121767	121220	121118
Oklahoma	35779	34074	33510	34652	34112	35344	35210	36534	37905	38571	39689
Oregon	26151	25018	24728	25765	25870	27273	27360	28416	29325	29467	29282
Pennsylvania	132923	123279	118093	119119	115891	119761	120208	122343	124569	125284	127079
Rhode Island	9914	9240	8965	8992	8772	9217	9382	9608	9797	9973	10162
South Carolina	38008	36484	35403	35517	34466	36563	36655	37444	38546	38915	39058
South Dakota	7892	7626	7705	8042	8153	8565	8712	9170	9616	9568	9551
Tennessee	47640	45220	44038	44239	42765	44810	45109	46413	47411	46980	46731
Texas	185297	178425	175286	179308	177844	185624	186186	193560	204035	211942	216017
Utah	22934	23094	23767	25544	26565	28942	29629	30583	31155	30675	30496
Vermont	6641	6210	5887	6094	5976	6251	6215	6414	6573	6766	6876
Virginia	65292	61094	59217	60422	59031	62149	63461	65499	67929	69383	71108
Washington	46568	43898	43746	45513	45702	48318	48910	50986	52924	53828	54307
West Virginia	22704	21457	20314	20708	19863	20453	20162	20115	20137	19237	18679
Wisconsin	57546	54139	53376	55387	54150	56506	57025	58566	60063	59581	59595
Wyoming	5981	5762	5742	6030	5992	6246	6279	6559	6752	6814	6786
United States	2581343	2442924	2386320	2443997	2405947	2516041	2536791	2616123	2709273	2750231	2782284

Table A.2—continued

Category: Public

State	1990	1991	1992	1993	1994	1995	1996	1997	1998	1999	2000
Alabama	41612	39780	38706	38858	37819	39521	39717	40659	41884	41900	41726
Alaska	5710	5535	5480	5703	5760	6065	6257	6648	6977	7351	7681
Arizona	29918	29269	29199	30654	30686	32683	33393	35185	37551	39403	40482
Arkansas	26718	25655	25344	25930	25319	26370	26362	27033	27964	27725	27621
California	234021	226270	224936	234288	234110	246670	249391	260944	275673	291277	298033
Colorado	32900	31279	30929	32132	31944	33865	34386	35928	37737	39092	40164
Connecticut	28767	26378	25422	25892	25281	26116	26361	27051	27892	28289	29114
Delaware	5574	5186	4993	5170	5087	5341	5475	5668	5795	5779	5868
D. of Columbia	3740	3424	3250	3262	3171	3332	3352	3442	3617	3904	3982
Florida	85164	81170	79507	81670	80650	85414	87039	90807	95862	100191	103136
Georgia	62917	60713	59258	59990	58639	61886	63168	65770	68704	69996	70620
Hawaii	9812	9488	9563	9890	10054	10564	10918	11402	12057	12428	12737
Idaho	11842	11567	12207	12207	12234	13086	13090	13617	13786	13578	13451
Illinois	108577	101478	97850	100134	98475	102044	101753	104591	109213	109515	108564
Indiana	60126	56453	54710	55513	53928	55806	55612	56628	57725	56535	55897
Iowa	31534	29115	28683	29875	29515	30947	31069	31559	32180	31248	30421
Kansas	24849	24005	23754	24814	24624	25774	25886	26649	27610	27995	28023
Kentucky	37312	35098	34019	34544	33857	35174	34872	34804	35819	35137	34575
Louisiana	38242	36408	35767	36339	36078	37866	37809	38804	40335	40510	40723
Maine	12842	11988	11616	11561	11337	11838	11949	12178	12479	12551	12721
Maryland	42497	38975	37369	38372	37977	39992	40944	42324	44250	45818	47545
Massachusetts	53280	49313	47024	47243	45731	47169	47805	48988	50242	51284	52922
Michigan	96002	89567	86551	86858	84503	87387	88439	90548	92059	90480	89764
Minnesota	47140	44104	43719	45573	45176	47455	48904	51134	52269	52932	53533
Mississippi	26185	25167	24515	24980	24515	25663	25811	26571	27500	27638	27426
Missouri	48630	45925	44692	46128	45455	47837	48515	50044	51835	52205	52323
Montana	9336	8826	8835	9212	9139	9547	9612	10022	10209	10205	10248
Nebraska	17046	16098	15912	16545	16138	16801	16839	17256	17871	17987	17987
Nevada	9208	8826	8697	9044	9191	9839	10017	10696	11337	11747	11943
New Hampshire	10985	10293	10033	10264	10067	10635	10900	11257	11677	12007	12333
New Jersey	70096	65603	63846	64822	63564	66042	66463	68191	70382	71038	72930
New Mexico	15441	15065	14948	15610	15767	16740	17080	18256	19583	20176	20773
New York	144627	136007	132374	135490	133330	138331	138019	139445	142662	142592	145036
North Carolina	67431	63974	62140	62678	60474	63429	64273	65652	67338	67653	68780
North Dakota	7263	7033	6905	7198	7238	7602	7794	7997	8176	8214	8301
Ohio	115429	106934	103124	104807	101511	104741	105050	107891	109624	109131	109039
Oklahoma	35171	33495	32940	34063	33532	34743	34612	35913	37261	37915	39014
Oregon	24775	23701	23427	24409	24509	25838	25920	26921	27782	27916	27741
Pennsylvania	112633	104461	100067	100936	98201	101480	101859	103668	105552	106160	107681
Rhode Island	8253	7692	7463	7486	7303	7673	7810	7998	8156	8302	8460
South Carolina	35696	34265	33249	33357	32369	34339	34425	35166	36201	36548	36682
South Dakota	7410	7160	7235	7551	7655	8042	8180	8610	9029	8984	8968
Tennessee	44648	42380	41272	41461	40079	41996	42276	43498	44433	44029	43796
Texas	175450	168943	165971	169779	168393	175760	176292	183274	193192	200679	204537
Utah	22593	22751	23414	25164	26170	28512	29188	30128	30692	30219	30042
Vermont	5679	5310	5034	5211	5110	5345	5314	5485	5621	5786	5880
Virginia	61419	57470	55704	56837	55529	58462	59696	61613	63899	65267	66890
Washington	43762	41253	41110	42770	42948	45406	45963	47914	49735	50584	51034
West Virginia	22024	20814	19705	20087	19268	19840	19558	19512	19534	18661	18119
Wisconsin	52033	48952	48262	50081	48962	51092	51562	52955	54309	53873	53885
Wyoming	5803	5591	5571	5851	5814	6060	6092	6364	6551	6611	6584
United States	2330122	2206207	2155751	2208293	2174186	2274160	2293071	2365312	2449824	2487070	2515735

Category: Private

Table A.2—continued

State	1990	1991	1992	1993	1994	1995	1996	1997	1998	1999	2000
Alabama	3398	3248	3160	3173	3088	3227	3243	3320	3420	3421	3407
Alaska	115	115	111	115	116	123	126	134	141	149	155
Arizona	950	930	928	974	975	1038	1061	1118	1193	1252	1286
Arkansas	820	788	778	796	777	810	810	830	859	851	848
California	23625	22842	22707	23652	23634	24902	25176	26342	27829	29405	30087
Colorado	2479	2357	2330	2421	2407	2552	2591	2707	2843	2946	3026
Connecticut	6291	5768	5559	5662	5528	5711	5764	5915	6099	6186	6367
Delaware	1548	1440	1387	1436	1412	1483	1520	1574	1609	1605	1629
D. of Columbia	953	872	828	831	808	849	854	877	922	995	1015
Florida	9752	9294	9104	9352	9235	9780	9966	10398	10977	11472	11809
Georgia	4462	4305	4202	4254	4158	4389	4480	4664	4872	4964	5008
Hawaii	2473	2391	2410	2493	2534	2663	2751	2874	3039	3132	3210
Idaho	234	229	230	241	242	259	259	269	273	268	266
Illinois	17524	16378	15792	16161	15894	16470	16422	16881	17626	17675	17522
Indiana	4050	3803	3585	3740	3633	3759	3746	3815	3889	3808	3765
Iowa	2571	2374	2339	2436	2407	2523	2533	2573	2624	2548	2481
Kansas	1561	1508	1492	1559	1547	1619	1626	1674	1735	1759	1761
Kentucky	3610	3396	3291	3342	3276	3403	3374	3431	3465	3400	3345
Louisiana	7997	7614	7479	7599	7544	7918	7907	8115	8435	8471	8516
Maine	1745	1628	1578	1570	1540	1608	1623	1654	1695	1705	1728
Maryland	6132	5624	5392	5537	5480	5770	5908	6107	6385	6611	6860
Massachusetts	9852	9119	8695	8736	8457	8722	8840	9059	9290	9483	9786
Michigan	10207	9522	9202	9235	8984	9291	9402	9627	9787	9619	9543
Minnesota	3773	3530	3499	3647	3616	3798	3914	4093	4183	4237	4285
Mississippi	2384	2292	2233	2275	2233	2337	2351	2420	2504	2517	2498
Missouri	5597	5285	5143	5309	5231	5505	5583	5759	5966	6011	6022
Montana	304	287	288	300	298	311	313	326	332	332	334
Nebraska	1866	1762	1741	1811	1766	1839	1843	1888	1956	1968	1969
Nevada	410	393	387	402	409	438	446	476	504	522	531
New Hampshire	1703	1595	1555	1591	1560	1648	1690	1745	1810	1861	1911
New Jersey	14182	13273	12918	13115	12860	13362	13447	13797	14240	14373	14755
New Mexico	1414	1380	1369	1430	1444	1533	1564	1672	1793	1848	1902
New York	27137	25520	24838	25423	25017	25956	25897	26165	26756	26756	27214
North Carolina	2880	2733	2654	2677	2583	2709	2745	2804	2876	2890	2938
North Dakota	515	498	489	510	513	539	552	566	579	582	588
Ohio	12786	11845	11423	11610	11245	11603	11637	11951	12143	12089	12079
Oklahoma	608	579	570	589	580	601	598	621	644	656	675
Oregon	1376	1317	1301	1356	1361	1435	1440	1495	1543	1551	1541
Pennsylvania	20290	18818	18026	18183	17690	18281	18349	18675	19014	19124	19398
Rhode Island	1661	1548	1502	1506	1469	1544	1572	1610	1641	1671	1702
South Carolina	2312	2219	2154	2160	2097	2224	2230	2278	2345	2367	2376
South Dakota	482	466	470	491	498	523	532	560	587	584	583
Tennessee	2992	2840	2766	2778	2686	2814	2833	2915	2978	2951	2935
Texas	9847	9482	9315	9529	9451	9864	9894	10286	10843	11263	11480
Utah	341	343	353	380	395	430	441	455	463	456	454
Vermont	962	900	853	883	866	906	901	929	952	980	996
Virginia	3873	3624	3513	3585	3502	3687	3765	3886	4030	4116	4218
Washington	2806	2645	2636	2743	2754	2912	2947	3072	3189	3244	3273
West Virginia	680	643	609	621	595	613	604	603	603	576	560
Wisconsin	5513	5187	5114	5306	5188	5414	5463	5611	5754	5708	5710
Wyoming	178	171	171	179	178	186	187	195	201	203	202
United States	251221	236717	230569	235704	231761	241881	243720	250811	259449	263161	266549

Table A.2—continued

Category: Male

State	1990	1991	1992	1993	1994	1995	1996	1997	1998	1999	2000
Alabama	21863	20899	20272	20482	19825	20893	20911	21375	21979	22029	21886
Alaska	3032	2912	2855	3006	3013	3204	3284	3479	3633	3866	4046
Arizona	15351	14935	15016	15724	15670	16688	17123	18117	19137	20192	20685
Arkansas	13670	13119	13040	13331	13018	13602	13496	13843	14401	14232	14234
California	128768	124365	124939	129289	128797	135923	137537	144167	151875	160306	164012
Colorado	17819	16933	16775	17476	17368	18410	18724	19498	20469	21253	21901
Connecticut	17427	16084	15496	15748	15301	16051	16051	16397	17127	17431	17840
Delaware	3476	3172	3020	3213	3109	3319	3363	3429	3521	3477	3500
D. of Columbia	2130	1915	1807	1833	1758	1862	1862	1926	2040	2192	2242
Florida	45763	43554	42749	43875	43340	45858	46759	48705	51590	53971	55438
Georgia	32423	31377	30499	30818	30350	32172	32625	34093	35627	36280	36700
Hawaii	6113	5961	6014	6190	6313	6624	6819	7076	7368	7704	7777
Idaho	6126	5956	6046	6260	6279	6764	6690	7057	7047	6963	6971
Illinois	62625	58520	56471	57836	56944	59009	58765	60395	62982	63243	62725
Indiana	31730	29892	29227	29658	28678	29840	29700	30101	30826	29898	29745
Iowa	17345	16012	15725	16458	16288	16915	17025	17354	17550	17194	16637
Kansas	13278	12705	12672	13215	13113	13760	13942	14295	14799	15095	15095
Kentucky	20277	19144	18462	18742	18472	19093	18960	19196	19360	18967	18595
Louisiana	22267	21110	20606	21267	20719	21879	21863	22472	23294	23473	23477
Maine	7378	6848	6644	6772	6521	6917	6939	7111	7306	7386	7411
Maryland	23660	21861	20857	21448	21267	22333	22879	23658	24661	25543	26651
Massachusetts	31118	28800	27471	27617	26622	27532	27742	28371	29318	29702	30858
Michigan	52675	49005	47518	47669	46344	47944	48452	49672	50242	49643	49095
Minnesota	25583	24050	24025	25040	24651	26043	26703	27879	28484	28843	29248
Mississippi	13740	13170	12939	13188	12933	13493	13602	13961	14418	14588	14431
Missouri	26877	25398	24550	25694	25257	26607	26726	27609	28732	28869	29002
Montana	4980	4680	4694	4870	4815	5022	5110	5312	5501	5453	5459
Nebraska	9607	9120	8947	9337	9018	9487	9435	9738	9976	10133	10099
Nevada	4866	4744	4652	4824	4938	5227	5343	5697	6086	6270	6340
New Hampshire	6339	6004	5837	5926	5824	6127	6218	6403	6759	6857	7049
New Jersey	41795	39244	38289	38848	38062	39621	39788	40763	42260	42671	43883
New Mexico	8351	8243	8134	8565	8608	9139	9284	9831	10663	10865	11244
New York	83712	79128	77165	79032	77615	80587	80167	80954	82643	83077	84362
North Carolina	34081	32045	31319	31535	30338	31805	32267	33058	33782	33979	34381
North Dakota	3956	3843	3743	3933	3949	4149	4227	4374	4424	4428	4541
Ohio	63946	59302	57230	58088	56116	57965	58211	59612	60635	60491	60109
Oklahoma	18060	17024	16816	17437	17243	17892	17682	18397	19156	19608	20259
Oregon	13131	12783	12514	13017	13098	13871	13896	14294	14828	14963	14846
Pennsylvania	66204	61296	58919	59146	57651	59846	59934	60899	61683	62274	63069
Rhode Island	4819	4449	4393	4310	4179	4388	4481	4574	4670	4693	4751
South Carolina	18185	17545	17216	17247	16773	17892	17927	18313	18957	18998	19066
South Dakota	3926	3787	3844	4044	4156	4279	4357	4597	4744	4808	4803
Tennessee	23065	21852	21374	21356	20747	21727	21865	22466	23046	22736	22705
Texas	90997	87664	86562	88184	87123	90843	90985	94668	99704	103577	105892
Utah	11424	11548	11846	12797	13304	14369	14861	15287	15632	15292	15390
Vermont	3342	3110	2984	3025	3047	3177	3157	3251	3345	3492	3532
Virginia	31825	29769	28887	29556	28837	30517	31122	31932	33132	33953	34831
Washington	23582	22292	22226	23314	23369	24601	24987	25810	27059	27492	27676
West Virginia	11456	10773	10194	10460	10100	10278	10075	10067	10123	9641	9434
Wisconsin	29032	27358	26914	28002	27321	28516	28770	29512	30237	30358	30185
Wyoming	3052	2924	2910	3013	3026	3183	3187	3315	3459	3477	3496
United States	1276247	1208222	1183304	1211715	1191212	1247243	1255894	1294360	1340290	1361926	1377604

Table A.2—continued

Category: Female

State	1990	1991	1992	1993	1994	1995	1996	1997	1998	1999	2000
Alabama	23147	22129	21594	21549	21082	21855	22049	22604	23325	23292	23247
Alaska	2793	2735	2736	2812	2863	2984	3099	3303	3485	3634	3790
Arizona	15517	15264	15111	15904	15991	17033	17331	18186	19607	20463	21083
Arkansas	13868	13324	13082	13395	13078	13578	13676	14020	14422	14344	14235
California	128878	124747	122704	128651	128947	135649	137030	143119	151627	160377	164108
Colorado	17560	16703	16484	17077	16983	18007	18253	19137	20111	20785	21289
Connecticut	17631	16062	15485	15806	15508	15776	16074	16569	16864	17044	17641
Delaware	3646	3454	3360	3393	3390	3505	3632	3813	3883	3907	3997
D. of Columbia	2563	2381	2271	2260	2221	2319	2244	2393	2499	2707	2755
Florida	49153	46910	45862	47147	46545	49336	50246	52500	55249	57692	59507
Georgia	34956	33641	32961	33426	32447	34103	35023	36341	37949	38680	38928
Hawaii	6172	5918	5959	6193	6275	6603	6850	7200	7728	7856	8170
Idaho	5950	5840	5841	6188	6197	6581	6659	6829	7012	6883	6746
Illinois	63476	59336	57171	58459	57425	59505	59410	61077	63857	63947	63361
Indiana	32446	30364	29168	29595	28883	29725	29652	30342	30788	30445	29917
Iowa	16760	15477	15297	15853	15634	16555	16577	16778	17254	16602	16265
Kansas	13132	12808	12574	13158	13053	13633	13570	14028	14546	14659	14689
Kentucky	20645	19352	18848	19144	18661	19484	19286	19693	19924	19570	19325
Louisiana	23972	22912	22640	22671	22903	23905	23853	24447	25476	25508	25762
Maine	7209	6768	6550	6359	6356	6529	6633	6721	6868	6870	7038
Maryland	24969	22738	21904	22461	22190	23429	23973	24773	25974	26886	27754
Massachusetts	32014	29632	28248	28362	27566	24354	28903	29676	30214	31065	31850
Michigan	53534	50084	48235	48424	47143	48734	49389	50503	51604	50456	50212
Minnesota	25330	23584	23193	24180	24141	25210	26115	27348	27968	28326	28570
Mississippi	14829	14289	13809	14067	13815	14507	14560	15030	15586	15567	15493
Missouri	27350	25812	25285	25743	25423	26735	27372	28194	29069	29371	29343
Montana	4660	4433	4429	4642	4622	4836	4815	5036	5040	5084	5123
Nebraska	9305	8740	8706	9019	8886	9153	9247	9406	9851	9822	9857
Nevada	4752	4475	4432	4622	4662	5050	5120	5475	5755	5999	6134
New Hampshire	6349	5884	5751	5929	5803	6156	6372	6599	6728	7011	7195
New Jersey	42483	39632	38475	39089	38362	39783	40122	41225	42362	42740	43802
New Mexico	8504	8202	8183	8475	8603	9134	9360	10097	10713	11159	11431
New York	88052	82399	80047	81881	80732	83700	83749	84656	86788	86271	87888
North Carolina	36230	34662	33475	33820	32719	34333	34751	35398	36432	36564	37337
North Dakota	3822	3688	3651	3775	3802	3992	4119	4189	4331	4368	4348
Ohio	64269	59477	57317	58329	56640	58379	58466	60230	61132	60729	61009
Oklahoma	17719	17050	16694	17215	16866	17452	17528	18137	18749	18963	19430
Oregon	13020	12235	12214	12748	12772	13402	13464	14122	14497	14504	14436
Pennsylvania	66719	61983	59174	59973	58240	59915	60274	61444	62886	63010	64010
Rhode Island	5095	4791	4572	4682	4593	4829	4901	5034	5127	5280	5411
South Carolina	19823	18939	18187	18270	17693	18671	18728	19131	19589	19917	19992
South Dakota	3966	3839	3861	3998	3997	4286	4355	4573	4872	4760	4748
Tennessee	24575	23368	22664	22883	22018	23083	23244	23947	24365	24244	24026
Texas	94300	90761	88724	91124	90721	94781	95201	98892	104331	108365	110125
Utah	11510	11546	11921	12747	13261	14573	14768	15296	15523	15383	15106
Vermont	3299	3100	2903	3069	2929	3074	3058	3163	3228	3274	3344
Virginia	33467	31325	30330	30866	30194	31632	32339	33567	34797	35430	36277
Washington	22986	21606	21520	22199	22333	23717	23923	25176	25865	26336	26631
West Virginia	11248	10684	10120	10248	9763	10175	10087	10048	10014	9596	9245
Wisconsin	28514	26781	26462	27385	26829	27990	28255	29054	29826	29223	29410
Wyoming	2929	2838	2832	3017	2966	3063	3092	3244	3293	3337	3290
United States	1305096	1234702	1203016	1232282	1214735	1268798	1280897	1321763	1368983	1388305	1404680

Category: White Non-Hispanic

Table A.2—continued

State	1990	1991	1992	1993	1994	1995	1996	1997	1998	1999	2000
Alabama	32219	30232	29622	29675	28776	30031	30231	30775	31698	32330	32172
Alaska	4332	4190	4061	4311	4334	4627	4724	4944	5214	5491	5668
Arizona	22958	22087	21882	23247	23249	25073	25429	26807	28789	30574	31209
Arkansas	22234	21040	20774	21208	20610	21391	21365	21743	22472	22556	22456
California	151526	141068	137602	144638	141834	151041	151111	158330	168518	175443	177027
Colorado	28212	26483	26036	27388	27037	28903	29336	30555	32154	33345	34148
Connecticut	29707	27048	25956	26443	25598	26333	26596	27068	28120	28472	29230
Delaware	5454	5033	4796	4951	4826	4995	5088	5179	5307	5277	5330
D. of Columbia	964	920	899	896	859	892	890	908	906	935	934
Florida	71370	67309	65955	68074	67289	71376	72621	76012	80621	84049	86196
Georgia	47739	45589	44552	45010	43827	46251	46983	48594	50876	52482	52897
Hawaii	2479	2375	2302	2384	2321	2517	2529	2567	2657	2781	2772
Idaho	11213	10954	11007	11540	11575	12414	12359	12793	12888	12618	12442
Illinois	91351	83711	80674	82934	80647	83421	83489	85289	88135	88042	86507
Indiana	57598	53690	51971	52733	50936	52784	52541	53384	54253	53210	52482
Iowa	32472	29889	29374	30694	30306	31725	31864	32312	32983	31963	31051
Kansas	23337	22353	22190	23103	22876	23925	23896	24532	25416	25731	25663
Kentucky	37411	35112	34081	34607	33857	35067	34820	35092	35492	34934	34314
Louisiana	30190	27966	27482	27840	27310	28449	28261	28720	29787	30466	30450
Maine	14369	13423	12985	12940	12681	13251	13353	13612	13945	14028	14211
Maryland	32702	29992	28654	29445	28732	29956	30608	31281	32673	33511	34613
Massachusetts	57200	52572	50031	50077	48245	49788	50346	51574	52901	53769	55418
Michigan	86654	79685	77373	78199	75662	78402	79371	81053	82399	81385	80404
Minnesota	47675	44328	43941	45758	45324	47687	48924	51104	52198	52997	53508
Mississippi	17452	16403	16063	16354	15860	16599	16677	17006	17584	17953	17782
Missouri	47409	44550	43528	44931	44332	46665	47348	48592	50469	50787	50808
Montana	8752	8220	8232	8614	8536	8862	8970	9249	9411	9522	9522
Nebraska	17342	16358	16121	16883	16371	17049	17070	17439	18030	18165	18123
Nevada	7754	7335	7194	7598	7670	8268	8404	8902	9402	9721	9833
New Hampshire	12476	11673	11364	11621	11390	12022	12319	12709	13180	13538	13892
New Jersey	62209	57205	55471	56537	55016	57093	57314	58259	60321	60443	61767
New Mexico	7452	6953	6711	7455	7546	8211	8375	8839	9865	10490	10650
New York	125273	115863	111588	113732	110332	113983	112567	113353	116245	115954	117183
North Carolina	51369	48301	46841	47214	45411	47687	48257	48865	50361	51104	51872
North Dakota	7243	6998	6875	7174	7178	7548	7751	7930	8115	8247	8323
Ohio	112010	103327	99881	101346	97886	100863	101017	103011	104650	104257	103944
Oklahoma	28795	27292	26801	27841	27248	28185	28014	28709	29739	30395	31077
Oregon	23811	22690	22313	23304	23288	24613	24488	25411	26171	26125	25852
Pennsylvania	117748	108823	104280	105248	101990	105133	105664	107434	109402	109871	111321
Rhode Island	9197	8552	8279	8300	8079	8458	8596	8789	8955	9085	9244
South Carolina	25202	23977	23201	23289	22445	23634	23820	24127	25028	25649	25723
South Dakota	6970	6688	6766	7081	7095	7478	7617	7998	8261	8459	8400
Tennessee	39291	37049	36099	36286	34969	36575	36809	37535	38280	38315	38067
Texas	114090	106882	103749	108550	106406	113097	113522	117954	125316	132055	133389
Utah	20826	20946	21542	23229	24118	26369	26869	27664	28101	27447	27167
Vermont	6502	6069	5766	5960	5853	6114	6072	6264	6423	6604	6702
Virginia	49461	46160	44877	45609	44249	46521	47220	48588	50377	51795	52908
Washington	40612	38003	37784	39378	39392	41790	42024	43782	45313	45832	46014
West Virginia	21788	20566	19520	19870	19063	19609	19358	19236	19309	18454	17903
Wisconsin	52204	48810	48159	50089	48846	50943	51359	52501	53801	53432	53318
Wyoming	5344	5077	5097	5340	5267	5522	5521	5701	5893	5936	5886
United States	1979948	1847819	1798302	1846928	1804567	1889113	1899757	1950075	2018404	2046024	2057772

Table A.2—continued

Category: Black Non-Hispanic

State	1990	1991	1992	1993	1994	1995	1996	1997	1998	1999	2000
Alabama	12142	12108	11569	11654	11436	12002	11994	12442	12819	12158	12093
Alaska	177	173	165	170	171	183	199	217	231	229	239
Arizona	1019	1054	1022	1035	1070	1130	1138	1243	1309	1375	1418
Arkansas	4758	4841	4754	4926	4864	5159	5158	5406	5620	5275	5242
California	25490	24525	24369	25366	25855	27508	27928	29721	31078	33223	34214
Colorado	1525	1482	1445	1476	1493	1604	1569	1678	1738	1741	1802
Connecticut	3011	2805	2668	2741	2789	2918	2969	3189	3168	3199	3334
Delaware	1424	1346	1329	1420	1419	1540	1619	1745	1768	1760	1807
D. of Columbia	3558	3214	3017	3038	2964	3127	3129	3230	3426	3747	3839
Florida	16318	15913	15439	15892	15735	16793	17209	17972	18856	19907	20714
Georgia	18447	18148	17618	17920	17677	18657	19219	20342	21120	20794	20975
Hawaii	162	156	149	150	132	167	152	142	164	165	169
Idaho	45	45	49	45	46	42	44	46	46	43	42
Illinois	22616	21586	20239	20178	20208	21214	20565	21713	23236	23194	23071
Indiana	4907	4835	4659	4734	4781	4922	4900	5079	5343	5020	5004
Iowa	738	724	760	700	731	794	796	836	865	845	837
Kansas	1473	1460	1380	1448	1472	1537	1587	1666	1719	1709	1725
Kentucky	3107	3005	2850	2911	2896	3115	3048	3382	3369	3167	3155
Louisiana	14377	14354	14083	14401	14571	15510	15655	16260	16924	16398	16601
Maine	24	27	27	25	26	25	24	28	25	24	24
Maryland	13534	12274	11770	12123	12249	13294	13665	14437	15121	15898	16617
Massachusetts	2886	2725	2536	2626	2633	2741	2846	2848	2975	3175	3287
Michigan	15525	15359	14330	13904	13782	14186	14016	14600	14933	14016	14054
Minnesota	854	816	747	793	807	866	867	944	954	990	1010
Mississippi	10615	10540	10176	10416	10372	10912	10983	11495	11877	11633	11544
Missouri	5688	5516	5172	5299	5199	5434	5459	5867	5960	5989	6016
Montana	27	25	23	20	22	24	22	20	24	23	24
Nebraska	771	717	720	677	703	745	733	809	812	789	796
Nevada	845	821	827	783	799	830	879	969	1059	1048	1067
New Hampshire	60	63	59	63	61	71	70	73	74	74	76
New Jersey	12941	12289	11659	11779	11634	12461	12406	13220	13543	13932	14403
New Mexico	378	383	385	400	456	484	515	539	579	580	591
New York	24692	23912	23479	24678	24799	26349	26383	26670	27585	27110	27773
North Carolina	16837	16234	15814	15995	15486	16290	16397	17098	17309	16821	17115
North Dakota	33	36	34	34	33	34	35	35	33	31	31
Ohio	13486	12726	11948	12215	12014	12558	12649	13698	13885	13612	13708
Oklahoma	2721	2606	2549	2626	2626	2710	2631	2866	2978	2928	3023
Oregon	488	468	464	478	483	504	575	564	577	582	583
Pennsylvania	11466	10783	10034	10112	10089	10770	10531	10825	11000	11160	11354
Rhode Island	324	308	289	287	301	327	330	340	339	353	359
South Carolina	12243	11873	11610	11620	11375	12294	12192	12641	12829	12539	12573
South Dakota	26	22	26	35	32	34	33	32	32	27	25
Tennessee	7805	7594	7396	7379	7227	7650	7697	8252	8473	7977	7950
Texas	24323	23745	23048	23000	23133	24442	24332	25946	27370	26736	27453
Utah	169	163	156	178	185	207	201	211	219	214	214
Vermont	27	29	29	29	27	30	29	34	30	32	34
Virginia	13065	12226	11627	12055	12012	12823	13300	13810	14357	14230	14693
Washington	1353	1242	1245	1286	1311	1354	1349	1394	1367	1343	1341
West Virginia	661	638	551	613	577	605	563	618	569	514	498
Wisconsin	3273	3234	3122	3137	3099	3283	3233	3474	3645	3545	3578
Wyoming	55	63	54	40	61	62	62	71	77	76	67
United States	332489	321231	309470	314894	313923	332320	334064	350737	363405	361950	368162

Table A.2—continued

Category: Other Non-Hispanic

State	1990	1991	1992	1993	1994	1995	1996	1997	1998	1999	2000
Alabama	321	323	344	356	357	376	389	404	428	463	484
Alaska	1166	1154	1209	1180	1236	1202	1295	1434	1476	1577	1719
Arizona	2253	2332	2378	2357	2423	2539	2647	2862	3105	2996	3207
Arkansas	335	337	351	351	367	374	392	418	457	463	480
California	28589	29083	29496	29751	30243	31386	32715	34974	37406	43474	45771
Colorado	999	999	1035	1024	1043	1064	1126	1218	1294	1392	1481
Connecticut	601	590	600	619	629	646	657	700	719	757	796
Delaware	101	105	110	96	109	116	129	129	150	162	169
D. of Columbia	63	59	59	55	53	51	55	57	55	60	61
Florida	1528	1617	1629	1680	1711	1761	1839	1984	2112	2292	2425
Georgia	645	676	708	739	733	773	810	868	910	993	1040
Hawaii	8507	8252	8345	8633	8790	9195	9571	10085	10752	11044	11380
Idaho	257	260	258	248	255	258	265	289	315	347	361
Illinois	3149	3195	3226	3221	3208	3315	3415	3524	3771	3879	3965
Indiana	610	627	634	627	623	633	655	694	706	761	773
Iowa	451	462	434	456	439	432	422	433	442	457	464
Kansas	761	784	798	844	848	884	912	962	1037	1103	1140
Kentucky	138	127	128	130	121	120	126	128	134	138	143
Louisiana	717	729	723	746	790	807	836	850	902	924	953
Maine	133	114	132	119	115	113	125	125	132	129	137
Maryland	1623	1604	1621	1655	1722	1734	1795	1923	1999	2151	2275
Massachusetts	1233	1274	1277	1322	1321	1384	1430	1545	1587	1686	1790
Michigan	1805	1860	1830	1880	1863	1900	1979	2088	2086	2197	2254
Minnesota	1827	1905	1927	2086	2021	2140	2294	2439	2571	2431	2522
Mississippi	234	251	255	242	253	243	256	256	266	283	302
Missouri	582	589	610	633	616	641	664	698	733	805	838
Montana	669	709	685	704	694	751	734	847	885	764	800
Nebraska	321	299	296	273	286	288	303	312	336	331	343
Nevada	495	507	516	508	525	563	593	657	698	797	844
New Hampshire	94	100	105	108	118	130	135	158	173	194	211
New Jersey	2648	2798	2883	2958	3076	3211	3336	3528	3754	3793	4007
New Mexico	2018	2062	2198	2167	2225	2349	2417	2626	2845	2620	2787
New York	6111	6217	6282	6294	6289	6471	6685	6946	7096	7156	7428
North Carolina	1532	1623	1555	1563	1608	1606	1714	1788	1809	1861	1947
North Dakota	435	429	407	415	450	476	462	479	517	425	438
Ohio	1068	1067	1137	1137	1137	1168	1214	1252	1308	1368	1411
Oklahoma	3420	3377	3319	3330	3350	3478	3542	3890	4079	4106	4405
Oregon	1131	1144	1188	1210	1283	1295	1371	1448	1541	1689	1735
Pennsylvania	1693	1744	1775	1785	1766	1823	1857	1928	2015	2032	2103
Rhode Island	238	222	228	234	228	253	269	279	292	318	333
South Carolina	250	277	261	269	274	279	300	306	322	349	371
South Dakota	833	854	850	856	956	972	988	1038	1219	975	1014
Tennessee	277	284	282	298	301	311	319	333	358	378	392
Texas	3413	3552	3526	3570	3603	3699	3800	4019	4238	4592	4806
Utah	1028	1050	1175	1126	1186	1255	1307	1393	1504	1637	1686
Vermont	82	86	72	82	72	78	84	88	99	108	117
Virginia	1825	1810	1809	1831	1830	1850	1924	2017	2115	2241	2350
Washington	3083	3114	3114	3204	3235	3348	3516	3790	4050	4388	4603
West Virginia	115	115	103	96	98	98	103	118	120	125	129
Wisconsin	1059	1044	988	1044	1006	1057	1095	1191	1248	1194	1237
Wyoming	182	196	207	211	210	226	220	245	262	265	276
United States	92648	93988	95018	96323	97693	101122	105087	111763	118428	126670	132703

Category: Hispanic

Table A.2—continued

State	1990	1991	1992	1993	1994	1995	1996	1997	1998	1999	2000
Alabama	328	365	331	346	338	339	346	358	359	370	384
Alaska	150	130	156	157	135	176	165	187	197	203	210
Arizona	4638	4726	4845	4989	4919	4979	5240	5391	5541	5710	5934
Arkansas	211	225	243	241	255	256	257	296	274	282	291
California	52041	54436	56176	58185	59812	61637	62813	64261	66500	68543	71108
Colorado	4643	4672	4743	4665	4778	4846	4946	5184	5394	5560	5759
Connecticut	1739	1703	1757	1751	1793	1930	1903	2009	1984	2047	2121
Delaware	143	142	145	139	145	173	159	189	179	185	191
D. of Columbia	108	103	103	104	103	111	132	124	152	157	163
Florida	5700	5625	5588	5376	5150	5264	5336	5237	5250	5415	5610
Georgia	548	605	582	575	560	594	636	630	670	691	716
Hawaii	1137	1096	1177	1216	1345	1348	1417	1482	1523	1570	1626
Idaho	561	537	573	615	600	631	681	758	810	838	872
Illinois	8985	9364	9503	9962	10306	10564	10706	10946	11697	12075	12543
Indiana	1061	1104	1131	1159	1221	1226	1262	1286	1312	1352	1403
Iowa	444	414	454	461	446	486	520	551	514	531	550
Kansas	839	916	878	978	975	1047	1117	1163	1173	1211	1256
Kentucky	266	250	251	238	259	275	252	287	289	298	308
Louisiana	955	973	958	951	951	1018	964	1089	1157	1193	1235
Maine	61	52	50	47	55	57	70	67	72	75	77
Maryland	770	729	716	686	754	778	784	790	842	869	900
Massachusetts	1813	1861	1875	1954	1989	1978	2023	2080	2069	2137	2213
Michigan	2225	2185	2220	2110	2180	2190	2296	2434	2428	2501	2595
Minnesota	557	585	603	583	640	670	733	740	729	751	778
Mississippi	268	265	254	243	263	246	246	234	277	286	296
Missouri	548	555	525	574	539	602	627	646	639	659	683
Montana	192	159	183	174	185	222	199	232	221	228	236
Nebraska	478	486	516	523	544	558	576	584	649	670	694
Nevada	524	556	547	557	606	616	587	644	682	703	730
New Hampshire	58	52	60	63	58	60	66	62	60	62	65
New Jersey	6480	6584	6751	6663	6698	6639	6854	6981	7004	7243	7508
New Mexico	7007	7047	7023	7018	6984	7229	7337	7924	8087	8334	8647
New York	15688	15535	15863	16209	16927	17484	18281	18641	18505	19128	19866
North Carolina	573	549	584	583	552	555	650	705	735	757	784
North Dakota	67	68	78	85	90	83	98	119	90	93	97
Ohio	1651	1659	1581	1719	1719	1755	1807	1881	1924	1983	2055
Oklahoma	843	799	841	871	888	971	1023	1069	1109	1142	1184
Oregon	721	716	763	773	816	861	926	993	1036	1071	1112
Pennsylvania	2016	1929	2004	1974	2046	2035	2156	2156	2152	2221	2301
Rhode Island	155	158	169	171	164	179	187	200	211	217	226
South Carolina	313	357	331	339	352	356	343	370	367	378	391
South Dakota	63	62	63	70	70	81	74	102	104	107	112
Tennessee	267	293	261	276	268	274	284	293	300	310	322
Texas	43471	44246	44963	44188	44702	44386	44532	45641	47111	48559	50369
Utah	911	935	954	1011	1076	1111	1252	1315	1331	1377	1429
Vermont	30	26	20	23	24	29	30	28	21	22	23
Virginia	941	898	904	927	940	955	1017	1084	1084	1117	1157
Washington	1520	1539	1603	1645	1764	1826	2021	2020	2194	2265	2349
West Virginia	140	138	140	129	127	141	138	143	139	144	149
Wisconsin	1010	1051	1107	1117	1199	1223	1338	1400	1369	1410	1462
Wyoming	400	426	384	439	454	436	476	542	520	537	557
United States	176258	179886	183530	185852	189764	193486	197883	203548	209036	215587	223647

nonmissing states in the same region, with the constant of proportionality determined from the observed 1986 ratios.

For 1987, we used the state counts of public school graduates to estimate the numbers of private school graduates by applying the assumption that each state's private/public ratio remained the same as it was in 1986 (except for California, where the actual 1987 counts were used). This reflects the finding from the WICHE data that there was almost no change in the private/public ratio between 1985 and 1986.

The resulting state estimates in Table A.1 indicate that the number of private school graduates changed little from 1980 to 1987, at a time when the 17–18 year age group was shrinking and the public schools were producing fewer and fewer graduates. Private schools accounted for approximately 9 percent of the nation's high school graduates in 1980 and 10 percent in 1986.

ESTIMATES OF AGE GROUP SIZES

To augment the data on high school graduates, detailed estimates and projections of age group sizes by state, sex, race, and Hispanic origin were compiled for each of the years 1980–2000. Table A.3 lists the estimates of the numbers of 17-year-olds for the years 1980–1989. All estimates are for July 1 in the reference years, except for 1980, where the census estimates as of April 1980 are listed. Table A.4 provides the analogous projections for 1990–2000.

For the most part, the entries in these tables are taken directly from Census Bureau estimates and projections listed on public use tapes. The age group estimates for 1980 come from a tape that provides revised county population estimates by age, sex, race, and Hispanic origin derived from the 1980 census (U.S. Bureau of the Census, 1983). The estimates for later years are taken from a tape listing estimates and projections for the years 1986–2010 by state, race, and sex (U.S. Bureau of the Census, 1988c).

Minor adjustments have been made to the Bureau's estimates to fill in disaggregated estimates by race/Hispanic category for 1981–1985 and to reconcile the estimates with more recent estimates for the U.S. and Hispanic populations. In brief, the state estimates by age, sex, and race for 1981–1985 were obtained by first interpolating between the relevant cell sizes in 1980 and 1986 (e.g., the number of 17-year-olds in 1982 is estimated by interpolating between the number of 15-year-olds in 1980 and the number of 21-year-olds in 1986). To provide age group breakdowns by Hispanic origin, the estimated Hispanic age group total for the U.S. was first allocated across states proportional to the 1980 state estimates for the corresponding age groups, and then the state's Hispanic total was allocated across race categories assuming that the proportions of Hispanics in the white, black, and other categories were the same as they were for that age group in 1980.

The Census Bureau estimates for 1980 reported in Table A.3 are the "OMB-consistent modified race" estimates, which means that the "Other Non-Hispanics" category corresponds to the union of two race categories—Native American (American Indians, Eskimos, and Aleuts) and Asian/Pacific Islander. State estimates for those categories were derived by dividing the "Other Non-Hispanics" estimate into two categories proportional to their relative population sizes in 1980.

Thus, although some changes were made to provide more detailed estimates of age group sizes for the purpose of generating detailed estimates of numbers of high school graduates by state, sex, race, and Hispanic origin, all estimates are tied to Census Bureau age

Table A.3

ESTIMATED NUMBERS OF 17-YEAR-OLDS BY STATE AND CATEGORY: 1980–1989

Category: All

State	1980	1981	1982	1983	1984	1985	1986	1987	1988	1989
Alabama	74987	74008	71385	67730	65088	64009	65172	67689	70289	66274
Alaska	7588	7627	7361	7115	6996	6981	8036	8044	8199	7671
Arizona	49699	49568	48216	46380	46461	46930	49420	50916	53230	50210
Arkansas	43594	42930	41151	37742	36319	35941	37680	37695	39073	36796
California	426119	422111	406906	385527	376818	373043	379960	399195	405029	374310
Colorado	52429	51573	49365	45826	45324	45297	48382	49040	50034	45939
Connecticut	58411	57493	55074	53316	50834	49220	49589	50759	49548	43703
Delaware	11675	11528	11071	10645	10318	9761	9438	10019	10215	9357
D. of Columbia	10508	10514	10293	9700	9156	8646	7316	8300	8725	8008
Florida	163278	161371	155819	148388	146506	144827	157871	158082	164717	155469
Georgia	105809	104576	101193	97976	96998	96183	99419	104599	109623	103772
Hawaii	16951	17819	17698	16517	15459	14932	15007	15304	15452	14624
Idaho	17620	17197	16227	15511	15289	15014	16377	15651	16295	15146
Illinois	215191	211254	201780	188114	181663	175193	175223	178060	181526	166205
Indiana	104554	102891	98305	91525	89727	86715	86761	89369	92771	85609
Iowa	55121	53890	50891	47322	45045	43040	43248	43591	43621	39420
Kansas	42796	41962	39806	36858	34999	33876	35423	35300	36220	33217
Kentucky	71050	69553	66230	61525	59688	58170	59329	60123	62660	58760
Louisiana	83775	82751	79947	75087	73410	71632	72518	73738	74427	70030
Maine	21895	21415	20313	19436	19027	18475	18566	18831	19117	17765
Maryland	81622	80808	78020	74357	72108	70672	69863	70310	70397	64081
Massachusetts	106765	105011	100465	96521	93251	90895	88767	88922	88352	79173
Michigan	180279	177590	169918	160660	157274	153449	150210	156083	158884	143663
Minnesota	81154	79329	74930	70145	65945	64060	65169	64546	64836	57919
Mississippi	51871	51129	49384	45782	44624	44016	44543	46753	47881	45534
Missouri	92799	90924	86543	79496	76990	73826	76128	76936	78761	72827
Montana	15441	15151	14274	12867	12425	11790	12412	12334	12606	11407
Nebraska	29288	28674	27103	24976	23615	22783	23627	23179	23896	22073
Nevada	14335	14207	13683	13295	13169	13046	12376	14105	14529	13576
New Hampshire	16791	16597	16018	15787	15829	15915	15759	16615	17379	16006
New Jersey	138595	136425	130710	125487	120772	116820	120191	118560	117265	104742
New Mexico	27176	27075	26338	24265	23163	22504	24210	23999	24444	23040
New York	322169	318036	306097	294511	282586	272241	271810	275386	273860	243051
North Carolina	109453	108232	104388	99462	98836	99117	100265	104093	108221	101006
North Dakota	12607	12301	11607	10611	10133	9407	10135	9846	9695	9132
Ohio	202028	198337	189060	178119	173561	168120	168369	173723	178497	162131
Oklahoma	55860	55043	52380	47895	46071	45941	50148	49228	50840	47759
Oregon	46187	45174	42712	40829	39463	38423	39742	40231	40005	36276
Pennsylvania	213609	210188	201051	191508	185686	180563	180351	180415	182746	165314
Rhode Island	16836	16614	16035	15528	15297	15197	14373	14992	15276	13844
South Carolina	62325	61624	59447	56367	56584	54209	54534	56743	59383	56411
South Dakota	13751	13569	12856	11623	10722	10272	10800	10185	10495	9677
Tennessee	84545	83401	80214	75961	73892	72879	74284	78321	81141	75733
Texas	268566	264846	255836	242493	241590	243785	259088	272936	282930	267056
Utah	27185	26668	25338	24385	25147	25047	26004	27342	29386	28412
Vermont	9747	9587	9169	8851	8625	8510	8546	8894	9118	8334
Virginia	99692	98361	94646	89356	87115	86234	88799	89670	91969	84910
Washington	74296	72979	69245	65350	63763	63727	67130	67504	67765	61052
West Virginia	34355	33691	32149	30250	29489	29411	30638	30583	31429	29650
Wisconsin	93134	91239	86639	81754	79127	75275	74324	75911	76235	68321
Wyoming	8337	8159	7714	7269	7023	6981	7486	7490	7706	7238
United States	4223848	4163000	3993000	3778000	3677000	3603000	3674816	3760140	3836698	3531633

Category: Male

Table A.3—continued

State	1980	1981	1982	1983	1984	1985	1986	1987	1988	1989
Alabama	38193	37813	36395	34825	33502	32852	33271	34803	36032	34145
Alaska	4008	4037	3874	3860	3720	3671	4178	4265	4274	4077
Arizona	25305	25293	24566	23737	23684	23971	25190	26097	27244	25676
Arkansas	22262	21965	21035	19350	18569	18486	19301	19322	20213	19082
California	218898	217023	208487	197943	192667	191704	195318	204566	207082	191120
Colorado	26756	26374	25223	23315	22974	22996	24679	25187	25840	23542
Connecticut	29729	29329	28035	27264	26125	25324	25317	26008	25385	22438
Delaware	5854	5795	5543	5436	5165	4837	4740	5052	5134	4759
D. of Columbia	5233	5237	5092	4922	4567	4268	3643	4150	4314	4023
Florida	83506	82644	79651	75925	74834	74045	80850	80917	84778	79934
Georgia	54980	54320	52316	50448	49983	49251	51674	53743	56462	53247
Hawaii	8606	9085	9024	8347	7815	7543	7479	7820	7906	7348
Idaho	9078	8845	8299	8020	7830	7717	8457	7955	8294	7795
Illinois	110147	108337	103189	96450	93108	89686	89987	91492	93182	85348
Indiana	53043	52368	49973	46494	45725	44655	44199	45866	47673	43813
Iowa	27908	27401	25900	24094	22977	21949	21993	22479	22689	20401
Kansas	21762	21380	20291	18742	17656	17265	18022	18045	18827	17152
Kentucky	37670	36791	34190	32307	31244	30089	31496	31159	32522	30584
Louisiana	42077	41729	40324	38125	37269	36321	36500	37568	38144	35926
Maine	11191	11005	10411	10118	9846	9581	9506	9817	9849	9270
Maryland	41408	41144	39670	37626	36793	35986	35490	36110	36111	32587
Massachusetts	54696	53782	51299	49062	47297	46142	45640	45159	45334	40369
Michigan	91578	90538	86531	82154	80255	78759	76616	80366	81769	73932
Minnesota	41497	40686	38355	35673	33736	33132	33464	33351	33445	29553
Mississippi	26570	26236	25281	23527	22823	22662	22858	23973	24633	23526
Missouri	47851	46932	44550	40680	39400	37467	39368	39600	40785	37402
Montana	8063	7921	7444	6721	6431	6150	6497	6431	6631	5967
Nebraska	14949	14677	13842	12908	12263	11757	12083	11948	12285	11423
Nevada	7463	7387	7093	6794	6795	6681	6446	7213	7568	7017
New Hampshire	8545	8491	8156	8107	8215	8248	8046	8551	8945	8294
New Jersey	71222	70120	66957	64063	61651	59700	61965	60513	60197	53585
New Mexico	13893	13849	13431	12327	11831	11415	12387	12250	12428	11630
New York	163299	161557	155308	149092	143660	138360	138318	140396	140321	123904
North Carolina	55808	55278	53175	50916	50108	50619	51055	53112	55348	51748
North Dakota	6361	6253	5893	5523	5298	4889	5109	5153	5940	4731
Ohio	102793	101284	96346	91375	89312	86709	86022	89671	91536	83297
Oklahoma	29120	28710	27248	25025	23707	23705	26170	25521	26546	25021
Oregon	23686	23221	21930	20752	20415	19702	20464	20772	20780	18592
Pennsylvania	109234	107716	102827	98165	94964	92700	92601	92755	94248	85144
Rhode Island	8474	8392	8080	7929	7748	7883	7254	7646	7742	7053
South Carolina	32396	31995	30701	28860	27951	27955	28301	29027	30468	28751
South Dakota	7065	6979	6574	5970	5426	5176	5558	5197	5311	4923
Tennessee	43371	42883	41095	39215	38046	37690	38210	40403	41563	39052
Texas	137581	135892	130905	124816	124185	125599	132846	140266	144920	137090
Utah	13955	13671	12904	12816	12801	12606	13388	13801	14791	14347
Vermont	4965	4895	4684	4516	4389	4381	4372	4595	4761	4339
Virginia	50787	50245	48182	45501	44399	44063	45032	46028	46818	43080
Washington	38037	37463	35487	33524	32689	34844	34382	34844	35006	31464
West Virginia	17499	17215	16440	15518	15000	14954	15673	15743	16399	15504
Wisconsin	47414	46599	44198	41813	40612	38578	38002	39101	39341	35182
Wyoming	4328	4218	3990	3680	3536	3506	3893	3784	4063	3740
United States	2160114	2133000	2041000	1934000	1881000	1846000	1883311	1929591	1970877	1811927

Table A.3—continued

Category: Female

State	1980	1981	1982	1983	1984	1985	1986	1987	1988	1989
Alabama	36794	36195	34990	32905	31586	31157	31901	32886	34257	32129
Alaska	3580	3590	3487	3255	3276	3310	3858	3779	3925	3594
Arizona	24394	24275	23650	22643	22777	22959	24230	24819	25986	24534
Arkansas	21332	20965	20116	18392	17750	17455	18373	18373	18860	17714
California	207221	205088	198419	187584	184151	181339	184642	194629	197947	183190
Colorado	25673	25199	24142	22511	22350	22301	23703	23853	24194	22397
Connecticut	28682	28164	27039	26052	24709	23896	24272	24751	24163	21265
Delaware	5821	5733	5528	5209	5153	4924	4698	4967	5081	4598
D. of Columbia	5275	5277	5201	4778	4589	4378	3673	4150	4411	3985
Florida	79772	78727	76168	72463	71672	70782	77021	77165	79939	75535
Georgia	50829	50256	48877	47528	47015	46932	47745	50856	53161	50525
Hawaii	8345	8734	8674	8170	7644	7389	7528	7484	7546	7276
Idaho	8542	8352	7928	7491	7459	7297	7920	7696	8001	7351
Illinois	105044	102917	98591	91664	88505	85507	85236	86568	88344	80857
Indiana	51511	50523	48332	45031	44002	42060	42562	43503	45098	41796
Iowa	27213	26489	24991	23228	22068	21091	21255	21112	20932	19019
Kansas	21034	20582	19515	18116	17343	16611	17401	17255	17393	16065
Kentucky	33380	32762	31434	29218	28444	28081	27833	28964	30138	28176
Louisiana	41698	41022	39623	36962	36141	35311	36018	36170	36283	34104
Maine	10704	10410	9902	9318	9181	8894	9060	9014	9268	8495
Maryland	40214	39664	38350	36731	35135	34686	34373	34200	34286	31494
Massachusetts	52069	51229	49166	47459	45954	44753	43127	43763	43018	38804
Michigan	88701	87052	83387	78506	77019	74690	73594	75717	77115	69731
Minnesota	39657	38643	36575	34472	32209	30928	31705	31195	31391	28366
Mississippi	25301	24893	24103	22255	21801	21354	21685	22780	23248	22008
Missouri	44948	43992	41993	38816	37590	36359	36760	37336	37976	35425
Montana	7378	7230	6830	6146	5994	5640	5915	5903	5975	5440
Nebraska	14339	13997	13261	12068	11352	11026	11544	11231	11611	10650
Nevada	6872	6820	6590	6501	6374	6365	5930	6892	6961	6559
New Hampshire	8246	8106	7862	7680	7614	7667	7713	8064	8434	7712
New Jersey	67373	66305	63753	61424	59121	57120	58226	58047	57068	51157
New Mexico	13283	13226	12907	11938	11332	11089	11823	11749	12016	11410
New York	158870	156479	150789	145419	138926	133881	133492	134990	133539	119147
North Carolina	53645	52954	51213	48546	48728	48498	49210	50981	52873	49258
North Dakota	6246	6048	5714	5088	4835	4518	5026	4693	4755	4401
Ohio	99235	97053	92714	86744	84249	81411	82347	84052	86961	78834
Oklahoma	26740	26333	25132	22870	22364	22236	23978	23707	24294	22738
Oregon	22501	21953	20782	20077	19048	18721	19278	19459	19225	17684
Pennsylvania	104375	102472	98224	93343	90722	87863	87750	87660	88498	80170
Rhode Island	8362	8222	7955	7599	7549	7314	7119	7346	7534	6791
South Carolina	29929	29629	28746	27507	26633	26254	26233	27716	28915	27660
South Dakota	6686	6590	6282	5653	5296	5096	5242	4988	5184	4754
Tennessee	41174	40518	39119	36746	35846	35189	36074	37918	39578	36681
Texas	130985	128954	124931	117677	117405	118186	126242	132670	138010	129966
Utah	13230	12997	12434	11939	12346	12441	12615	13541	14595	14065
Vermont	4782	4692	4485	4335	4236	4129	4174	4299	4357	3995
Virginia	48905	48116	46464	43855	42716	42171	43767	43642	45151	41830
Washington	36259	35516	33758	31826	31074	31112	32748	32640	32759	29588
West Virginia	16856	16476	15709	14732	14485	14457	14965	14840	15030	14146
Wisconsin	45720	44640	42441	39941	38515	36697	36322	36810	36894	33139
Wyoming	4009	3941	3724	3589	3487	3475	3593	3706	3643	3498
United States	2063734	2030000	1952000	1844000	1796000	1757000	1791505	1830549	1865821	1719706

Table A.3—continued

Category: White Non-Hispanic

State	1980	1981	1982	1983	1984	1985	1986	1987	1988	1989
Alabama	50671	49757	47511	45073	43684	43297	44367	46759	47739	44338
Alaska	5358	5228	4941	4698	4700	4809	5677	5718	5722	5241
Arizona	33549	32995	31588	29912	29832	30159	32780	34120	35728	32441
Arkansas	33830	33189	31564	28771	27905	27598	29465	29632	30394	28574
California	262155	258664	246663	224925	215603	209087	209644	224365	225543	196235
Colorado	41446	40462	38406	35142	34788	34588	37292	37839	38457	34457
Connecticut	49986	48904	46493	44408	41787	40501	40502	41694	40162	34940
Delaware	9120	8943	8481	8058	7804	7229	7010	7449	7450	6860
D. of Columbia	1019	1031	1041	1013	1249	1337	1263	1534	1507	1359
Florida	113542	112385	107888	101773	100742	100893	112087	113330	117224	107646
Georgia	70745	69607	66406	63418	63729	63897	66587	71240	73544	68227
Hawaii	4447	4327	4153	3641	3420	3171	3355	3350	3343	2880
Idaho	16311	15902	14971	14272	14042	13706	15046	14351	14900	13713
Illinois	161751	158352	149520	137051	131146	124716	123856	125614	125368	110336
Indiana	92796	91157	86627	80478	78750	75694	75841	78226	80521	73731
Iowa	53263	51962	48977	45349	43090	41089	41099	41393	41341	37120
Kansas	38079	37128	35038	32281	30529	29419	30569	30556	31059	28241
Kentucky	63954	62608	59483	55256	53820	52298	53383	54238	56247	52493
Louisiana	52299	51274	48739	44742	44147	42737	44300	46057	45410	41989
Maine	21583	21059	19978	19125	18691	18149	18240	18516	18763	17397
Maryland	57167	56163	53414	50420	48779	46839	46119	46470	45544	40782
Massachusetts	97595	95633	91048	86924	83621	80999	78966	79076	78000	69024
Michigan	150485	147422	139826	130437	126836	121971	118406	123307	123128	109411
Minnesota	78000	76068	71581	66796	62550	60506	61348	60496	60496	53557
Mississippi	29216	28601	27167	25148	24608	24487	24863	26747	26821	25143
Missouri	79113	77409	73248	66857	64919	62230	64314	65065	66155	60638
Montana	14144	13749	12878	11555	11182	10571	11104	11062	11242	10075
Nebraska	27158	26542	24924	22807	21945	20757	21479	21058	21682	19821
Nevada	11287	11161	10692	10398	10239	10180	9543	11045	11308	10396
New Hampshire	16553	16320	15756	15474	15500	15573	15441	16268	17024	15622
New Jersey	105384	103014	97371	91742	87599	83449	85581	84399	81479	71274
New Mexico	12107	11982	11384	9821	8830	8333	9815	9699	10053	8655
New York	230042	225036	213449	201895	192176	182058	180769	183713	178902	155847
North Carolina	76637	75326	71818	67922	68824	68834	70057	73390	75475	69346
North Dakota	11894	11567	10841	9908	9480	8702	9435	9135	8985	8329
Ohio	175491	171662	162849	153002	149268	144183	143393	148248	151046	136012
Oklahoma	45440	44363	41653	37882	36522	36235	39389	38934	39735	36764
Oregon	42501	41484	39108	37226	35884	34711	35864	36228	35937	32151
Pennsylvania	185779	182243	173432	164806	159922	154898	154681	155166	155939	140481
Rhode Island	15652	15379	14777	14280	13972	13848	12989	13546	13735	12348
South Carolina	38486	37828	35992	33781	33443	33415	34129	35992	37104	34566
South Dakota	12445	12139	11413	10190	9405	8933	9316	8811	9008	8195
Tennessee	66919	65795	62913	59281	58397	57558	58777	62405	63839	59347
Texas	160734	157500	147556	135138	133174	134065	146584	158858	164482	147599
Utah	24439	23844	22618	21858	22387	22321	23171	24362	26204	25156
Vermont	9628	9469	9053	8711	8479	8351	8358	8682	8901	8095
Virginia	74588	73135	69548	65134	64116	63343	65375	66876	67629	61731
Washington	66158	64702	60975	57435	55766	55452	58131	58330	58352	51773
West Virginia	32634	31913	30448	28636	27989	27950	29085	29193	29909	28208
Wisconsin	86434	84410	79939	74887	72235	67988	67168	68398	68214	60482
Wyoming	7568	7386	6938	6464	6208	6105	6585	6597	6792	6267
United States	3217587	3154179	2993077	2796201	2713463	2639219	2692598	2767537	2793542	2515313

Table A.3—continued

Category: Black Non-Hispanic

State	1980	1981	1982	1983	1984	1985	1986	1987	1988	1989
Alabama	23232	23222	22840	21577	20320	19632	19700	19799	21349	20772
Alaska	197	195	196	182	170	191	211	205	235	231
Arizona	1600	1615	1593	1535	1452	1466	1576	1593	1674	1608
Arkansas	9029	9005	8848	8216	7637	7524	7316	7191	7796	7351
California	38974	39004	38514	37885	36164	35267	36215	37184	39045	35946
Colorado	2019	2042	2026	1872	1772	1808	1939	1916	2154	1997
Connecticut	5180	5253	5216	5325	5093	4861	5105	5056	5367	4727
Delaware	2267	2283	2269	2279	2184	2183	2094	2179	2371	2118
D. of Columbia	9161	9160	8948	8370	7580	7011	5787	6482	6909	6328
Florida	30629	30619	30337	29632	29130	28142	30189	28931	31918	31940
Georgia	33117	33275	32963	32757	31447	30407	30846	31290	33826	33345
Hawaii	142	155	153	167	187	145	186	185	214	198
Idaho	50	39	29	43	38	40	50	53	66	59
Illinois	37581	37447	36844	35438	34724	33828	33790	34052	37386	35907
Indiana	9301	9348	9219	8664	8476	8360	8281	8219	9273	8796
Iowa	931	928	925	932	930	872	976	1039	1079	1045
Kansas	2859	2850	2819	2607	2395	2323	2415	2288	2544	2358
Kentucky	6191	6153	5951	5486	5153	5105	5198	5138	5694	5504
Louisiana	28656	28625	28309	27391	26201	25921	25233	24627	25966	24975
Maine	42	47	34	33	35	37	43	40	44	41
Maryland	21862	21989	21853	21158	20481	20789	20629	20574	21511	19877
Massachusetts	5170	5142	5115	5121	4898	5060	4998	4854	5269	4819
Michigan	24296	24447	24313	24349	24294	25035	25187	25921	28636	27074
Minnesota	1056	1051	1045	1035	975	1017	1024	1098	1185	1152
Mississippi	21789	21695	21348	19745	19159	18610	18704	19083	20094	19419
Missouri	11770	11667	11527	10857	10314	9817	9965	9934	10635	10168
Montana	14	24	20	30	28	27	29	37	39	32
Nebraska	1184	1185	1172	1107	1069	971	1044	1028	1120	1090
Nevada	1210	1207	1186	1182	1207	1107	1047	1180	1237	1246
New Hampshire	67	67	69	96	95	90	90	104	117	112
New Jersey	21122	21233	21035	20922	19951	19940	20856	20218	21386	19088
New Mexico	501	507	505	488	427	479	456	475	529	463
New York	51430	51447	51356	49985	47268	46379	47247	47254	50084	44129
North Carolina	29939	29956	29556	28616	27011	27175	26966	27399	29259	28005
North Dakota	31	15	19	34	25	22	35	33	49	48
Ohio	22980	22955	22586	21322	20491	20068	20830	21247	23142	21698
Oklahoma	4718	4683	4602	4235	3878	3760	4171	3924	4391	4158
Oregon	826	816	797	828	748	703	720	749	781	729
Pennsylvania	23178	23193	22816	21548	20572	20031	19862	19458	20670	18650
Rhode Island	649	665	666	642	650	640	644	661	727	679
South Carolina	22747	22759	22433	21598	20134	19747	19379	19738	21206	20835
South Dakota	20	18	20	25	23	27	27	37	41	40
Tennessee	16561	16570	16295	15673	14488	14335	14451	14818	16202	15286
Texas	37104	37150	36697	35528	34723	34416	35273	35834	39456	37919
Utah	338	329	299	221	243	228	207	222	229	220
Vermont	16	17	16	31	29	33	38	40	54	48
Virginia	22351	22426	22251	21295	19894	19509	19821	19051	20443	19202
Washington	2138	2116	2086	1866	1791	1812	1944	1995	2125	1871
West Virginia	1425	1403	1380	1241	1131	1062	1125	1014	1134	1029
Wisconsin	4260	4271	4203	4268	4230	4550	4364	4594	5061	4748
Wyoming	67	64	66	42	67	53	76	59	75	68
United States	591977	592312	585365	565479	541382	532615	538359	540100	581797	549148

Table A.3—continued

Category: Other Non-Hispanic

State	1980	1981	1982	1983	1984	1985	1986	1987	1988	1989
Alabama	288	310	317	356	336	382	411	454	480	511
Alaska	1853	2026	2061	2061	1970	1808	1966	1920	2025	1944
Arizona	4232	4668	4766	4580	4674	4733	4640	4681	5021	5075
Arkansas	310	345	357	367	376	425	467	466	480	501
California	25045	27481	28043	28409	29187	31108	33238	35410	37445	38386
Colorado	860	976	982	991	985	1042	1186	1231	1332	1373
Connecticut	370	404	425	435	541	582	630	729	737	797
Delaware	65	77	87	94	89	113	112	136	139	140
D. of Columbia	90	100	98	126	100	90	75	87	94	99
Florida	1181	1322	1364	1414	1635	1872	2196	2275	2512	2639
Georgia	484	528	539	558	588	671	770	875	969	1040
Hawaii	10752	11704	11885	11140	10240	10032	9903	10020	10145	9788
Idaho	343	379	394	378	399	384	429	392	443	392
Illinois	2420	2666	2719	2744	2918	3209	3650	3903	4129	4228
Indiana	476	529	555	498	606	672	740	875	887	942
Iowa	388	418	428	465	447	485	582	551	596	583
Kansas	522	584	626	608	759	811	989	978	1053	1141
Kentucky	214	242	238	218	196	258	225	204	220	218
Louisiana	630	708	747	778	906	904	1003	1058	1114	1139
Maine	164	182	184	164	179	181	169	172	184	205
Maryland	1221	1344	1361	1474	1455	1712	1800	2003	2023	2153
Massachusetts	957	1054	1070	1142	1238	1364	1398	1462	1553	1685
Michigan	1747	1910	1950	2018	2099	2323	2345	2606	2721	2841
Minnesota	1414	1542	1594	1603	1675	1775	2023	2126	2309	2404
Mississippi	257	285	301	302	274	325	384	375	407	398
Missouri	635	692	706	673	673	739	803	845	880	920
Montana	1034	1125	1146	1047	971	974	1023	994	1070	1009
Nebraska	309	343	364	384	417	437	407	402	415	436
Nevada	587	650	670	596	621	626	680	752	807	810
New Hampshire	75	82	78	96	109	110	100	113	120	142
New Jersey	1392	1524	1586	1811	1968	2294	2833	2881	3177	3305
New Mexico	2716	2997	3068	2883	2738	2766	3075	2996	3120	3106
New York	5490	6059	6148	6397	6632	7132	7773	8046	8594	8708
North Carolina	1763	1938	1951	1901	1949	2038	2178	2297	2419	2560
North Dakota	600	649	662	586	549	605	591	595	581	651
Ohio	888	986	995	1077	1131	1210	1317	1408	1459	1489
Oklahoma	4324	4750	4857	4532	4414	4678	5315	5015	5357	5391
Oregon	1273	1399	1417	1385	1427	1489	1635	1716	1736	1825
Pennsylvania	1194	1305	1338	1424	1458	1699	1943	2039	2226	2271
Rhode Island	167	189	199	220	234	267	326	353	375	403
South Carolina	264	287	304	272	283	343	326	358	397	389
South Dakota	1189	1299	1331	1322	1206	1208	1369	1233	1342	1338
Tennessee	286	323	328	308	363	368	415	445	474	481
Texas	2465	2697	2732	2984	3248	3564	4190	4410	4752	4854
Utah	979	1066	1095	988	1082	1116	1202	1298	1389	1488
Vermont	34	42	47	50	55	65	81	103	101	125
Virginia	1198	1322	1359	1425	1581	1827	2061	2177	2325	2429
Washington	3261	3586	3638	3497	3616	3751	4210	4305	4425	4481
West Virginia	70	79	81	100	122	118	164	153	164	164
Wisconsin	1043	1132	1163	1202	1218	1235	1270	1344	1372	1504
Wyoming	184	204	204	237	218	246	247	236	271	272
United States	89703	98509	100558	100320	102155	108166	116859	121503	128366	131173

Table A.3—continued

Category: Hispanic

State	1980	1981	1982	1983	1984	1985	1986	1987	1988	1989
Alabama	796	719	717	724	748	698	694	677	721	653
Alaska	180	178	163	174	156	173	182	201	217	255
Arizona	10318	10290	10269	10353	10503	10572	10424	10522	10807	11086
Arkansas	425	391	382	388	401	394	432	406	403	370
California	99945	96962	93686	94308	95864	97581	100863	102236	102996	103743
Colorado	8104	8093	7951	7821	7779	7859	7965	8054	8091	8112
Connecticut	2875	2932	2940	3148	3213	3276	3352	3280	3282	3239
Delaware	223	225	234	214	241	236	222	255	255	239
D. of Columbia	238	223	206	191	227	208	191	197	215	222
Florida	17926	17045	16230	15569	14999	13920	13399	13546	13063	13244
Georgia	1463	1166	1285	1243	1234	1208	1216	1194	1284	1160
Hawaii	1610	1633	1507	1569	1610	1584	1563	1749	1750	1758
Idaho	916	877	833	818	810	684	852	855	886	982
Illinois	13439	12789	12697	12881	12875	13440	13927	14491	14643	15734
Indiana	1981	1857	1904	1885	1895	1989	1899	2049	2090	2140
Iowa	539	582	561	576	578	594	591	608	605	672
Kansas	1336	1400	1323	1362	1316	1323	1450	1478	1564	1477
Kentucky	691	550	558	565	519	509	523	543	499	545
Louisiana	2190	2144	2152	2176	2156	2070	1982	1996	1937	1927
Maine	106	127	117	114	122	108	114	103	126	122
Maryland	1372	1312	1392	1305	1393	1332	1315	1263	1319	1269
Massachusetts	3043	3182	3232	3334	3494	3472	3405	3530	3530	3645
Michigan	3751	3811	3829	3856	4045	4120	4272	4249	4399	4337
Minnesota	684	668	710	711	745	762	774	826	846	806
Mississippi	609	548	568	587	583	594	592	548	559	574
Missouri	1281	1156	1062	1109	1084	1040	1046	1092	1091	1101
Montana	249	253	230	235	244	218	256	241	255	291
Nebraska	637	604	643	678	634	618	697	691	679	726
Nevada	1251	1189	1135	1119	1102	1133	1106	1128	1177	1124
New Hampshire	96	128	115	121	125	142	128	130	118	130
New Jersey	10692	10654	10718	11012	11254	11137	10921	11062	11223	11075
New Mexico	11852	11589	11381	11073	11168	10926	10864	10829	10742	10816
New York	35207	35494	35144	36234	36510	36672	36021	36373	36280	34367
North Carolina	1114	1032	1063	1023	1052	1070	1064	1007	1068	1095
North Dakota	82	70	85	83	79	78	74	83	80	104
Ohio	2669	2734	2630	2718	2671	2659	2829	2820	2850	2932
Oklahoma	1378	1247	1268	1246	1257	1268	1273	1355	1357	1446
Oregon	1587	1475	1390	1390	1404	1520	1523	1538	1551	1571
Pennsylvania	3458	3447	3465	3730	3734	3935	3865	3752	3911	3912
Rhode Island	368	381	393	386	441	442	420	432	439	414
South Carolina	828	750	718	716	724	704	700	655	676	621
South Dakota	97	113	92	86	88	104	88	104	104	104
Tennessee	779	713	678	699	644	618	641	653	626	619
Texas	68263	67499	68851	68843	70445	71740	73041	73834	74240	76684
Utah	1429	1429	1326	1318	1435	1382	1424	1460	1564	1548
Vermont	69	59	53	59	62	61	69	69	62	66
Virginia	1555	1478	1488	1502	1524	1555	1542	1566	1572	1548
Washington	2739	2575	2546	2552	2590	2712	2845	2874	2863	2927
West Virginia	226	296	240	273	247	281	264	223	222	249
Wisconsin	1397	1426	1334	1397	1444	1502	1522	1575	1588	1587
Wyoming	518	505	506	526	530	577	578	598	568	631
United States	324581	318000	314000	316000	320000	323000	327000	331000	332993	335999

Table A.4

PROJECTED NUMBERS OF 17-YEAR-OLDS BY STATE AND CATEGORY: 1990-2000

Category: All

State	1990	1991	1992	1993	1994	1995	1996	1997	1998	1999	2000
Alabama	63350	61521	61769	60112	62819	63089	64590	66510	66345	66065	65841
Alaska	7437	7362	7626	7704	8090	8341	8867	9290	9789	10227	10525
Arizona	49120	49004	51251	51289	54343	55527	58455	62212	64981	66758	67856
Arkansas	35334	34903	35706	34867	36312	36298	37222	38502	38103	37960	37881
California	361972	359768	374521	374241	393412	397754	415287	437809	461657	472364	477514
Colorado	43674	43182	44726	44468	47019	47741	49881	52365	54234	55723	56057
Connecticut	40071	38619	39325	38397	39664	40007	41058	42244	42848	44098	45022
Delaware	8701	8381	8676	8536	8964	9182	9509	9716	9690	9838	9966
D. of Columbia	7307	6921	6947	6748	7095	7136	7325	7700	8309	8477	8551
Florida	148184	145141	148816	146854	155410	158368	164970	173916	181773	187118	191753
Georgia	100132	97682	98889	96666	102013	104130	108422	113215	115095	116119	117271
Hawaii	14138	14251	14738	14985	15724	16247	16966	17922	18475	18933	19577
Idaho	14790	14908	15610	15638	16718	16722	17396	17614	17344	17182	16911
Illinois	155339	149785	153226	150689	156154	155592	159943	166997	167470	166008	164768
Indiana	80381	77900	79040	78786	79428	79152	80600	82162	80403	79500	78786
Iowa	36398	35856	37322	36876	38662	38814	39427	40186	39022	37988	36983
Kansas	32088	31721	33138	32882	34419	34567	35587	36862	37376	37415	37155
Kentucky	55274	53538	54359	53281	55354	54845	55769	56317	55210	54325	53526
Louisiana	66673	65462	66512	66029	69307	69202	71026	73823	73985	74374	73998
Maine	16573	16059	15983	15670	16365	16519	16836	17250	17350	17582	17774
Maryland	58770	56347	57841	57247	60285	61718	63800	66699	69065	71668	73646
Massachusetts	73277	69879	70205	67956	70063	71008	72747	74601	76155	78587	80096
Michigan	134033	129372	129536	126024	130245	131798	134950	137161	134649	133594	132744
Minnesota	54189	53713	55993	55503	58303	60084	62824	64219	65014	65752	64878
Mississippi	43762	42627	43424	42618	44606	44862	46185	47797	47949	47581	46955
Missouri	68776	66801	68952	67907	71465	72444	74728	77336	77922	78063	78251
Montana	10785	10795	11246	11156	11654	11721	12219	12446	12403	12458	12295
Nebraska	20845	20602	21399	20874	21731	21780	22320	23114	23264	23265	22998
Nevada	13016	12826	13309	13524	14453	14691	15688	16627	17227	17517	17530
New Hampshire	14996	14618	14995	14664	14495	15876	16392	17006	17480	17953	18358
New Jersey	98025	95401	96747	94873	98519	99150	101729	104884	105862	108686	111666
New Mexico	22482	22305	23135	23342	24709	25202	26938	28759	29512	30384	31111
New York	228569	222458	227692	224067	232463	231945	234334	239354	239239	243339	245897
North Carolina	95830	93082	93884	90586	95014	96277	98342	100751	101108	102794	103721
North Dakota	8844	8681	9045	9097	9549	9786	10042	10259	10277	10384	10203
Ohio	150207	144710	147076	142455	146984	147417	151402	153128	153001	153001	150903
Oklahoma	45483	44730	46220	45502	47142	46963	48733	50557	51431	52925	53297
Oregon	34705	34305	35720	35865	37805	37929	39388	40651	40847	40589	40115
Pennsylvania	153320	146863	148082	144072	148887	149402	152055	154768	155662	157889	157696
Rhode Island	12907	12521	12547	12442	12862	13094	13407	13673	13919	14180	14343
South Carolina	54148	52543	52698	51140	54251	54346	55517	57114	57499	57711	57619
South Dakota	9349	9443	9855	9989	10479	10654	11213	11758	11612	11589	11535
Tennessee	71884	70006	70282	67943	71190	71662	73740	75324	74443	74050	73694
Texas	257148	252625	257473	255371	265569	266346	276787	291285	301990	307818	309569
Utah	28609	29443	31625	32891	35789	36644	37820	38529	37936	37714	36929
Vermont	7794	7385	7643	7495	7838	7797	8043	8234	8475	8615	8697
Virginia	79449	76992	78558	76750	80804	82510	85159	88319	90139	92380	93873
Washington	57556	57354	59661	59909	63297	64072	66749	69289	70471	71098	70923
West Virginia	28021	26519	27029	26254	26694	26302	26242	26263	25085	24357	23691
Wisconsin	64276	63361	65717	64254	67044	67663	69493	71266	70695	70711	70190
Wyoming	6974	6936	7286	7238	7533	7576	7913	8135	8208	8175	7967
United States	3344905	3267207	3343015	3291201	3439994	3467952	3576035	3702621	3758125	3802881	3819105

Table A.4—continued

Category: Male

State	1990	1991	1992	1993	1994	1995	1996	1997	1998	1999	2000
Alabama	32672	31576	31918	30896	32541	32548	33283	34191	34145	33924	33863
Alaska	3921	3835	4024	4034	4282	4383	4651	4839	5150	5387	5518
Arizona	25037	25009	26232	26180	27751	28416	30045	31684	33259	34077	35014
Arkansas	18310	18199	18586	18165	18980	18839	19321	20087	19813	19811	19746
California	184678	184580	191663	191112	201135	203782	212957	224132	236076	241409	244423
Colorado	22319	22086	22964	22861	24129	24531	25595	26837	27851	28689	28827
Connecticut	20663	19908	20251	19677	20622	20628	21069	21937	22314	22841	23258
Delaware	4347	4141	4407	4260	4552	4604	4701	4825	4766	4800	4869
D. of Columbia	3614	3395	3444	3301	3504	3505	3615	3835	4124	4217	4198
Florida	76074	74595	76506	75517	79828	81442	84711	89600	93737	96295	98602
Georgia	51525	50079	50593	49829	52766	53555	55965	58441	59366	60093	60533
Hawaii	7162	7222	7450	7587	7954	8202	8507	8849	9248	9339	9694
Idaho	7579	7682	7963	7988	8591	8511	8965	8967	8857	8862	8663
Illinois	79817	76933	78842	77636	80413	80058	82233	85828	86160	85423	84694
Indiana	41240	40309	40915	39576	41147	40968	41556	42511	41214	40991	40661
Iowa	18840	18502	19351	19137	19890	20020	20402	20634	20208	19555	19020
Kansas	16429	16340	17041	16927	17761	18003	18464	19102	19485	19486	19402
Kentucky	28870	27824	28247	27840	28790	28548	28923	29161	28549	27995	27720
Louisiana	34110	33281	34302	33464	35325	35314	36281	37641	37825	37846	37785
Maine	8602	8343	8498	8187	8684	8711	8924	9167	9264	9297	9552
Maryland	30089	28727	29519	29267	30743	31501	32585	33975	35189	36705	37523
Massachusetts	37337	35610	35804	34515	35698	35983	36778	37987	38499	39975	40742
Michigan	68791	66586	66631	64807	66997	67690	69421	70211	69249	68497	68294
Minnesota	27779	27738	28922	28461	30068	30831	32195	32894	33298	33765	33458
Mississippi	22569	22158	22565	22143	23109	23299	23919	24723	24931	24665	24406
Missouri	35359	34097	35660	35042	36897	37078	38303	39795	39996	40177	40307
Montana	5604	5622	5828	5761	6012	6110	6341	6567	6498	6506	6431
Nebraska	10837	10625	11091	10706	11262	11206	11554	11852	12032	11992	11830
Nevada	6823	6696	6941	7087	7502	7659	8164	8709	8972	9077	9159
New Hampshire	7844	7627	7749	7607	8014	8126	8374	8831	8959	9208	9501
New Jersey	50294	49021	49738	48746	50691	50937	52201	54023	54538	56071	57505
New Mexico	11456	11303	11811	11859	12572	12764	13539	14588	14817	15319	15827
New York	117010	113796	116763	114775	119155	118632	119786	122012	122538	124401	125770
North Carolina	48690	47553	47920	46072	48338	49035	50223	51232	51490	52111	52668
North Dakota	4593	4474	4694	4712	4947	5034	5208	5263	5254	5385	5241
Ohio	77279	74427	75580	73041	75411	75770	77583	78895	78708	78230	77548
Oklahoma	23597	23318	24150	23879	24755	24487	25480	26511	27115	28012	27979
Oregon	18062	17698	18418	18522	19622	19660	20230	20973	21160	20992	20963
Pennsylvania	78806	75690	76016	74066	76866	76969	78218	79209	79945	80962	80924
Rhode Island	6511	6414	6293	6109	6413	6542	6682	6822	6858	6946	7041
South Carolina	27719	27194	27230	26481	28251	28294	28879	29875	29841	29948	30015
South Dakota	4735	4805	5058	5184	5349	5421	5722	5912	5946	5940	5912
Tennessee	37037	36228	36168	35127	36801	37025	38080	39038	38407	38344	38113
Texas	132016	129872	132237	130703	135803	136145	141665	148867	154275	157605	158868
Utah	14510	14869	16063	16709	18031	18627	19163	19601	19181	19293	18888
Vermont	4039	3872	3930	3952	4122	4100	4219	4334	4522	4576	4589
Virginia	40290	39090	39995	39045	41302	42123	43239	44876	45937	47123	47851
Washington	29736	29634	31082	31185	32815	33287	34390	36021	36594	36840	36846
West Virginia	14579	13794	14146	13658	13902	13628	13614	13688	13033	12748	12258
Wisconsin	33173	32607	33914	33081	34533	34829	35751	36642	36769	36565	36217
Wyoming	3580	3555	3684	3699	3888	3892	4047	4215	4236	4259	4173
United States	1716553	1678539	1718797	1690175	1768514	1781252	1835724	1900409	1930198	1952524	1962889

Table A.4—continued

Category: Female

State	1990	1991	1992	1993	1994	1995	1996	1997	1998	1999	2000
Alabama	30678	29945	29851	29216	30278	30541	31307	32319	32200	32141	31978
Alaska	3516	3527	3602	3670	3808	3958	4216	4451	4639	4840	5007
Arizona	24083	23995	25019	25109	26592	27111	28410	30528	31722	32681	32842
Arkansas	17024	16704	17120	16702	17332	17459	17901	18415	18290	18149	18135
California	177234	175188	182858	183129	192277	193972	202330	213677	225581	230955	233091
Colorado	21355	21096	21762	21607	22890	23210	24286	25528	26383	27034	27230
Connecticut	19408	18711	19074	18720	19042	19379	19989	20307	20534	21257	21764
Delaware	4354	4240	4269	4276	4412	4578	4808	4891	4924	5038	5097
D. of Columbia	3693	3526	3503	3447	3591	3631	3710	3865	4185	4260	4353
Florida	72110	70546	72310	71337	75582	76926	80256	84316	88036	90823	93151
Georgia	48607	47603	48296	46837	49247	50575	52457	54774	55729	56076	56738
Hawaii	6976	7029	7288	7398	7770	8045	8459	9073	9227	9594	9883
Idaho	7211	7226	7647	7650	8127	8211	8431	8647	8487	8320	8248
Illinois	75522	72852	74384	73053	75741	75534	77710	81169	81310	80585	80074
Indiana	39141	37591	38125	37210	38281	38184	39044	39651	39189	38509	38125
Iowa	17558	17354	17971	17739	18772	18794	19025	19552	18814	18433	17963
Kansas	15659	15381	16097	15955	16658	16564	17123	17760	17891	17929	17753
Kentucky	26404	25714	26112	25441	26564	26297	26846	27156	26661	26330	25806
Louisiana	32563	32181	32210	32565	33982	33888	34745	36182	36160	36528	36213
Maine	7971	7716	7485	7483	7982	7808	7912	8086	8086	8285	8222
Maryland	28681	27620	28322	27980	29542	30217	31215	32724	33876	34963	36123
Massachusetts	35940	34269	34401	33441	34365	35025	35969	36614	37656	38612	39354
Michigan	65242	62786	62905	61217	63248	64108	65529	66950	65400	65097	64450
Minnesota	26410	25975	27071	27042	28235	29253	30629	31325	31716	31987	31420
Mississippi	21193	20469	20859	20475	21497	21563	22266	23074	23018	22916	22549
Missouri	33417	32704	33292	32865	34568	35366	36425	37541	37926	37886	37944
Montana	5181	5173	5418	5395	5642	5611	5878	5879	5905	5952	5864
Nebraska	10008	9977	10308	10168	10469	10574	10766	11262	11232	11273	11168
Nevada	6193	6130	6368	6437	6951	7032	7524	7918	8255	8440	8371
New Hampshire	7152	6991	7206	7057	7481	7750	8018	8175	8521	8745	8857
New Jersey	47731	46380	47009	46127	47828	48213	49528	50861	51324	52615	54161
New Mexico	11026	11002	11324	11483	12137	12438	13399	14171	14695	15065	15284
New York	111559	108662	110929	109292	113308	113313	114548	117342	116701	118938	120127
North Carolina	47140	45529	45964	44514	46676	47242	48119	49519	49618	50683	51053
North Dakota	4251	4207	4351	4385	4602	4752	4834	4996	5023	4999	4962
Ohio	72928	70283	71496	69414	71573	71647	73819	74936	74420	74771	73355
Oklahoma	21886	21412	22070	21643	22387	22476	23253	24046	24316	24911	25318
Oregon	16643	16607	17302	17343	18183	18269	19158	19678	19687	19597	19152
Pennsylvania	74514	71173	72066	70006	72021	72433	73837	75559	75717	76927	76772
Rhode Island	6396	6107	6254	6133	6449	6552	6725	6851	7061	7234	7302
South Carolina	26429	25349	25468	24659	26000	26052	26638	27239	27658	27763	27604
South Dakota	4614	4638	4797	4805	5130	5233	5491	5846	5666	5649	5623
Tennessee	34847	33778	34114	32816	34389	34637	35660	36286	36036	35706	35581
Texas	125132	122753	125236	124668	129766	130201	135660	142418	147715	150706	150701
Utah	14099	14574	15562	16182	17758	18017	18657	18928	18755	18421	18041
Vermont	3755	3513	3713	3543	3716	3697	3824	3900	3953	4039	4108
Virginia	39159	37902	38563	37705	39502	40387	41920	43443	44202	45257	46022
Washington	27820	27720	28579	28724	30482	30785	32359	33268	33877	34258	34077
West Virginia	13442	12725	12883	12271	12792	12674	12628	12575	12052	11609	11433
Wisconsin	31103	30754	31803	31173	32511	32834	33742	34624	33926	34146	33973
Wyoming	3394	3381	3602	3539	3645	3684	3866	3920	3972	3916	3794
United States	1628352	1588668	1624218	1601026	1671480	1686700	1740311	1802212	1827927	1850357	1856216

Category: White Non-Hispanic

Table A.4—continued

State	1990	1991	1992	1993	1994	1995	1996	1997	1998	1999	2000
Alabama	41471	40641	40688	39442	41156	41424	42135	43401	44266	44045	43989
Alaska	5066	4892	5194	5217	5571	5680	5929	6253	6583	6780	6860
Arizona	31059	30715	32620	32616	35173	35589	37520	40284	42788	43591	43162
Arkansas	26993	26639	27201	26405	27392	27351	27809	28745	28847	28714	28707
California	181615	176763	185735	181702	193509	193431	202692	215704	224569	226358	217876
Colorado	32269	31687	33332	32855	35124	35644	37107	39050	40498	41457	40927
Connecticut	31763	30439	31007	29959	30783	31081	31582	32820	33224	34093	34579
Delaware	6324	6020	6208	6049	6247	6363	6475	6625	6585	6647	6718
D. of Columbia	1295	1268	1261	1209	1253	1250	1275	1269	1306	1304	1300
Florida	101334	99288	102457	101276	107430	109255	114345	121292	126416	129569	131871
Georgia	65042	63546	64202	62459	65930	66917	69156	72407	74681	75257	76145
Hawaii	2758	2670	2764	2687	2913	2925	2969	3073	3216	3205	3141
Idaho	13395	13450	14098	14140	15167	15075	15583	15674	15322	15088	14683
Illinois	100750	97082	99792	96850	100176	100249	102340	105581	105412	103430	100880
Indiana	68583	66354	67318	64902	67268	66936	67958	69022	67675	66699	65858
Iowa	34147	33539	35048	34604	36250	36362	36860	37619	36444	35387	34341
Kansas	26985	26796	27872	27580	28835	28754	29502	30566	30933	30825	30364
Kentucky	49240	47785	48521	47438	49103	48764	49045	49599	48815	47929	47192
Louisiana	38745	38067	38558	37783	39320	39040	39627	41069	42006	41956	41488
Maine	16249	15711	15665	15341	16033	16146	16461	16863	16963	17179	17349
Maryland	37405	35716	36709	35773	37266	38065	38863	40584	41602	42952	44006
Massachusetts	63303	60200	60184	57896	59750	60386	61856	63462	64443	66408	67434
Michigan	100293	97392	98429	95096	98540	99755	101796	103472	102213	100887	99718
Minnesota	49745	49310	51344	50848	53369	54860	57296	58522	59417	59974	58967
Mississippi	23565	23083	23507	22760	23817	23917	24372	25182	25721	25474	25212
Missouri	56895	55581	57367	56597	59578	60431	61931	64333	64720	64721	64826
Montana	9448	9462	9902	9809	10169	10295	10590	10774	10899	10890	10676
Nebraska	18690	18410	19280	18677	19450	19469	19884	20544	20702	20644	20308
Nevada	9801	9609	10146	10222	11017	11199	11849	12511	12928	13063	12914
New Hampshire	14613	14219	14535	14248	15031	15398	15883	16477	16917	17355	17720
New Jersey	65382	63358	64567	62771	65145	65367	66390	68747	68816	70294	71528
New Mexico	8057	7765	8627	8732	9500	9690	10216	11405	12124	12299	11710
New York	143656	138058	140560	135890	140284	138209	139101	142650	142181	143511	142417
North Carolina	65137	63144	63621	61198	64253	64995	65736	67750	68736	69757	70409
North Dakota	8045	7902	8247	8243	8667	8900	9100	9309	9461	9545	9331
Ohio	125333	121162	122868	118592	122175	122310	124537	126523	126051	125616	123583
Oklahoma	34823	34174	35506	34718	35902	35660	36481	37784	38626	39344	39344
Oregon	30613	30052	31385	31325	33110	32879	34096	35100	34992	34584	33856
Pennsylvania	129753	124333	125465	121450	125136	125760	127851	130171	130681	132365	131960
Rhode Island	11467	11089	11106	10802	11289	11714	11714	11930	12092	12295	12377
South Carolina	32848	31759	31881	30726	32287	32535	32939	34110	35007	35106	35168
South Dakota	7853	7945	8317	8311	8755	8920	9361	9632	9866	9786	9652
Tennessee	55849	54421	54692	52685	55071	55425	56403	57517	57550	57161	56900
Texas	137789	133621	139693	136737	145323	145839	151528	160995	169650	171206	165593
Utah	25291	26010	28048	29109	31821	32383	33322	33834	32994	32625	31591
Vermont	7553	7179	7415	7285	7604	7548	7786	7986	8207	8326	8390
Virginia	57604	56000	56890	55141	57960	58799	60476	62703	64471	65834	66797
Washington	48372	48059	50090	50046	53089	53296	55515	57410	58021	58200	57472
West Virginia	26619	25264	25710	24668	25364	25033	24858	24954	23847	23131	22489
Wisconsin	56469	55716	57951	56483	58900	59366	60626	62117	61701	61540	60849
Wyoming	5937	5960	6238	6145	6443	6435	6628	6853	6899	6834	6554
United States	2343291	2279307	2339821	2283497	2390698	2402829	2465344	2552317	2588084	2601352	2577181

Table A.4—continued

Category: Black Non-Hispanic

State	1990	1991	1992	1993	1994	1995	1996	1997	1998	1999	2000
Alabama	20646	19687	19834	19443	20403	20371	21115	21731	20623	20506	20247
Alaska	225	212	219	221	236	256	278	296	293	305	301
Arizona	1651	1597	1618	1673	1766	1775	1939	2041	2143	2205	2206
Arkansas	7447	7319	7563	7472	7922	7919	8280	8607	8084	8033	7873
California	34339	34003	35385	35960	38268	38819	41306	43198	46175	47485	47557
Colorado	1934	1883	1924	1943	2089	2041	2181	2259	2263	2341	2323
Connecticut	4383	4154	4276	4326	4516	4594	4917	4885	4925	5126	5211
Delaware	1996	1968	2108	2099	2272	2384	2557	2593	2580	2647	2663
D. of Columbia	5705	5350	5385	5246	5530	5526	5706	6034	6589	6746	6798
Florida	31035	30131	31009	30698	32758	33597	35090	36827	38878	40410	41479
Georgia	32731	31775	32288	31853	33596	34579	36552	37944	37372	37698	37762
Hawaii	191	182	183	162	204	185	173	200	201	206	201
Idaho	59	65	60	61	56	57	60	60	55	55	54
Illinois	34057	31924	31839	31764	33331	32300	34067	36331	36215	35913	35326
Indiana	8625	8317	8445	8499	8750	8702	9023	9462	8887	8848	8714
Iowa	1024	1068	987	1032	1119	1120	1176	1220	1188	1175	1146
Kansas	2323	2198	2302	2338	2439	2513	2636	2723	2710	2731	2694
Kentucky	5319	5039	5147	5124	5495	5367	5938	5922	5572	5546	5431
Louisiana	24825	24333	24870	25097	26686	26921	27896	29037	28156	28469	28325
Maine	45	46	44	44	42	40	47	42	40	41	41
Maryland	18039	17305	17809	17961	19451	19994	21109	22101	23209	24250	24876
Massachusetts	4525	4210	4345	4337	4521	4685	4686	4904	5219	5400	5412
Michigan	26600	24822	24527	23812	24514	24527	25211	25760	24191	24207	24006
Minnesota	1099	1005	1067	1083	1164	1164	1279	1330	1357	1336	1336
Mississippi	19204	18570	18987	18868	19850	19988	20880	21575	21140	20969	20537
Missouri	9839	9204	9440	9258	9672	9710	10411	10578	10627	10669	10607
Montana	30	28	24	27	28	27	24	29	28	29	29
Nebraska	1015	1011	958	990	1049	1032	1136	1137	1104	1113	1083
Nevada	1206	1211	1149	1169	1214	1285	1413	1547	1529	1555	1546
New Hampshire	116	108	117	113	132	130	134	137	137	141	147
New Jersey	17995	17046	17229	16980	18194	18093	19223	19717	20225	20888	21325
New Mexico	469	470	488	555	588	625	654	703	705	718	712
New York	42409	41442	43446	43303	45972	45785	46226	47802	46889	47900	47845
North Carolina	26930	26235	26543	25655	27028	27185	28299	28597	27840	28309	28304
North Dakota	52	48	49	47	48	49	50	47	44	44	45
Ohio	20449	19174	19588	19245	20095	20237	21827	22117	21699	21828	21404
Oklahoma	3970	3891	3980	3997	4125	3998	4345	4510	4444	4583	4569
Oregon	696	690	711	717	749	856	836	857	861	862	848
Pennsylvania	17491	16285	16403	16309	17399	17008	17473	17768	18006	18305	18078
Rhode Island	640	599	593	619	674	680	702	698	724	737	740
South Carolina	20168	19731	19732	19298	20837	20676	21387	21732	21215	21270	21031
South Dakota	34	39	55	50	52	49	49	39	43	39	39
Tennessee	14870	14492	14436	14112	14947	15026	16082	16490	15521	15466	15289
Texas	36813	35655	35590	35694	37725	37531	40020	42217	41247	42288	42287
Utah	211	202	231	241	268	261	273	283	275	275	277
Vermont	52	52	51	48	53	52	61	52	57	61	64
Virginia	17959	17098	17708	17633	18824	19492	20230	21029	20861	21532	21770
Washington	1713	1718	1776	1808	1868	1857	1919	1881	1844	1841	1800
West Virginia	995	860	957	901	943	881	966	893	808	782	734
Wisconsin	4681	4514	4542	4473	4738	4662	5003	5254	5110	5151	5098
Wyoming	77	66	50	75	76	76	87	94	93	82	75
United States	528907	509032	517620	514433	544276	546689	572921	593250	589974	599137	598265

Table A.4—continued

Category: Other Non-Hispanic

State	1990	1991	1992	1993	1994	1995	1996	1997	1998	1999	2000
Alabama	512	546	566	565	595	614	640	676	732	765	795
Alaska	1925	1995	1947	2037	1986	2127	2346	2413	2575	2794	2987
Arizona	5215	5293	5246	5392	5654	5872	6340	6882	6647	7092	7488
Arkansas	503	522	524	548	557	583	621	678	686	711	758
California	38807	39245	39581	40137	41648	43376	46373	49595	57632	60611	62926
Colorado	1367	1414	1398	1424	1452	1534	1658	1763	1895	2015	2088
Connecticut	780	793	818	829	849	863	918	941	991	1042	1081
Delaware	143	151	130	147	157	174	176	203	220	229	245
D. of Columbia	92	92	85	81	80	86	89	84	92	94	93
Florida	2782	2804	2892	2945	3031	3163	3413	3634	3942	4167	4373
Georgia	1085	1136	1185	1176	1238	1298	1390	1456	1591	1663	1740
Hawaii	9495	9588	9917	10077	10542	10967	11555	12318	12655	13036	13547
Idaho	396	394	378	389	393	404	439	478	522	543	556
Illinois	4270	4309	4304	4275	4416	4548	4691	5005	5146	5249	5401
Indiana	968	975	963	956	970	1002	1060	1077	1160	1178	1214
Iowa	600	561	589	568	557	545	559	590	590	598	600
Kansas	1173	1194	1260	1265	1318	1357	1431	1541	1639	1691	1753
Kentucky	203	202	204	191	190	199	201	210	219	225	228
Louisiana	1153	1143	1179	1245	1271	1315	1337	1416	1451	1495	1531
Maine	175	201	181	174	174	192	192	201	197	208	217
Maryland	2128	2150	2195	2278	2295	2374	2540	2640	2837	3000	3179
Massachusetts	1736	1739	1798	1790	1877	1936	2094	2149	2281	2422	2537
Michigan	2910	2866	2945	2908	2966	3089	3257	3254	3428	3514	3628
Minnesota	2500	2530	2741	2651	2806	3006	3194	3367	3184	3300	3363
Mississippi	426	434	411	430	414	434	435	452	481	511	527
Missouri	931	963	998	972	1012	1047	1098	1154	1266	1318	1353
Montana	1068	1029	1057	1042	1124	1100	1260	1315	1138	1189	1212
Nebraska	407	402	371	387	391	411	422	454	448	463	477
Nevada	827	842	828	851	915	961	1064	1130	1288	1364	1411
New Hampshire	151	158	162	176	197	203	237	260	290	315	338
New Jersey	3477	3579	3671	3812	3980	4131	4365	4644	4684	4945	5231
New Mexico	3153	3343	3300	3389	3575	3679	3984	4319	3974	4217	4465
New York	8812	8870	8878	8822	9066	9337	9693	9001	9972	10334	10649
North Carolina	2712	2592	2606	2682	2675	2854	2967	3004	3089	3236	3394
North Dakota	642	610	619	667	707	686	711	765	630	647	668
Ohio	1484	1580	1579	1579	1621	1683	1732	1809	1892	1950	2014
Oklahoma	5321	5222	5238	5265	5460	5556	6087	6380	6420	6878	7213
Oregon	1844	1912	1946	2060	2079	2197	2317	2465	2697	2765	2840
Pennsylvania	2338	2378	2391	2361	2435	2479	2575	2692	2711	2806	2887
Rhode Island	377	385	394	385	426	453	469	491	533	557	587
South Carolina	431	405	418	425	433	464	472	498	541	574	596
South Dakota	1362	1356	1368	1515	1541	1564	1639	1909	1530	1585	1650
Tennessee	491	488	516	522	537	552	576	618	651	676	697
Texas	5028	4980	5041	5078	5214	5358	5664	5973	6472	6764	6990
Utah	1518	1613	1629	1713	1812	1883	2005	2163	2350	2416	2467
Vermont	131	110	125	110	119	131	135	151	164	180	190
Virginia	2409	2407	2435	2430	2456	2554	2676	2807	2973	3116	3254
Washington	4519	4511	4645	4680	4845	5075	5469	5837	6317	6619	6851
West Virginia	164	147	136	137	139	145	167	170	176	182	183
Wisconsin	1478	1397	1476	1423	1493	1546	1677	1758	1682	1741	1778
Wyoming	291	307	311	310	333	323	359	383	387	402	411
United States	132710	133863	135575	137271	142021	147430	156769	166054	177068	185392	192661

Table A.4—continued

Category: Hispanic

State	1990	1991	1992	1993	1994	1995	1996	1997	1998	1999	2000
Alabama	721	647	681	662	665	680	700	702	724	749	810
Alaska	221	263	266	229	297	278	314	328	338	348	377
Arizona	11195	11399	11767	11608	11750	12291	12656	13005	13403	13870	15000
Arkansas	391	423	418	442	441	445	512	472	486	502	543
California	107151	109757	113820	116442	119987	122128	124916	129312	133281	137910	149155
Colorado	8104	8198	8072	8246	8354	8522	8935	9293	9578	9910	10719
Connecticut	3145	3233	3224	3283	3516	3469	3641	3598	3708	3837	4151
Delaware	238	242	230	241	288	261	255	295	305	315	340
D. of Columbia	215	211	216	212	232	274	255	313	322	333	360
Florida	13033	12918	12458	11935	12191	12353	12122	12163	12537	12972	14030
Georgia	1274	1225	1214	1178	1249	1336	1324	1408	1451	1501	1624
Hawaii	1694	1811	1874	2049	2065	2170	2269	2331	2403	2486	2688
Idaho	940	999	1074	1048	1102	1186	1314	1402	1445	1496	1618
Illinois	16262	16470	17291	17800	18231	18495	18845	20080	20697	21476	23161
Indiana	2205	2254	2314	2429	2440	2512	2559	2601	2681	2775	3000
Iowa	627	688	698	672	736	787	832	776	800	828	896
Kansas	1607	1533	1704	1699	1827	1943	2018	2032	2094	2168	2344
Kentucky	512	512	487	528	566	515	585	586	604	625	675
Louisiana	1950	1919	1905	1904	2030	1926	2166	2301	2372	2454	2654
Maine	104	101	95	111	116	141	136	144	150	154	167
Maryland	1198	1176	1128	1235	1273	1285	1288	1374	1417	1466	1585
Massachusetts	3713	3730	3878	3933	3915	4001	4111	4086	4212	4357	4713
Michigan	4230	4292	4080	4208	4225	4427	4686	4675	4817	4986	5392
Minnesota	845	868	841	921	964	1054	1066	1051	1083	1121	1212
Mississippi	567	540	519	560	525	523	498	588	607	627	679
Missouri	1111	1053	1147	1080	1203	1256	1288	1271	1309	1355	1465
Montana	239	276	263	278	333	299	345	328	338	350	378
Nebraska	733	779	790	820	841	868	878	979	1010	1045	1130
Nevada	1182	1164	1186	1282	1307	1246	1362	1439	1482	1535	1659
New Hampshire	116	133	141	127	135	145	138	132	136	142	153
New Jersey	11171	11418	11280	11310	11200	11559	11751	11776	12137	12559	13582
New Mexico	10803	10727	10720	10666	11046	11208	12084	12332	12709	13150	14224
New York	33692	34088	34808	36052	37141	38614	39314	39001	40197	41594	44986
North Carolina	1051	1111	1114	1051	1058	1243	1340	1400	1443	1492	1614
North Dakota	105	121	130	140	127	151	181	138	142	148	159
Ohio	2941	2794	3041	3039	3093	3187	3306	3382	3486	3607	3902
Oklahoma	1369	1443	1496	1522	1655	1749	1820	1883	1941	2008	2171
Oregon	1552	1651	1678	1763	1867	1997	2139	2229	2297	2378	2571
Pennsylvania	3738	3867	3823	3952	3917	4155	4156	4137	4264	4413	4771
Rhode Island	423	448	454	436	473	492	522	554	570	591	639
South Carolina	701	648	667	691	694	671	719	714	736	761	824
South Dakota	100	103	115	113	131	119	164	167	173	179	194
Tennessee	674	605	638	624	635	659	679	699	721	747	808
Texas	77518	78369	77149	77862	77307	77618	79575	82100	84621	87560	94699
Utah	1589	1618	1717	1828	1888	2117	2220	2249	2317	2398	2594
Vermont	58	44	52	52	62	66	61	45	47	48	53
Virginia	1477	1485	1525	1546	1564	1665	1777	1780	1834	1898	2052
Washington	2952	3066	3150	3375	3495	3844	3846	4161	4289	4438	4800
West Virginia	243	248	226	223	248	243	251	246	254	262	285
Wisconsin	1648	1734	1748	1875	1913	2089	2187	2137	2202	2279	2465
Wyoming	669	603	687	708	681	742	839	805	829	857	927
United States	339997	345005	349999	356000	362999	371004	381001	391000	402999	417000	450998

114

group estimates for the resident population. None of the age group estimates were adjusted for "census undercount," because those adjustments are small except for blacks of ages 1–9 and 21 and up (U.S. Bureau of the Census, 1988d).

SELF-REPORTED EDUCATIONAL ATTAINMENT BY REGION AND RACE

The U.S. high school graduation rate in 1980 was 71.5 percent—69.3 for males, 73.6 for females. The 71.5 percent figure is close to the percentage of 19-year-olds who reported having completed four years of high school on the 1980 census, which was 75.9 percent (72.3 for males, 79.5 percent for females).

Table A.5 shows how the reported school completion rates varied across regions and race/Hispanic categories in 1980. The race-specific percentages are remarkably uniform across regions. The main exceptions are the black and Asian/Pacific Islander percentages in the West, which are much higher than in other regions. As one might expect, the pattern of school completion rates across regions is similar to the pattern of high school graduation rates: Northeast, 77.3; North Central, 77.2; South, 65.9; West, 66.9. This suggests that the educational attainment rates can be used as proxies for the analogous high school graduation rates, provided that the former are scaled down to agree with the observed graduation rates in each region.

Table A.5

PERCENTAGES OF 19-YEAR-OLDS WHO REPORTED HAVING COMPLETED FOUR YEARS OF HIGH SCHOOL BY SEX, REGION, RACE, AND HISPANIC ORIGIN: APRIL 1980

	Total	White	Black	Asian	Native American	Hispanic Origin
Both sexes						
Northeast	80.0	83.4	62.5	77.0	62.6	52.5
North Central	78.7	81.3	61.2	74.5	55.7	55.0
South	71.8	75.1	63.0	72.2	59.3	55.0
West	74.8	77.6	74.0	81.4	53.2	54.4
U.S.	75.9	79.1	63.6	78.8	55.8	54.3
Males						
Northeast	76.3	80.1	55.5	75.1	58.1	47.9
North Central	75.7	78.6	54.5	72.1	52.4	51.2
South	67.6	71.5	55.9	72.0	55.4	51.3
West	71.8	74.9	70.5	79.2	48.2	50.4
U.S.	72.3	76.0	57.0	76.9	51.4	50.3
Females						
Northeast	83.5	86.6	69.1	79.0	67.0	56.9
North Central	81.7	84.0	67.4	77.1	58.9	58.9
South	76.1	78.7	69.9	72.5	63.6	59.1
West	77.9	80.5	78.1	83.6	58.1	58.7
U.S.	79.5	82.3	69.9	80.8	60.1	58.5

SOURCES: U.S. Bureau of the Census, *1980 Census of Population*, Detailed Population Characteristics, United States Summary, Section B: Regions, PC80-1-D1-B, March 1984. The U.S. figures are from Section A: United States, PC80-1-D1-A, April 1983, Table 262.

To spell out the rescaling procedure for a given region, consider filling the entries of a 2x10 contingency table with two rows (for "Graduates" and "Nongraduates") and ten columns (corresponding to the cells that result from crossing sex with five race/Hispanic categories) by multiplying the number of 17-year-olds in each category by the appropriate regional rate in Table A.5. Then the column entries of the contingency table will add up to the numbers of 17-year-olds in the ten categories, but the row sums will differ from the numbers of graduates and nongraduates in the region. Since the latter can be determined from state totals, the problem reduces to adjusting the entries in the contingency table to accord with prescribed marginal totals.

There is a standard method for carrying out this adjustment called "iterative proportional fitting" or "raking" (U.S. Bureau of the Census, 1971, p. 707). The method entails finding row and column multipliers such that, when the table entries are rescaled using those multipliers, the resulting entries will sum correctly along both rows and columns. The iterative procedure to accomplish the rescaling is equivalent to shifting the logits of the graduation rates (i.e., the logarithms of the odds ratios) for the race/Hispanic categories by the same constant so that the weighted average of the category graduation rates will conform to the overall graduation rate. Hence, from a logistic regression perspective, iterative proportional fitting amounts to shifting the constant term in the regression equation so that the fitted proportions are consistent with the population proportion.

DISAGGREGATED ESTIMATES OF NUMBERS OF GRADUATES

To provide state high school graduation rates by sex, race, and Hispanic origin that are consistent with the overall state rates for each of the years 1980–1987, we applied iterative proportional fitting using the regional rates in Table A.5 as first approximations for the state rates in the ten sex/race/Hispanic categories. That is, in each state, the numbers of 17-year-olds in the ten categories were multiplied by the appropriate regional rates to generate preliminary estimates of the numbers of graduates and nongraduates in each category. These estimates were then "raked" to make them conform with the actual (or estimated) number of high school graduates in that state and year.

To a certain extent, this method relies on an implicit assumption that the pattern of graduation rates across sex/race cells has remained relatively stable over time. As partial evidence on that score, we can compare the reported school completion rates in Table A.5 derived from the 1980 census with analogous rates for 1987 derived from the Current Population Survey (U.S. Bureau of the Census, 1988a). Whereas 75.9 percent of the persons of age 19 reported having completed four years of high school in 1980, the 1987 figure was 77.6 percent, an increase that is commensurate with the change in graduation rates reported in this study. The 1980 and 1987 rates for males were 72.3 and 73.4; for females, 79.5 and 81.7; whites, 79.1 and 80.4; blacks, 63.6 and 62.8; and Hispanics, 54.3 and 57.6. Taking into account the sampling errors associated with the 1987 estimates, we see little evidence of changes in the overall pattern of school completion rates in terms of differences across sex and race/Hispanic categories.

EXTENDING THE ESTIMATES BEYOND 1987

The estimated numbers of high school graduates for 1988–1989 and the projections for 1990–2000 result from applying the assumption that the observed stability in the overall graduation rates from 1983 to 1987 will persist through 2000. Partly because of uncertainties about the numbers of private high school graduates in 1985 and 1987 but also because of questions about some of the 1987 public school estimates, the projected graduation rate for each state was taken to be the average of the observed rates for 1985 through 1987. Applying the projected rate to the 17-year age group estimates for the years after 1987 yields projections of total numbers of graduates for each state, which are then disaggregated by sex and race using the same raking procedure that was used for the 1980–1987 estimates.

The assumption that the states' graduation rates will remain stable as the composition of the school age population changes to include higher percentages of minority students (with lower graduation rates) implies that the race-specific rates will rise. To assure that the state projections would reflect this condition of nondecreasing race-specific rates, a slight modification of the above scheme was used. For each state, the scheme was implemented sequentially, storing each year's rates by sex and race as they were generated. In those cases where the race-specific rates would drop under the uniform rate assumption, the state projections were modified to keep the sex/race rates at the same level that they were the previous year, thereby leading to a slight increase in the state's overall rate.

Given that the U.S. population is projected to shift to the South and West during the 1990s and that the states in those regions tend to have lower than average graduation rates, a scheme that keeps the state rates completely fixed at the 1987 rates would imply steadily decreasing U.S. rates. With the modification indicated above, the U.S. graduation rates remain almost flat at around 73 percent between 1987 and 2000 (73.3 in 1987, 73.2 in 2000). The overall Hispanic rates rise from 51.7 percent in 1987 to 53.6 in 2000, the black rates go from 60.4 to 61.4, and the white (non-Hispanic) rates increase from 78.6 to 79.1.

PROJECTIONS OF GRADUATES FROM PRIVATE SCHOOLS

Motivated by the apparent stability in the regional private/public ratios between 1985 and 1986, we projected overall numbers of private school graduates in each state by applying the most recently observed private proportion to the state's projected total numbers of high school graduates. To provide breakdowns of the state estimates by sex, race, and Hispanic origin, we used the percentages of high school students enrolled in private schools in Table A.6. Applying these estimates to the estimated state totals in each of the ten sex/race/Hispanic cells in any year leads to preliminary estimates of the numbers of private school graduates in those cells. Those estimates and the corresponding estimated numbers of public school graduates were then raked to match the prescribed private and public totals in those years.

The assumption that the state private proportions will remain stable over time implies a gradual reduction in the U.S. proportion of private school graduates—from 9.9 percent in 1986 to 9.6 in 2000. The main reason for this decline is the population shift into southern and western states where the private schools account for smaller proportions of high school graduates.

117

Table A.6

PERCENTAGES OF HIGH SCHOOL STUDENTS ENROLLED IN
PRIVATE SCHOOLS BY REGION, RACE, AND
HISPANIC ORIGIN: APRIL 1980

	Total	White	Black	Asian	Native American	Hispanic Origin
Northeast	12.68	13.53	7.73	9.92	14.25	11.70
North Central	9.17	9.50	6.26	7.67	12.72	12.75
South	7.18	8.63	2.96	6.00	8.81	7.65
West	6.91	6.92	6.40	6.89	9.15	7.00
U.S.	8.90	9.73	5.07	6.99	10.18	8.57

SOURCES: U.S. Bureau of the Census, *1980 Census of Population*, Vol. I: Characteristics of the Population, Chapter C: General Social and Economic Characteristics, PC80-1-C1, December 1983, pp. 71, 97–99, and 223–224.

ACCORDANCE WITH WICHE PROJECTIONS

The WICHE cohort survival method for projecting numbers of high school graduates by state depends mainly on the state estimates of enrollment by grade levels, whereas the projections reported here are tied to Census Bureau estimates of age group sizes. The two sets of projections for the years 1990–2000 agree closely in terms of projected U.S. totals, but the two sets of projections imply quite different growth rates for certain states and for the private schools.

WICHE's projected U.S. total for 2000 is 2,823,928, which is only 1.5 percent above our projection of 2,782,284, but their projection for California (355,087) is 8.2 percent above ours (328,120). WICHE's projection of 218,176 private school graduates in 2000 portends a steep deline in the proportion of private school graduates—from 9.9 percent in 1986 to 7.7 percent in 2000.

As an indication that WICHE's long-term public/private projections lack coherence, they project that the number of private school graduates in California will fall from 24,548 in 1987 to 12,916 in 2000, while the number of public school graduates will increase from 224,896 to 342,171. If there are forces at play in California that would lead to such a rapid decline in the private schools, we are not aware of them. Our projections indicate that the number of private high school graduates in California will increase from 25,507 in 1987 to 30,087 in 2000, and the number of public school graduates will increase from 237,414 to 298,033.

Appendix B

THE HS&B/DMDC DATA BASE

In addition to compiling a micro-level data base that provides detailed information on the postsecondary activities of over 26,000 young adults from the Classes of 1980 and 1982, we have brought together several supplemental data sources that permitted us to extend the scope of the study and link our research findings to national and state statistics bearing on the postsecondary activities of recent high school graduates and dropouts. This appendix describes the main features of the data base and provides summary statistics profiling the student populations of special interest in this study.

HIGH SCHOOL AND BEYOND

The main source of micro-level data on postsecondary activities is HS&B, a large-scale longitudinal study of the Classes of 1980 and 1982 that was conducted by NCES. The base year survey for HS&B was fielded in Spring 1980 to gather comprehensive information on 28,240 seniors and 30,030 sophomores from 1015 high schools. The survey was conducted using a two-stage cluster sample in which the first-stage sampling units were secondary schools stratified by school type, census division, and degree of urbanization (with three levels—urban, suburban, and rural). Within strata, schools were chosen with probabilities proportional to total sophomore and senior enrollment (Frankel et al., 1981).

In each selected school, completely random samples of up to 36 sophomores and 36 seniors were chosen to participate in the study. The participants were administered a battery of cognitive tests and asked to fill in questionnaires eliciting personal information. Additional data were gathered from the students' teachers, school administrators, and a subsample of the students' parents. The resulting student files provide a rich array of demographic and background measures on the students, including cognitive test scores, measures of socioeconomic status, rank in class, high school curriculum, and attitudinal information. They also contain data on the students' postsecondary plans, educational and career aspirations, and plans regarding family formation.

The First Follow-Up Survey of 11,995 seniors and 29,737 sophomores was conducted in February 1982. The sophomores who were still enrolled in their base year schools were administered a second battery of tests and resurveyed using questionnaires similar to those administered to the seniors in 1980. The other sophomores—dropouts, early graduates, and transfers to other schools—were mailed questionnaires to ascertain their current student and employment statuses.

The Second and Third Follow-Ups were fielded in February 1984 and February 1986 using the same 11,995 senior participants and a subsample of 14,825 sophomores. The mailed questionnaires for these follow-ups asked the participants to fill in several items about each episode of employment and educational activity that they had experienced between surveys, including the dates that the activity began and ended, thereby providing key information for tracking the participants' activities through February 1986. For full documentation of the longitudinal files, including further information on the survey design and a complete listing of data elements, see the HS&B user's manuals (National Opinion Research Center, 1987a, b).

The base year survey was well designed to profile the Classes of 1980 and 1982, providing extensive baseline data derived from large samples of schools and students stratified by census division, school type, and degree of urbanization. The sampling allocation scheme for the follow-up surveys was tailored to provide longitudinal data on sufficiently large samples of participants to support detailed analyses for special categories of students. The follow-up participants were chosen using a highly nonrepresentative sample allocation scheme in which most minority base year participants were selected to participate, as were most students whose parents participated in the base year parents' survey.

In theory, this lack of representativeness can be handled in analyses by incorporating case weights that are inversely proportional to the sampling inclusion probabilities, with appropriate adjustments for nonresponse so that the case weight totals in each cell match the cell population sizes. However, the specification of case weights for HS&B was confounded by the incompleteness of the school sampling frame, the lack of reliable population counts to specify stratum sizes, and other complications associated with selecting and enlisting schools to participate in the study.[1] The case weights on the follow-up files (but not the base year file) appear to have been calculated incorrectly, with widely varying weights for students in the same school having similar demographic characteristics. Hence, the use of HS&B follow-up data to estimate population means (such as the proportions of the Class of 1980 attending college at various times after graduation) entails special handling to allow for the nonrepresentativeness of the student samples.

With four public school types, five private school types, and a total school sample size of about 1000, the survey designers could not choose representative samples of schools in all cells defined by census division, school type, and degree of urbanization. Given the way the base year cluster samples were chosen and the nonrepresentativeness of the follow-up samples, we found it necessary to reconstruct the high school graduate populations for 1980 and 1982 to provide a basis (and stratum weights) for analyzing the follow-ups as a stratified two-stage probability sample within cells defined by school control (public or private), census division, sex, and race/Hispanic category.

The estimated numbers of high school graduates in these cells for the Classes of 1980 and 1982 are listed in Tables B.1 and B.2. These estimates are derived from the corresponding state estimates reported in Appendix A. So that the total case weights in each cell for majority (white non-Hispanic) and minority students would agree with the stratum sizes and would reflect the unequal school selection probabilities, the base year weights for all students in each cell were first summed and then rescaled to agree with the corresponding stratum cell sizes. In essence, adopting this reweighting procedure in analyses amounts to adjusting the base year weights to make them agree with known population sizes and treating the unsampled students at follow-up in each cell as missing observations.

---

[1]As an indication of the operational and statistical problems inherent in fielding and analyzing a large-scale panel study of this type, of the 1122 schools selected in the initial HS&B school sample, 104 were ineligible to participate for various reasons, and 298 others refused to participate (Frankel et al., 1981).

Table B.1

NUMBERS OF HIGH SCHOOL GRADUATES BY RACE, HISPANIC ORIGIN, CONTROL OF SCHOOL, AND CENSUS DIVISION: 1980

	Total	Male						Female					
		All	White	Black	Asian	Indian	Hisp.	All	White	Black	Asian	Indian	Hisp.
New England													
Public	156249	75918	71564	2588	447	92	1227	80331	74982	3288	463	104	1494
Private	25490	12362	11874	244	49	11	184	13128	12519	317	52	14	226
Total	181739	88280	83438	2832	496	103	1411	93459	87501	3605	515	118	1720
Middle Atlantic													
Public	445086	219662	183102	23856	2513	221	9970	225424	183693	28263	2252	215	11001
Private	72703	35884	31871	2208	304	40	1461	36819	32244	2637	273	38	1627
Total	517789	255546	214973	26064	2817	261	11431	262243	215937	30900	2525	253	12628
East North Central													
Public	546539	269033	238464	23696	1549	443	4881	277506	241500	28918	1505	461	5122
Private	57029	28053	25319	1701	140	60	833	28976	25785	2107	138	63	883
Total	603568	297086	263783	25397	1689	503	5714	306482	267285	31025	1643	524	6005
West North Central													
Public	244535	121835	114668	4410	656	939	1162	122700	114826	5209	626	884	1155
Private	18818	9377	8894	239	35	90	119	9441	8920	284	33	85	119
Total	263353	131212	123562	4649	691	1029	1281	132141	123746	5493	659	969	1274
South Atlantic													
Public	415305	199286	150284	42192	1356	518	4936	216019	156641	52502	1304	556	5016
Private	33092	15834	13697	1510	97	34	496	17258	14658	1955	92	38	515
Total	448397	215120	163981	43702	1453	552	5432	233277	171299	54457	1396	594	5531
East South Central													
Public	163824	78884	62850	15131	219	86	598	84940	65327	18806	174	81	552
Private	13173	6351	5828	459	12	6	46	6822	6177	587	8	6	44
Total	176997	85235	68678	15590	231	92	644	91762	71504	19393	182	87	596
West South Central													
Public	286103	140901	99608	20807	1014	1345	18127	145202	100410	24516	847	1379	18050
Private	19182	9229	7456	698	49	40	986	9953	7965	904	41	39	1004
Total	305285	150130	107064	21505	1063	1385	19113	155155	108375	25420	888	1418	19054
Mountain													
Public	143763	71529	58862	1909	815	1850	8093	72234	58934	1801	802	2119	8578
Private	5227	2598	2108	69	24	77	320	2629	2109	68	23	87	342
Total	148990	74127	60970	1978	839	1927	8413	74863	61043	1869	825	2206	8920
Pacific													
Public	346274	173643	126657	12402	12254	1328	21002	172631	126120	12758	11796	1447	20510
Private	28815	14457	9920	989	1528	106	1914	14358	9847	1017	1497	112	1885
Total	375089	188100	136577	13391	13782	1434	22916	186989	135967	13775	13293	1559	22395
United States													
Public	2747678	1350691	1106059	146991	20823	6822	69996	1396987	1122433	176061	19769	7246	71478
Private	273529	134145	116967	8117	2238	464	6359	139384	120224	9876	2157	482	6645
Total	3021207	1484836	1223026	155108	23061	7286	76355	1536371	1242657	185937	21926	7728	78123

Table B.2

NUMBERS OF HIGH SCHOOL GRADUATES BY RACE, HISPANIC ORIGIN, CONTROL OF SCHOOL, AND CENSUS DIVISION: 1982

	Total	Male						Female					
		All	White	Black	Asian	Indian	Hisp.	All	White	Black	Asian	Indian	Hisp.
New England													
Public	154611	76378	71581	2824	508	101	1364	78233	72822	3247	498	111	1555
Private	26123	12903	12323	285	63	18	214	13220	12567	326	63	19	245
Total	180734	89281	83904	3109	571	119	1578	91453	85389	3573	561	130	1800
Middle Atlantic													
Public	431711	212254	176445	23261	2681	231	9636	219457	178109	27923	2452	232	10741
Private	73623	36211	32033	2286	345	45	1502	37412	32638	2741	315	44	1674
Total	505334	248465	208478	25547	3026	276	11138	256869	210747	30664	2767	276	12415
East North Central													
Public	538804	266312	235063	24171	1728	486	4864	272492	236035	29135	1662	492	5168
Private	57687	28525	25607	1817	169	70	862	29162	25816	2197	162	72	915
Total	596491	294837	260670	25998	1897	556	5726	301654	261851	31332	1824	564	6083
West North Central													
Public	232219	115626	108871	4137	692	926	1000	116593	108974	4964	653	889	1113
Private	18704	9316	8824	244	42	95	111	9388	8843	290	41	90	124
Total	250923	124942	117695	4381	734	1021	1111	125981	117817	5254	694	979	1237
South Atlantic													
Public	423116	205205	153549	44677	1577	598	4804	217911	156950	53696	1437	619	5209
Private	33707	16307	13995	1659	118	45	490	17400	14695	2015	107	46	537
Total	456823	221512	167544	46336	1695	643	5294	235311	171645	55711	1544	665	5746
East South Central													
Public	167410	81360	64591	15898	248	99	524	86050	65817	19392	200	93	548
Private	13258	6457	5897	492	17	9	42	6801	6136	600	12	8	45
Total	180668	87817	70488	16390	265	108	566	92851	71953	19992	212	101	593
West South Central													
Public	280037	136388	96239	19852	1105	1453	17739	143649	98524	23895	928	1507	18795
Private	18723	8975	7195	706	58	46	970	9748	7733	894	46	45	1030
Total	298760	145363	103434	20558	1163	1499	18709	153397	106257	24789	974	1552	19825
Mountain													
Public	139539	70105	57442	1929	905	1996	7833	69434	56417	1814	870	2181	8152
Private	5996	3011	2365	87	36	113	410	2985	2317	83	35	125	425
Total	145535	73116	59807	2016	941	2109	8243	72419	58734	1897	905	2306	8577
Pacific													
Public	337311	169191	123460	12060	13131	1501	19039	168120	121517	12553	12551	1566	19933
Private	31150	15616	10749	1092	1685	131	1959	15534	10578	1136	1623	138	2059
Total	368461	184807	134209	13152	14816	1632	20998	183654	132095	13689	14174	1704	21992
United States													
Public	2704758	1332819	1087241	148809	22575	7391	66803	1371939	1095165	176619	21251	7690	71214
Private	278971	137321	118988	8668	2533	572	6560	141650	121323	10282	2404	587	7054
Total	2983729	1470140	1206229	157477	25108	7963	73363	1513589	1216488	186901	23655	8277	78268

INFORMATION ON MILITARY SERVICE

To provide more detailed and reliable data on the military service of the HS&B participants, the social security numbers (SSNs) of the 10,925 senior and 13,682 sophomore respondents to the Second Follow-Up Survey were passed through DMDC's accession, master, and loss files for Fiscal Years 1979–1985 to extract records of military personnel having the same SSNs as those reported by the HS&B participants.

This search turned up matches on SSNs for 857 seniors and 950 sophomores, of which 833 seniors and 913 sophomores also matched on dates of birth. A closer examination of the matched records indicated that some of the matches on SSN but not on date on birth did not match on demographic characteristics (e.g., sex, race, and age), so that only matches on both criteria were deemed valid. Of the 833 senior matches, 752 had served on active duty, the others only in the reserves. Of the 913 sophomore matches, 761 served on active duty.

A comparison of the military service items reported on HS&B with analogous items on the DMDC file for matched cases revealed that the HS&B data on military service are quite reliable, including the reported dates of service entry and separation.[2] However, a few participants (46 seniors and 73 sophomores) whose HS&B records showed some active duty served only in the reserves, according to DMDC records. Moreover, 18 seniors and 39 sophomores whose HS&B records indicated no active duty showed up on the DMDC file as having entered the military.

In addition to the 752 seniors and 761 sophomores whose service statuses were verified on the DMDC file through matches on SSN and date of birth, there were 273 other seniors and 281 sophomores who reported having some active duty but whose SSNs did not turn up on the DMDC file, perhaps because their SSNs were erroneously recorded or missing on their HS&B records. Altogether, 1025 (8.5 percent) of the senior participants and 1042 (7.0 percent) of the sophomores were identified as having spent some time on active duty.

INFORMATION ON OTHER ACTIVITIES

Using the individual HS&B episodic data on employment, student activities, and military service (and substituting DMDC data when available), we constructed vectors of educational, employment, and military service measures indicating each HS&B participant's status on these dimensions for each month between January 1980 and February 1986. In particular, the components of the education vector included separate codes to reflect four levels of schooling (high school, four-year college, two-year college, and vocational-technical school) and student status (full-time or part-time).

Creating these vectors of activity measures from longitudinal data is a major undertaking due to myriad problems presented by missing and sometimes conflicting data elements, which necessitate leaving some individuals' activities unclassified. In brief, we began by using the reported school-leaving date to fill in the components for the months when the participant was still in high school. Then, proceeding sequentially across episodes of educational activities reported on the follow-ups, we first used the data on each episode to encode the participant's student status. Then we determined the months (components) in that status

---

[2]The reliability of military service data reported on mailed questionnaires was documented earlier by Kolstad (1986), who used SSN matches on NLS72 participants to create a linked NLS72/DMDC file analogous to our HS&B/DMDC file. In examining the concordance of data elements derived from NLS72 data by Kanouse et al. (1980) with items drawn from DMDC records, Kolstad found very close agreement. In particular, he reported a correlation of .97 between the service entry dates reported on the two files.

using the reported beginning and ending dates for the episode, except in cases where the students reported being "still enrolled" as of the follow-up date, in which case the latter date was used as the episode ending date. In cases of overlapping sojourns of student activity, we opted for full-time student data over part-time data. And we opted for the data on earlier surveys over later surveys, but we substituted the latter when the former were not available. Insofar as possible, we tried to use the same coding scheme for classifying employment and educational activities that was used in an earlier study based on NLS72 (Kanouse et al., 1980, Appendix B).

By combining these activity vectors with information available in other items, we then constructed a "track" vector for each participant with monthly components indicating his or her main activity each month from January 1980 to February 1986. To reconcile cases in which two full-time activities were reported (e.g., military service and full-time student status), we adopted a priority scheme, beginning with a determination of military status. For those on active duty during a given month, the main activity was classified as "military service." Otherwise, student status was checked to determine whether a "full-time student" assignment was appropriate. If not, employment status was checked next, leading to a "not employed" assignment if the participant was jobless, or to "civilian employment" if the participant was employed full-time or if he or she worked part-time and was not enrolled part-time. The remaining cases were assigned to the "unclassified" category, including the part-time students who held part-time jobs and the participants whose student statuses were unclassified.

One of the implications of this scheme is that the main activities of nonrespondents to a particular follow-up were typically not classified during the months spanned by the follow-up unless, for example, they entered military service and their dates of service included some of the months in question. Fortunately, HS&B maintained very high response rates throughout (94 percent on the First Follow-Up Survey), and a substantial portion of the nonrespondents were high school dropouts. Since this study focuses almost entirely on the postsecondary behavior of the graduates in the Classes of 1980 and 1982, nonresponse is not a major concern in this study.

SOCIOECONOMIC STATUS AND ACADEMIC APTITUDE

Earlier studies have pinpointed socioeconomic status and academic aptitude as important determinants of college entrance among high school graduates. The HS&B student files provide measures of these attributes that we shall refer to as SES and TEST. Except for changes of scale, these measures coincide with the base year composite measures BYSES and BYTEST for members of the senior cohort, and the First Follow-Up composites FUSES and FUTEST for the sophomores. In cases where FUSES or FUTEST were missing and the quartile codes SESQ and TESTQ derived from the sophomores' base year scores were available, we used the latter to estimate missing values of SES and TEST.

The SES composite score is based on student-reported information on five components: (1) father's occupation, (2) father's education, (3) mother's education, (4) family income, and (5) material possessions in the household. To calculate SES, the students' responses were first scored on each component using standardized scales having mean 0 and variance 1. Then each student's composite score was calculated using the unweighted average of the student's nonmissing standardized scores on the five components. To provide a more convenient scale for SES, we multiplied the resulting composite score by 100 and added 500.

124

The academic aptitude TEST score was derived using an unweighted average of the nonmissing standardized scores on three cognitive tests of vocabulary, reading, and mathematics. A similar rescaling like that used for SES was adopted to provide TEST scores that have an overall mean close to 500.

Table B.3 provides summary statistics on the SES and TEST scores with breakdowns by graduate status for all participants and for the military entrants in the two classes. As the table shows, TEST scores were available for 10,259 of the 11,995 members of the senior cohort and for 14,392 of the 14,825 members of the sophomore cohort. For the enlistees whose records were available from DMDC files, we also had AFQT scores. Our examination of the complete pairs of TEST and AFQT scores showed that the correlation coefficients between TEST and the normalized score corresponding to the AFQT percentile were .54 for the senior cohort and .56 for the sophomores.

LINKAGES TO OTHER DATA BASES

Other extensions of the HS&B/DMDC data base have enhanced its utility for studying the sorting-out process in the 1980s. To permit examining how seniors' postsecondary plans and activities are affected by regional variations in labor market conditions and educational opportunities, an effort was undertaken to pinpoint the locations of the high schools and colleges attended by the HS&B participants. HS&B provides institutional codes for the colleges that the participants planned to attend as seniors and those that they actually attended after graduation. By linking these items to a Department of Education file on institutional characteristics (including state and county codes) and making use of other information on the HS&B file, we have identified the locations of all HS&B schools by state and urban/rural category.

To incorporate information on local economic conditions into our analyses, we used the derived state codes for the HS&B schools to link the student files to state-level data on four factors: (1) unemployment rate among high school graduates of age 16–19 not enrolled in school, April 1980; (2) unemployment rates, 1980–1984; (3) per capita personal income, 1980–1984; and (4) average hourly earnings of production workers on manufacturing payrolls, 1980–1983.[3] While the availability of the state codes permits appending other state-level economic and population characteristics to the file, our findings in Section III indicate that neither the seniors' postsecondary plans nor their activities after graduation appear to be sensitive to these characteristics once one controls for individual and school attributes.

HS&B's principal shortcoming for the purposes of this study is that its coverage is limited to two high school classes in the early 1980s. To offset that disadvantage and to permit linking the findings of this study to national time series that provide continual updates on youth employment, college enrollment, and educational attainment, we have linked our estimation procedures throughout to population estimates of high school graduates by state, race, and sex for the Classes of 1980 and 1982. The comparable estimates and projections for the years 1980–2000 in Appendix A provide a basis for estimating changes in the demographics of high school graduating classes since 1982. Insofar as changes over time in the postsecondary flows of graduates and dropouts are concerned, we have presented numerous time

[3]The sources of these data are: (1) U.S. Bureau of the Census, *1980 Census of Population*, Vol. 1—Characteristics of the Population, Chapter 3: General Social and Economic Characteristics, U.S. Summary, PC80-1-C1, December 1983, Table 239; (2) *State and Metropolitan Area Data Book, 1986*, pp. 551–552; (3) *County and City Data Book, 1983*, p. 9; and (4) *Handbook of Labor Statistics*, Bulletin 2217, June 1985, p. 219.

Table B.3

SUMMARY STATISTICS FOR MEASURES OF SOCIOECONOMIC STATUS AND ACADEMIC APTITUDE BY GRADUATION AND MILITARY SERVICE STATUSES

	Senior Cohort						Sophomore Cohort					
	All Participants			Military Entrants			All Participants			Military Entrants		
	HSGs	Dropouts	All	HSGs	Dropouts	All	HSGs	Dropouts	All	HSGs	Dropouts	All
SOCIOECONOMIC STATUS												
No. of cases	10773	357	11130	930	19	949	11880	2341	14221	857	145	1002
Sum of weights/1000	2752	77	2828	214	5	219	2944	630	3575	220	42	262
Mean	496	472	496	479	443	478	500	464	494	478	476	477
Standard deviation	75	80	75	72	50	72	73	65	73	66	64	66
First quartile	442	418	441	430	422	429	448	400	440	430	401	429
Median	491	461	490	474	447	474	496	465	489	473	465	468
Third quartile	550	527	550	527	468	526	553	515	545	521	515	516
TEST SCORE												
No. of cases	9946	313	10259	877	15	892	11807	2585	14392	851	153	1004
Sum of weights/1000	2525	67	2592	201	36	205	2922	687	3609	218	45	262
Mean	510	462	509	507	438	506	521	446	507	517	483	512
Standard deviation	88	82	88	88	55	88	88	77,	91	79	72	79
First quartile	441	391	439	438	423	436	455	381	435	462	431	457
Median	512	450	510	506	432	505	528	435	510	519	473	513
Third quartile	580	522	579	576	473	574	592	497	579	571	532	563
STATISTICS FOR COMPLETE PAIRS												
No. of pairs	9664	291	9955	846	15	861	11703	2255	13958	846	138	984
Sum of weights/1000	2469	63	2532	195	4	198	2899	605	3504	217	40	257
Means SES score	495	471	495	480	438	479	500	465	494	478	476	477
Test score	512	466	511	510	438	508	522	451	510	518	485	513
Standard deviations SES Score	74	76	75	72	52	72	73	66	73	67	65	66
Test score	87	82	87	87	55	87	88	77	91	79	71	79
Correlation coeff.	.32	.40	.33	.27	.39	.27	.38	.26	.39	.27	.27	.27

126

series indicating that, except for the increases in military entrance rates in the early 1980s and the closing of the gender gap in college entrance rates, patterns of postsecondary activities have been quite stable for the last 20 years.

BIBLIOGRAPHY

Adkins, Douglas L., *The Great American Degree Machine*, Carnegie Commission on Higher Education, Berkeley, CA, 1975.

Black, Matthew, and Thomas Fraker, "An Analysis of the Success of High School Graduates in the Military," Mathematica Policy Research, Inc., Washington, DC, January 1984.

Bureau of Labor Statistics, *Handbook of Labor Statistics*, Bulletin 2340, August 1989a.

Bureau of Labor Statistics, *Employment and Earnings*, U.S. Government Printing Office, Washington, DC, November 1989b.

Carnegie Council on Policy Studies in Higher Education, *Giving Youth a Better Chance*, Jossey-Bass Publishers, San Francisco, 1979.

Carroll, C. Dennis, *College Persistence and Degree Attainment for 1980 High School Graduates: Hazards for Transfers, Stopouts, and Part-Timers*, National Center for Education Statistics, CS 89-302, U.S. Government Printing Office, Washington, DC, January 1989.

Cox, D. R., *The Analysis of Binary Data*, Chapman and Hall, London, 1970.

Department of Defense, *Selected Manpower Statistics, Fiscal Year 1985*, Directorate for Information Operations and Reports, U.S. Government Printing Office, Washington, DC, 1985.

Fernandez, R. L., *Enlistment Effects and Policy Implications of the Educational Assistance Test Program*, RAND, R-2935-MRAL, September 1982.

Finn, Chester E., Jr., "The High School Dropout Puzzle," *The Public Interest*, No. 87, Spring 1987, pp. 3–22.

Flanagan, John C., et al., *Project TALENT: Five Years After High School*, American Institutes for Research and University of Pittsburgh, 1971.

Folger, John K., Helen S. Astin, and Alan E. Bayer, *Human Resources and Higher Education*, Russell Sage Foundation, New York, 1970.

Folger, John K., and Charles B. Nam, *Education of the American Population*, U.S. Bureau of the Census, U.S. Government Printing Office, Washington, DC, 1967.

Frankel, M. R., et al., *Sample Design Report*, National Opinion Research Center, Chicago, December 1981.

Haggstrom, Gus W., "The Growth of Higher Education in the United States," Carnegie Commission on Higher Education, Berkeley, CA, 1971.

Haggstrom, Gus W., et al., *The Multiple Option Recruiting Experiment*, RAND, R-2671-MRAL, November 1981.

Haggstrom, Gus W., "Logistic Regression and Discriminant Analysis by Ordinary Least Squares," *Journal of Business and Economic Statistics*, Vol. 1, 1983, pp. 229–238.

Haggstrom, Gus W., Linda Darling-Hammond, and David W. Grissmer, *Assessing Teacher Supply and Demand*, RAND, R-3633-ED/CSTP, May 1988.

Hexter, Holly, and Elaine El-Khawas, *Joining Forces: The Military's Impact on College Enrollments*, American Council of Education, October 1988.

Holden, Constance, "Wanted: 675,000 Future Scientists and Engineers," *Science*, Vol. 244, 30 June 1989, pp. 1536–1537.

Hosek, J. R., and C. E. Peterson, *Enlistment Decisions of Young Men*, RAND, R-3238-MIL, July 1985.

Hosek, J. R., C. E. Peterson, and R. A. Eden, *Educational Expectations and Enlistment Decisions*, RAND, R-3350-FMP, March 1986.

Jaffe, A. J., and Walter Adams, "Trends in College Enrollment," *College Board Review*, Winter, 1964–65, pp. 27–32.

Johnston, Jerome, and Jerald G. Bachman, *Youth in Transition*, Vol. V (*Young Men and Military Service*), Institute for Social Research, University of Michigan, Ann Arbor, 1972.

Kanouse, D. E., et al., *Effects of Postsecondary Experiences on Aspirations, Attitudes, and Self-Conceptions*, RAND, R-2616-HEW, April 1980.

Kolstad, Andrew, "The Educational Enrollments of Military Veterans: Evidence from a Longitudinal Study," National Center for Education Statistics, Washington, DC, February 1986.

Kutscher, Ronald E., "Projections Summary and Emerging Issues," *Monthly Labor Review*, November 1989, pp. 66–74.

Manski, Charles F., and David A. Wise, *College Choice in America*, Harvard University Press, Cambridge, MA, 1983.

National Center for Education Statistics, *Digest of Education Statistics, 1988*, U.S. Government Printing Office, Washington, DC, 1988.

National Center for Education Statistics, *Digest of Education Statistics, 1989*, U.S. Government Printing Office, Washington, DC, 1989.

National Center for Education Statistics, *Projections of Education Statistics to 2000*, U.S. Government Printing Office, Washington, DC, 1989.

National Opinion Research Center, *High School and Beyond 1980 Sophomore Cohort Third Follow-Up (1986) Data File User's Manual*, Vols. I and II, National Center for Education Statistics, October 1987.

National Opinion Research Center, *High School and Beyond 1980 Senior Cohort Third Follow-Up (1986) Data File User's Manual*, Vols. I and II, National Center for Education Statistics, October 1987.

Office of the Assistant Secretary of Defense (Force Management and Personnel), *Population Representation in the Military Services: Fiscal Year 1987*, Washington, DC, August 1988.

Ornstein, Michael D., *Entry into the American Labor Force*, Academic Press, New York, 1976.

Pallas, Aaron M., "School Dropouts in the United States," in *The Condition of Education*, 1986 Edition, Center for Education Statistics, Washington, DC, 1986.

Panel to Study the NSF Scientific and Technical Personnel Data System, *Surveying the Nation's Scientists and Engineers*, National Academy Press, Washington, DC, 1989.

Peng, Samuel S., William B. Fetters, and Andrew J. Kolstad, *High School and Beyond: A Capsule Description of High School Students*, National Center for Education Statistics, Washington, DC, April 1981.

Porter, Oscar F., *Undergraduate Completion and Persistence at Four-Year Colleges and Universities*, National Institute of Independent Colleges and Universities, Washington, DC, 1989.

Robert, Marc., et al., *What to Do about the Nursing Shortage*, Commonwealth Fund, New York, 1989.

Shapiro, Gary M., and Donna Kostanich, "High Response Error and Poor Coverage are Severely Hurting the Value of Household Survey Data," paper presented at American Statistical Association Meetings, U.S. Bureau of the Census, August, 1988.

Shavelson, R. J., et al., "Enlistment Decisionmaking: Choice Among Competing Alternatives," in Bray, R. M., et al. (eds.), *Youth Attitude Study II, Fall 1985*, Research Triangle Institute, Research Triangle Park, NC, 1986.

Shavelson, R. J., G. W. Haggstrom, and J. D. Winkler, *Potential for Military Recruiting from Two-year Colleges and Postsecondary Vocational Schools*, RAND, N-1946-MRAL, January 1983.

Shavelson, R. J., G. W. Haggstrom, and T. J. Blaschke, *Two-year Colleges and Vocational Schools as Sources of Military Manpower*, RAND, N-2193-MIL, October 1984.

U.S. Bureau of the Census, *The Methods and Materials of Demography*, Vol. 2, U.S. Government Printing Office, Washington, DC, 1971.

U.S. Bureau of the Census, *Current Population Reports*, Series P-25, No. 917, "Preliminary Estimates of the Population of the United States, by Age, Sex, and Race: 1970 to 1981," July 1982.

U.S. Bureau of the Census, "Census of Population and Housing, 1980: County Population by Age, Sex, Race, and Spanish Origin (Preliminary OMB-Consistent Modified Race)," Tape Technical Documentation, Washington, DC, 1983.

U.S. Bureau of the Census, *Current Population Reports*, Series P-25, No. 995, "Projections of the Hispanic Population: 1983 to 2080," November 1986.

U.S. Bureau of the Census, *Current Population Reports*, Series P-20, No. 428, "Educational Attainment in the United States: March 1987 and 1986," August 1988a.

U.S. Bureau of the Census, *Current Population Reports*, Series P-20, No. 429, "School Enrollment—Social and Economic Characteristics of Students: October 1986," August 1988b.

U.S. Bureau of the Census, *Current Population Reports*, Series P-25, No. 1017, "Projections of the Population of States, by Age, Sex, and Race: 1988 to 2010," October 1988c.

U.S. Bureau of the Census, *Current Population Reports*, Series P-25, No. 1022, "United States Population Estimates, by Age, Sex, and Race: 1980 to 1987," March 1988d.

U.S. Bureau of the Census, *Current Population Reports*, Series P-25, No. 1024, "State Population and Household Estimates, With Age, Sex, and Components of Change: 1981–87," May 1988e.

U.S. Bureau of the Census, *Statistical Abstract of the United States: 1989* (109th edition), U.S. Government Printing Office, Washington, DC, 1989.

Western Interstate Commission for Higher Education, *High School Graduates: Projections by State, 1986 to 2004*, Boulder, CO, 1988.